# BARBARIAN
# SENTIMENTS

## Also by William Pfaff

The Wrath of Nations:
Civilization and the Furies of Nationalism *(1993)*

Condemned to Freedom *(1971)*


*(with Edmund Stillman)*

Power and Impotence:
The Failure of America's Foreign Policy *(1966)*

The Politics of Hysteria:
The Sources of Twentieth-Century Conflict *(1964)*

The New Politics:
America and the End of the Postwar World *(1961)*

# BARBARIAN SENTIMENTS

## America in the New Century

Revised Edition, with a
New Foreword and Afterword

## William Pfaff

🔥 Hill and Wang
A division of Farrar, Straus and Giroux
New York

Hill and Wang
A division of Farrar, Straus and Giroux
19 Union Square West, New York 10003

Much of this book first appeared, in different form, in
*The New Yorker*. Portions of additional materials in this edition first
appeared, in different forms, in *World Policy Journal*, *Du* magazine,
the *International Herald Tribune*, and the *Los Angeles Times*.

"Thermopylae," from *The Complete Poems of Cavafy*, translation
copyright © 1948, 1949, 1959, 1961 by Rae Dalven, reprinted by
permission of Harcourt Brace Jovanovich, Inc.

Library of Congress Cataloging-in-Publication Data

Pfaff, William, 1928–
    Barbarian sentiments : America in the new century / William Pfaff.—
Rev. ed. with a new foreword and afterword.
        p.    cm.
    Includes index.
    ISBN 0-8090-2806-9 (alk. paper)
    1. United States—Foreign relations—1989–    I. Title.
E840 .P43 2000
327.73—dc21                                                    00–035014

Designed by Thomas Frank

For Carolyn, Alix, and Nick

In order to handle barbarian affairs, you have to know
barbarian sentiments: in order to know barbarian sentiments,
you have to know barbarian conditions.

—WEI YUAN, *Member of the Grand Secretariat of the*
*Imperial Manchu Court, and one of the founders of*
*Western learning in China, introducing a collection*
*of documents on European practices published*
*shortly before the first Opium War*


## THERMOPYLAE

Honor to those who in their lives
are committed and guard their Thermopylae.
Never stirring from duty;
just and upright in all their deeds,
but with pity and compassion too;
generous whenever they are rich, and when
they are poor, again a little generous,
again helping as much as they are able;
always speaking the truth,
but without rancor for those who lie.

And they merit greater honor
when they foresee (and many do foresee)
that Ephialtes will finally appear,
and in the end the Medes will go through.

—C. P. CAVAFY

*Translated by Rae Dalven*

# CONTENTS

# FOREWORD TO THE REVISED EDITION

One rereads a book published a decade earlier with surprise that one actually wrote these things in quite this way about national and international situations that since have so fundamentally changed. *Barbarian Sentiments* came out just before the collapse of the Soviet Union and the Communist bloc, a moment of great historical significance. Communism had been the most important modern manifestation of Enlightenment ambition, or hubris, an attempt to transform human beings and human society through the power of human will, in pursuit of the millennium. It was an effort to replace intemporal salvation with a temporal paradise, usurping God—a very European idea. The effort was not a success, although that is no assurance that it will not be tried again.

In the aftermath, we have entered a new century and a new millennium. The United States bestrides the stage, professing that secular millenarianism which is the nation's style, as well as its essential assumption. *Barbarian Sentiments* appraised the old epoch as it ended. In this new volume, I reconsider what I wrote then, wrapping the old text in an assessment of what has happened since 1989 and of what now may follow. This new edition is thus double-minded, and the tension between the two parts may prove suggestive.

The afterword with which I conclude describes the situation of the United States as it begins the new century, largely unaware that it may prove to be a century unkind to Americans.

I have slightly edited the original text of *Barbarian Sentiments* to make it run smoothly for the reader today. Thus a line that originally said "current Soviet foreign policy is . . ." I have now changed to "Soviet foreign policy in 1989 was . . . ," and so forth. I have cut nothing, and no change whatever has been made to the sense of original text or to the judgments I made in 1989, even when they were wrong.

The concluding pages of chapters 3 and 4, dealing with Central Europe and the Soviet Union, as it then was, have not been edited at all. They were written urgently at a moment of impending crisis and change, and I meant them to influence not only American policy but that of elites in Western and Central Europe and in the Soviet Union, where, thanks to my column in the *International Herald Tribune,* I knew I had an audience. I was trying to weigh in the balance, and what I wrote then cannot be taken out of its historical context.

I have added at the end of the chapters new comments, usually brief, in which I reconsider what I wrote a decade ago and what has followed since. My judgments on what has happened since 1989 to Russia and what was then the Soviet bloc, the subjects of chapters 3 and 4, follow chapter 4. I have made no attempt to bring all of the issues I originally discussed up to date, which would have produced another book of the same size or larger.

In the afterword I write about the United States today, its new political character and foreign policy, and its policy debate, in an effort to understand what may lie in the future.

*Barbarian Sentiments* was written for American readers, but with German, French, and Portuguese translations it found an unexpectedly large international audience in Europe and Latin America. A substantial part of the original text was adapted from the "Reflections" articles I wrote for *The New Yorker* between 1971 and 1992, under the editorships of William Shawn and Robert Gottlieb. As the former is now dead and the magazine they edited has been changed into just another magazine, I feel that I should add a particular expression of thanks to them both. I can imagine no other general magazine that would have permitted me to write on political matters in what Mr. Shawn called "a literary form of [my] own invention," in which historical and cultural considerations were intimately connected to the discussion of current issues, doing so with complete freedom in form and matter, saying things that often were surely not the views of my editors. I consider myself very fortunate, and I am grateful to them.

William Pfaff

# BARBARIAN
# SENTIMENTS

# DEAD STARS

The accounts that history presents have to be paid. Past has to be reconciled with present in the life of a nation. History is an insistent force: the past is what put us where we are. The past cannot be put behind until it is settled with.

The force of the past is commonly underestimated, even denied, in American discussion. It has been characteristic of American culture to think history mostly bunk, and certainly to act as though it were—possibly because the United States has enjoyed a relatively happy history. The past does not stalk us—or so we are inclined to think. Yet the legacy of the worst things in our past, slavery and the casual decimation of American Indian society, is still unresolved. It is true that slavery itself and Jim Crow, which followed, were eventually undone because of the working of the national conscience. Thus, the American majority lives with this past without undue discomfort. The evidence all about us that, in crucial respects, the United States remains an economically and socially divided nation is taken as the other side of our prized individualism.

The capacity of Americans for forgetting the past or acting as if the past had no relevance follows from the conviction of a special Providence, which is, as Tocqueville noted, a "doctrine of necessity." Democracy, he said, denies the "aristocratic" notion that individuals shape history, and is inclined to assume that "each nation is indissolubly bound by its position, its origin, its antecedents, and its character." Thus, historians in a democracy find it "not enough to show what events have occurred: they wish to show that events could not have occurred otherwise." The United States and the

Soviet Union, each of which claimed to be the democratic nation par excellence, had a common belief in inevitability—which the evidence contradicts. Things *could* have been otherwise.

The fact that they could have been, and can be, otherwise is a troubling consideration; but while Americans may assume inevitability, at least they do not claim infallibility. The Soviet Union rested on just that claim: of an unfailingly correct "general line." It is a claim by which Mikhail Gorbachev found himself dangerously bound. His society, like any other, needed to connect with its past in order to deal with its present: to make moral sense of the past in order to possess moral confidence in itself and in its future. What went on in the Soviet Union before 1989 was an affair of consequence because it happened in a nation that more than any other had committed itself to the future, justifying everything by what it was supposed to become, and by what it triumphantly claimed to have left behind. The discovery that nothing is left behind until the truth about it has been told is as radically unsettling as the fact that the truth about the future is unforeseeable.

The American belief in the inevitability of the past is accompanied by the conviction that anything is possible in the future, which is a different thing from believing in the future's foreseeability. When President Ronald Reagan described the Soviet Union as an "Evil Empire," he was implying that the U.S.S.R. need not be that. It could change and become something else, if it chose. Conversion was possible. The view that whatever the Russians—or the Europeans, or the people of Asia's great civilizations—are, they have been for a very long time, and are very likely to continue to be, implies a fatalism that it goes against the American grain to accept.

Such fatalism would imply a fatalistic foreign policy as well, in which other nations are accepted for what they are, or for what history has made them into. But the American insistence that human freedom implies history's malleability has engendered an activist foreign policy that presumes that nations and international society can be changed into something more acceptable to Americans. This is the sense of the American Century: that in it history has been achieving its democratic fulfillment. It is the American temper to force matters to a conclusion, to settle, win, put it all behind, move on to something else. It is crucially hard to accept that history does not have a stop: that there are problems at the heart of American national security that might have no solution.

There are exhausted ideas, like dead stars, in the American political atmosphere, which nonetheless remain central to the way certain subjects are discussed and to the formulation of national policy. These are ideas that people want or need to be true. They are ideas about political change, about the correlation between political and economic progress, and about the universal relevance of certain values and political institutions, which are held to merely because it would be bewildering to be without them. Theoretical formulations that are generally conceded to be false but have become conventional, and for which no replacement is evident, continue to be employed by people who certainly know better. A very large discrepancy exists between, on the one hand, what serious Americans observe in certain matters and actually think about them and, on the other hand, the propositions that are repeatedly put forward as the basis for national policy. There is a real dissociation of perception from analysis and decision, and one looks for an explanation in American political culture.

There are some false ideas, derived from a partial perception or oversimplified generalization from a particular situation, which then enter into the political fashion. In the 1940s it was convenient as well as expedient to think that Soviet Russia was, at least potentially, a democratic power: that it was a "new" nation and in that respect closer to the United States than the "old" nations of Europe. Despite the intervening Cold War identification of the U.S.S.R. with totalitarian evil, many Americans were willing to believe as late as the 1960s and early 1970s that the United States and the U.S.S.R. were "converging" toward some new model of advanced industrial or postindustrial society in which the two would emerge into a new and progressive social order. Yet the Soviet Union even then was stagnant, and Western Europe and

Japan, then dismissed as minor forces in world affairs, were actually overtaking the United States in industrial dynamism.

Americans in the 1950s were impressed, and disturbed, by China's "Great Leap Forward" and a decade later were convinced that China was already a world power capable of mobilizing the radical forces of non-Western, "rural" society to besiege the "urban" West. It was the fear of a unitary "Asian Communism," supposedly controlled by China, that sent the United States into the Vietnam War. This perception of China as a threat has since vanished, but Americans continue to think of China as a great power, even as becoming a "superpower" as early as the year 2000. Yet the total of industrial production in China at the end of the 1980s was probably half that in Britain, even less than that in France, and in technological sophistication, scientific advance, education, and standard of living, China was far, far behind Britain or France. The sheer physical scale of China and of its population causes people to think that size must inevitably become quality. Yet modern China has never been able to transform its human and material resources into real national power; this has been its problem since the Manchu decline began. Why should one assume that there has been a decisive change? Perhaps there has been, but the case remains unproven.

The example of Japan's brilliant, if bloody, self-transformation from feudal hermit kingdom into a superbly powerful modern industrial feudalism is taken to demonstrate that the same thing will happen not only in China but in the rest of the Pacific Basin. The reasons which might cause one to think that the Japanese precedent is not readily reproducible are widely ignored. The fact that the total gross industrial output in the 1980s of South Korea, Singapore, Taiwan, and Hong Kong—the other four rapidly industrializing East Asian powers—was still, all together, not a great deal larger than that of the Netherlands alone, did not check people from assuming that the day of the Pacific Basin's world preeminence had already dawned. There simply is a will to believe. There was such a will in the early and mid-1970s to believe, on even less evidence, that Iran was about to become the world's "fifth superpower."

. . .

A second kind of false belief reflects the cultural assumptions of the society holding it; it is what, for reasons embedded in its own history, a people needs or wants to believe. American belief about Europe has always included a powerful component of the desire to believe that Europe has been left behind by the United States, the "new" world having succeeded the "old," an American Century by now in place. Americans have wished to believe that the United States has a missionary destiny in Asia, religious in the nineteenth century, secular in the twentieth. These convictions reflect a progressive outlook on history that is, one might think paradoxically, one of the engines driving the United States—a nation otherwise very conservative in its political outlook.

Americans in modern times, whether they consider themselves liberals, conservatives, neoconservatives, or radicals, have had only the vocabulary of optimism with which to deal with international affairs. We recoil from acknowledging the complexities and perversities of history's workings, since to do so would threaten the optimism that has been indispensable to the development of the United States itself. The denial that there are wolves at the door has made us go forward. Other societies are obsessed by the wolves. "The illusions of eternal strength and health, and of the essential goodness of people—they were the illusions of a nation, the lies of generations of frontier mothers," wrote F. Scott Fitzgerald.

Freud has written of the "psychical reaction-formations"—sexual repression being the most important—with which civilization has attempted to check human aggressiveness. In the United States, there has been another kind of repression of reality—this generalized political optimism maintained in the teeth of evidence. Woodrow Wilson said: "Am I an idealist? That is how I know that I am an American." Freud, of course, also noted the degree to which repression may be a doomed effort. At one point in his *Civilization and Its Discontents* he wrote, bleakly: "Perhaps we may also familiarize ourselves with the idea that there are difficulties attaching to the nature of civilization which will not yield to any attempt at reform"—a deeply un-American thought.

Although its origins are in the eighteenth century, the American vocabulary of optimism developed its present political form in the years before the First World War, replacing a conception of progressive imperialism that was associated with Theodore Roosevelt and Alfred Thayer Mahan, and which Americans had never wholeheartedly accepted, because of their own experience of colonial victimization. Woodrow Wilson proposed a utopian internationalism in which aim and purpose were everything; means, method, and even analysis were discounted. Having seized the attention of the world with his Fourteen Points for ending the First World War, he proved at the peace conference at Versailles in 1919 to have no clear notion of what he wanted, trusting that everything could be solved by fresh thought and the application of general principles. His confidence was representative of that of other Americans of the time. Theirs was a political utopianism which derived from that religious tradition by which the United States was considered (as it continues to be today by many Protestant fundamentalists) the secular expression of God's redemptive action—a secular fulfillment of God's promises. (The sociologist Robert Nisbet has remarked that Wilson's religion, "like America's, began as Calvinism but was transformed into Americanism.") This tradition found its modern political expression in the liberal internationalism of American foreign policy from the time of Wilson through that of Franklin Roosevelt and his successors, up to the disabling event of the Vietnam War.

Today, not much American enthusiasm survives for schematic world reform, nor is there much optimism about the evolution of "world order." Liberal foreign policy thought has become more narrowly focused, emphasizing arms control in Soviet-American relations, pressing the allies on security "burden-sharing," and expressing a "neoliberal" nationalism and economic protectionism, while abandoning little of the old language of progressive internationalism and of American leadership of the free world. There is nothing intellectually new in this, nor much sign of recognition that the basic problems of the end of this century might arise outside the narrow terms of the bilateral Soviet-American relationship.

The conversion of many American intellectuals to conservatism, to the support of the Reagan presidency and the Bush candidacy in 1988—their rallying to a straightforward and sometimes hectoring patriotism, and proud renunciation of the "adversary culture"—has not produced on their part any serious reexamination of the ideas on which American foreign policy has been made for more than three-quarters of a century. There is, rather, celebration of the conventional wisdom. Irving Kristol has said that the task of the neoconservative intellectual is "to explain to the American people why they are right, and to the intellectuals why they are wrong." What sentiment, for an intellectual, could be more American?

In place of a reexamination of the old liberal political ideas, there is, in essential respects, their reiteration. The United States still is aggressively described as model for mankind, source of idealism, seat of justice. Challenged to rewrite policy for Central America, the Kissinger Commission, a group under conservative leadership that presented its report in 1984, could do no better than to propose a large aid program to help Central Americans achieve "the vision of the future that our ideals represent." How could Lyndon Johnson or Hubert Humphrey have disagreed? It was President Johnson who said of the United States and Latin America that "we want for the peoples of this hemisphere only what they want for themselves—liberty, justice, dignity, a better life for all." There had been no change in twenty years. There has been very little change in seventy years. Wilson held that the American flag "is the flag not only of America but of humanity," and after the bombardment of Veracruz, in 1914, he said that "the United States had gone to Mexico to serve mankind." Ronald Reagan could have put it no better of Grenada, El Salvador, Nicaragua.

We are in an odd situation. At one level of intelligence, or consciousness, Americans—conservatives, liberals, the rest—know that their political language is false and that their ideas are sentimental and self-aggrandizing. People recognize perfectly well that the Lebanese, Iranians, Nicaraguans, Salvadorans, Filipinos, Africans—not to speak of the Europeans, Japanese, and Chinese—all lead lives more or less remote from the American national experience, with different perceptions and national ambitions, motivated by different values. This is evident to those who make American policy; it is the main obstacle to the success of that policy. There would be no problem in the Middle East or Central America—or in any of the other places where the United States finds itself in collision with local feelings—if it were really true that American values are universally admired and sought, or would be if these were properly explained. That we are the norm of the world is simply an ancient and self-serving theme of American political rhetoric, of interest, these days, only to ourselves.

Americans and their government are perfectly able to identify the material and political interests of the United States abroad, and distinguish these from the interests of others, and to recognize as well that others' interests not only may conflict with American interests but may do so legitimately. We are willing to press our interests quite unsentimentally, to reject U.N. votes or decline to acknowledge World Court jurisdiction over American actions, when to do so suits us. We aggressively defend our trade interests, to the point of protectionism (or beyond it), yet at another level the language of liberal idealism seems indispensable to Americans. It is the only language we have—drained of content though it may be. Keynes said of political and economic ideas: "Both when they are right and when they are wrong, [they] are more powerful than is commonly understood. Indeed the world is ruled by little else. Practical men, who believe themselves to be quite exempt from any intellectual influences, are usually the slaves of some defunct economist. Madmen in authority, who hear voices in the air, are distilling their frenzy from some academic scribbler of a few years back. I am sure that the power of vested interests is vastly exaggerated compared with the gradual encroachment of ideas." America's problem is how to free itself from the grip of its exhausted ideas.

These are the ideas that justified abandoning the isolationism of the first hundred and fifty years of the country's existence. The original American position was that of exemplary isolation; the United States held itself aloof as—in Jefferson's phrase—"the world's best hope." From Jefferson (who urged cancellation of all our treaties) to Franklin Roosevelt (with Wilson the dazzling exception), the mainstream of American liberal thought remained isolationist, concerned to preserve America—this special dispensation—from the foreign corruptions America had been founded to defy. The conversion to internationalism came only with the two world wars, when events seemed to render isolationism impossible. Once the country had taken up an active part in world affairs in 1917, and reconfirmed this in the 1940s, the idea of the United States as exemplar of the world had to be given a new practical expression, and that is what liberal internationalism accomplished. Collective security; international organization on a parliamentary model, with universal representation of the world's nations; the rule, and enlargement, of international law became the ideas at the center of American foreign policy, and remained so for three-quarters of a century. Liberal ideas they certainly were, but American ideas as well. Senator Robert A. Taft, leader of the conservative and nationalist wing of the Republican party in the 1940s and early 1950s, an isolationist, a progenitor of the conservative Republican Party of the present day, contested the NATO Treaty in 1949 on the grounds that it involved unforeseeable commitments, but he also said that international peace, in his view, ultimately depended upon "an international law defining the duties and obligations of nations . . . international courts to determine whether nations are abiding by that law . . . joint armed force to enforce that law and the decisions of that court . . . It is quite true that the United Nations Charter as drafted does not yet reach the ideals of international peace and justice which I have described, but it goes a long way in that direction . . ."

The United States' conversion to internationalism, and to the program of world intervention that emerged in the late 1940s and the 1950s, was a turning of the mind but not of the heart. Superficially, American foreign policy had been reversed from the old isolationism; but the new policies betrayed their inner resemblance to what had gone before. The earliest postwar programs possessed a modest objective: to reestablish a balance of power in Central and Southern Europe. But "balance" was an objective too mild, too detached, for a nation that had to be cajoled from its insular assumptions and its established contempt for "power politics." The popular support for these policies took on a rather different character, and the Manichaean moralism that John Foster Dulles subsequently supplied to American policy found warm response among a people with little time for the self-conscious declaration of political and military limits that distinguished the work of the first postwar generation of policymakers.

American world policy, American internationalism and interventionism, initially sponsored by the liberal elites of the country and then taken over—at first uneasily but later with undiscriminating enthusiasm—by Republican converts from isolationism, became a new and grand campaign in the crusade both Wilson and Roosevelt had waged against what they had called the enemies of democracy, and what Ronald Reagan more boisterously and disingenuously reidentified as the Evil Empire. It became a program avowedly to institute world democracy—to establish in every nation the crucial American institutions: law, representative government, human rights, a free-trade capitalist economy.

The unspoken but unmistakable assumption behind all of this was that the world would be a safe place for America only when the world was made very much like America. The corollary assumptions—that to make it so was possible and a reasonable goal of foreign policy—derived from the breathtaking conviction that people everywhere shared the fundamental ambitions and values of Americans. Or that they would, once they were told about them—and Americans were not reluctant to tell them. Our bitterest official and popular resentments were reserved not for our enemies but for those supposed friends, like the French, who perversely refused to admit that American policies were uniquely altruistic or American institutions worth special emulation. But then the West Europeans as a whole were thought limited in outlook. Assistant Secretary of State George Ball, a distinguished advocate of European-American cooperation, could nonetheless declare in 1965, when Britain's empire had been ended and France had surrendered Equatorial and West Africa, Indochina, Tunisia, Morocco, and Algeria, while America was plunging into the night of Vietnam, that the American world role was "unique in world history" because it was disinterested. The Europeans, he said, were unqualified to share world responsibility with the United States because "they have little experience in the exercise of responsibility divorced from the defense of territories or the advancement of quite narrow and specific national interests. To undertake—alongside the United States—to play a role of responsibility in a world where colonial empires have largely disappeared would require them to develop a whole new set of attitudes towards world affairs."

American interventionism from the 1950s to the 1980s expressed precisely the attitudes that had lain behind the isolationism of the past, giving them a new practical outlet. Americans now dealt with the "power politics" and the "jealousies and rivalries of the complicated politics of Europe" (to use Wilson's words) by attempting to remake Europe: thus American enthusiasm for the creation of a "united states" of Europe. In the past, Americans had held themselves apart from Europe, avoiding an involvement feared to be corrupting. When that no longer seemed possible, the aim became to make over that Europe in ways that would remove or neutralize those corruptive powers. It was, of course, an ambition sure to fail.

There was in the United States in 1988 a turning away from the engagements that lay at the center of the system of collective security developed since 1945. The effect was one of "progressively reducing Europe's military dependence on us and insulating ourselves from conflict in Europe," as Earl Ravenal of Georgetown University formulated what was, for him, the appropriate policy objective. The drift was toward an American unilateralism. The United States would set its own priorities and act as it deemed necessary. The views of the European allies expressed by Americans reflected a reemergence of that distrust of Europeans which has been a lasting factor in the American outlook—of that Europe which is commonly thought (as the then presidential candidate Senator Gary Hart felicitously put it in 1984) inclined to "radical extremes" and "corruption," and "less idealistic generally." In the new enthusiasm expressed for development in the Pacific Basin there is evident an American preference, going back to the nineteenth century, for Asian entanglements over European ones, reflecting the assumption (which is wrong) that Asia is more tractable, less demanding, potentially more susceptible to American influence.

Years of Atlanticism, of American emphasis on American leadership in the defense of Europe, have meanwhile tended to obscure exactly what we are doing in Europe, and why and how it all began. American policy originated not in benevolence but in fear of another war, and in concern about Germany and German rearmament, as well as about the Soviet Union. The American commitment to Europe arose from a strategic decision to prevent the Soviet Union from acquiring control over the industrial plant, the skilled manpower, and the war-making capacity of the West European states. This commitment was fully in the policy tradition of that other maritime power, from which the United States had inherited its European role, Great Britain, which since the Hundred Years' War had made strategic interventions on the Continent, conducting a diplomacy of coalition and division meant to prevent any single power from dominating Europe. The American strategic interest in the autonomy and independence of Western Europe remains identical. The Atlantic Alliance is the instrument by which the congruent European interest in its own autonomy is safeguarded. It has been a useful instrument; it is not an indispensable one. The political ambitions that have become attached to it should not be permitted to obscure its primary function.

The defense of the West was a spontaneous choice and a common cause for most West Europeans during the early 1950s, when Stalin was alive and the Soviet Union remained dark, driven, seemingly unreconcilable. The United States then possessed a solid moral as well as military claim to the leadership of the West—a claim that rested upon its conduct in the Second World War and the generosity and gravity of its postwar policies. In 1988 the defense of the West was a conception that had come to possess new political complexities and a different moral dimension.

Europeans who in 1988 were under the age of forty had few memories of the United States as liberator and as rebuilder of the European economies and of a democratic polity. To them, the United States had instead come often to seem the oppressor, in Vietnam and Cambodia; the sponsor of military dictatorship in Greece, and of the Shah in Iran; the destabilizer of socialist Chile; the interventionist in Central America and the past patron of corrupt oligarchies or of generals there and in the Philippines, Argentina, Brazil, South Korea. The Soviet Union seemed an unchanging quantity: fixed, bleakly predictable, unlovable, but latterly, suddenly interesting. The United States seemed unstable, mercurial in its national moods, even a little hysterical when it treated Colonel Qaddafi and Fidel Castro as if they were major figures in the world's affairs, made the overturn of a black Caligula in pitiable Grenada occasion for triumphal celebration of the power of the free world, or elevated the internal struggles in Central American states to the level of international crisis. Europeans will concede that America's is the better record than the Soviet Union's, but such a comparison is held to be irrelevant. We are theirs, a part of their moral responsibility. The Russians are alien.

What has been happening in the European-American relationship is ordinarily taken to add up to a bad thing. One might ask, however, if it may not in the end prove to have been a good thing—or, at least, a necessary thing. It is making explicit a fundamental, and undoubtedly inevitable, change in the American security relationship with Western Europe, which was never a complete union of minds but, rather, a practical association to deal with the problems of a particular time. It may be that what is happening at the end of the 1980s can compel the governments of the West to do what they have so stubbornly resisted doing, which is to look for a creative way out of their blocked, corroded, and extremely dangerous politico-military confrontation with the Soviet Union in Central Europe.

The Western governments might ask, at last, what might be put in its place to leave the United States, the Soviet Union, and the European nations on both sides of the German divide more secure rather than less. Such an intellectual enterprise would necessarily consider whether a European reassumption of primary responsibility for Europe's defense and the reduction or withdrawal of American ground forces from Europe—ordinarily opposed as opening the way to Soviet domination of what Mikhail Gorbachev described as "the common European house"—might actually provide the crucial element in the unlocking of a larger political settlement on the Continent. This settlement would certainly not cause world peace to break out; the global Soviet-Western political competition would undoubtedly continue, being a basic competition of *Weltanschauungen*, of visions of history. The risks merely might be reduced.

A central argument of this book is that Europe still is crucially important, and even rather dangerous. It can't be counted out, as Americans have been inclined to do since the 1940s. It is more important to the American future than Asia or the Soviet Union or Latin America. It is more important to the civilization in which Americans live because that civilization remains fundamentally a European one. It is true that the ethnic makeup of the United States has drastically changed in recent years, and that non-Western civilizations have had an increasing influence on American society, but that still has changed nothing fundamental, and is not going to do so in the foreseeable future.

It is a book about the character and motivations of that non-Western world, because the countries there have been made the vehicles, or victims, of American as well as Soviet ambitions during the years of Cold War, while their actual conditions and sentiments have been treated with large indifference.

This is, inevitably, a book about the Soviet Union as well, because the U.S.S.R. is and will remain the focus of Americans' attention, and also because what happens next in the Soviet Union, and the peaceful (or unpeaceful) resolution of an unsustainable and intolerable Soviet domination of the eastern half of Europe, are crucial issues of the years before us—probably the most important of all.

The salient fact about Central and Eastern Europe in 1988 is that nothing was settled. Everything was supposed to have been settled forty years earlier. Stalin told Tito that in "this war [w]hoever occupies territory also imposes on it his own social system. Everyone imposes his own system as far as his Army can reach." History decided otherwise. Soviet political control of Eastern and East-Central Europe has been a historical parenthesis, being closed; nothing fundamental or lasting has been changed by it.

Because the Soviet Union's domination of Eastern and East-Central Europe contributed to the solution of the "problem" of Europe for the United States as well as the Soviet Union, closing that parenthesis will reopen for everyone questions to which they have given virtually no thought for forty years. East-Central, Eastern, and Balkan Europe is a region of unachieved nationalisms, unresolved ethnic tensions, challenged frontiers and irredentisms, out of which both world wars came. If Soviet-dominated Europe is reunited with Western Europe, which now seems sure eventually—and perhaps sooner than one thinks—Europe is changed in a fundamental way, and so is the American relationship to Europe.

The partition of Germany was the crucial geopolitical consequence of the Second World War—it was what the war, in the end, had been all about. If the Soviet presence now is removed from Central Europe, the question of Germany is again posed. Since its unification in 1871, Germany has been, by way of the two world wars it instigated, the main force acting on modern history. Without those wars, it is reasonable to think that there would have been no Russian Revolution, no Chinese Revolution, no Cold War, no American world role. What there would have been we cannot know.

Today is not yesterday, of course, and the terrible experiences the people of Central and Eastern Europe have undergone in the first half of this century—horrors unrivaled since the Thirty Years' War—have certainly altered political values and sobered national and ideological enthusiasms. Nonetheless, the simple material forces pushing an underdeveloped East toward the productive West are overwhelming. Western Europe has reemerged from its own period of postwar trauma and withdrawal. The recovery is economic much more than it is political, which is perhaps just as well, although the political life of the individual West European countries is vigorous and seriously conducted. The 1992 Single European Market, on its way in 1989, completes the work of the original Common Market and, on present trends, will make of Western Europe the richest, most populous, and most productive industrial community on earth. The harmonization of fiscal and monetary policy in the Community, pulling social policy after it, will produce a higher level of effective political integration than anyone has foreseen since the early and enthusiastic days of Jean Monnet. Western Europe's magnetism to the Europeans of the East will consequently be tremendous.

Mikhail Gorbachev's perestroika and "new thinking" in foreign policy, moreover, has sharply accelerated the return of Europe to what it was before by making evident the failure of the Soviet Union's attempt to change it. Old patterns of historical and cultural formation and commitment, which Stalin meant to suppress or kill, are now, again, dominant forces in a political situation of mounting change and real instabilities. Poland, Hungary, Czechoslovakia, and East Germany (formerly Saxony, Brandenburg, a part of Prussia), all are part of an ancient Central European civilization whose crucial attachments are to Western Europe: to Roman or Reformation Christianity, Renaissance thought and Baroque art, the Enlightenment, the experience of Romanticism. The Balkan states (Bulgaria, Romania, and also Greece, Albania, and Yugoslavia) are part of Eastern (or Southeastern) Europe, formerly under the domination of the Ottoman Empire, and before that, part of the Byzantine Eastern Roman Empire. The civilizations of Central and Eastern Europe, integrally linked to the civilization of Western Europe—Baroque variant to the Renaissance West, Byzantine variant to its medieval predecessor—were stifled and politically repressed for forty years but have never lost their connection to the West. As the Communist political and economic system imposed on the region in the 1950s falters, slipping into crisis, what always has existed there asserts itself with more and more force. The problem becomes what to do about the politically obsolescent, intellectually discredited, economically unworkable structure that has linked the eastern part of Europe to the Soviet Union. The structure of relations becomes increasingly dangerous precisely because it failed to work. It is, in 1989, the most serious problem in international affairs.

For a third of a century, the conduct of the international system rested upon a belief that neither the United States nor the Soviet Union wanted war, and that our rivalries, while irreducible in principle, were negotiable in practice. After Stalin, negotiations covered a great deal of ground. But diplomatic accommodation of East-West differences was helped by the fact that, once Europe was partitioned in the 1940s, not much was really at issue between the Soviet Union and the United States. It was possible, on both sides, to ignore the essential logic of the conflict. We struggled, of course, over the fate of the whole world, but that was not half so serious as the struggle over Greece had been in the 1940s, or the struggle over Berlin, while Stalin was alive. The diplomats could always defer settlement of the fate of the world; history would in any case see to it. But when the drama of glasnost and perestroika in the Soviet Union, and "new thought" on Soviet foreign relations, unsettled the inherently impermanent situation of East-Central, Eastern, and Balkan Europe, things became rather more serious—

and potentially more dangerous, although this is not widely recognized. The ostensibly closed issues of Central and Eastern Europe were reopened. Western Europe's economic and industrial resurgence is accompanied by a new sense of political possibilities, and a new assumption of strategic responsibilities, distanced from those of a United States no longer confident of its own direction. Fortune shows her power—as Machiavelli said—when no wise measures are taken to resist her. This is a warning.

Dead stars those ideas were, black holes in the intellectual firmament. During the years since 1988 they have continued to extinguish original thought. The policy conceptions and conventions of that earlier time have survived into the new century and new millennium largely unquestioned, despite the transformation during the 1990s of the international system, and the complacency with which they are held has been reinforced. They have distorted the nation's perception not only of the world abroad but of the American past, and of what our national past reveals about American possibility.

The American notion of special providence was fatefully reinforced by the disintegration of the Soviet system, which most American policymakers of the time were convinced constituted an international power in some sense equivalent to the United States itself, a dynamic threat to liberal democracy. That was an error which might have prompted subsequent reflection on how realistic the American conception was of the rest of the international scene, beyond the Soviet Union and the Warsaw Pact, but it did not. There was, instead, self-congratulation. The Soviet Union's self-induced collapse was audaciously appropriated as America's victory (Star Wars did it). There was no reappraisal of the degree to which we had collaborated for a half-century in a Russian millenarian fantasy, validating it by the scale and intensity of our response, turning the Russians' fantasy to the support of a certain millenarianism of our own, which survives.

The Soviet collapse reinforced America's international ambitions at a moment when internationalism seemed to be fading as a force in American opinion. The United States had become inextricably involved in the world, above all by commercial links, but during the Reagan years its government had increasingly resorted to overt or covert protectionism and trade unilateralism to defend its economic interests, and had launched its program to create a space-based missile defense system covering the North American continent, an ambition profoundly isolationist in conception and in emotional resonance.

The end of Soviet power encouraged Americans to think that history itself had validated American virtues and given the country a new mandate to improve the world, not by providing it with an edifying example, as once believed, but through action. The lack of interest in "schematic world reform" which I noted in the chapter vanished when there suddenly seemed an opportunity for just that. This revived international activism concerned Russia first of all, which was to be reformed according to American ideas and brought into a "strategic partnership"; this later was to become the aim with China as well. Germany's reunification, a development handled with skill and discretion by the Bush administration, suddenly made Central Europe a much more interesting place. It was decided that it should be incorporated into the American alliance system.

The Gulf War inspired Mr. Bush's seemingly ambitious promise of a New World Order, which the Clinton administration turned into a New Multilateralism, quickly abandoned for what should be called the New Unilateralism, antiseptically militarized, by which the United States fired cruise missiles into the Middle East, Central Asia, and the Balkans (at sometimes phantasmagoric targets), while usually keeping its land forces at a distance that guaranteed them against risk.

From this have come various formulations for a new hegemonism. NATO expansion is an expression of the concept, melding a muscular form of idealistic Wilsonian federalism with guiltless self-interest. The Pentagon has promoted a strategy of "preponderance" over any possible military rival or combination of rivals, while Congress has voted billions of dollars to continue the search for workable defensive missile systems and to prepare to counter what the president, his advisers, and various official commissions announced as dramatic new threats to the nation from electronic, bacteriological, chemical, and nuclear terrorism, wielded by rogue states or individual terrorist entrepreneurs, justifying ever greater efforts. The United States began the new millennium as the most heavily militarized nation on earth.

The political policy community debates the merits of "traditional leadership" or "multilateralism" as against global "primacism" (*hegemony* being excluded from the government's vocabulary). Confirmed in its self-esteem, proud of victory in the Cold War and the singularity of its power, Washington proclaims the United States the "indispensable nation," which "sees farther because it stands taller," to cite Secretary of State Madeleine Albright's description of the nation during her watch. One says "Washington" advisedly, since all this is primarily an affair of the governing and policy classes rather than of the public, relieved to be rid of the Cold War.

A note on the statistics of power. In 1989, in the discussion of China and the Pacific Basin in the original chapter, the following footnote appeared on what is page 6 of this edition:

Gross domestic product (GDP)—roughly speaking, the sum of the value of the goods and services produced in a country—is the standard statistical measure of the economic strength of a nation. In 1987, the most recent year for which internationally comparable figures were available at the time of writing, the GDP of South Korea was $121.31 billion; that of Taiwan, $80.42 billion; of Hong Kong (1986), $38.44 billion; and of Singapore, $20.20 billion, for a total of $260.37 billion. The GDP of the Netherlands in 1987 was $214.32 billion.

China's GDP is a disputed figure, generally placed by Western specialists at less than $500 billion. The International Institute for Strategic Studies estimates it at $293.57 billion for 1987. The 1987 GDP of France was $877.05 billion, and that of Britain, $609.69 billion. For comparison, the 1986–87 GDP of Japan was $2,119.6 billion and that of the U.S. in 1987 was $4,461.2 billion; the U.S.S.R. was estimated to be in the $1,800–$2,310 billion range; and the total figure for the European Community was $4,213.33 billion in 1987. Changing currency exchange rates artificially affect these comparisons from year to year, but the relationships above are grossly true. (Sources: International Institute for Strategic Studies, London, and Hong Kong government.)

The figures obviously are now out of date, but the comparisons are worth reviewing, using the latest edition of the same source used in 1989, the International Institute for Strategic Studies' authoritative annual, *The Military Balance.*

*The Military Balance* estimates in its 1999–2000 edition that China's GDP was $703 billion in 1998 (the latest year for which the figure could be calculated) as against the $293.57 billion given above for 1987. In 1987 American GDP was roughly 15 times the size of China's; in 1998 it is 12 times larger, although a high continuing growth rate is generally attributed to the Chinese economy. Japan's 1998 GDP of $3.8 trillion is 1.79 times its 1986–87 GDP of (roughly) $2.120 trillion.

The IISS figure for French GDP in 1998 is $1.4 trillion; France has also nearly doubled in economic size during the same period (even though the 1990s were a decade of very low growth in France, as in most of Western Europe). Its GDP remains approximately twice that (1.99 percent) of China's. For the United Kingdom, the 1998 GDP figure is $1.3 trillion. The ratios in economic power between China and each of these European states remain roughly what they were eleven years earlier—while China in 1998 had something like 21 times the population of each, up from 19.7 in 1987.

The power relationships have changed, but not by as much as often thought.

# 2 | THE CHALLENGE OF EUROPE

For four hundred years European civilization has dominated the world—for better or for worse. It is convenient, and flattering, for Americans to assume that this is all over; but it is very rash to do so. Although two European civil wars—world wars, since European wars become world wars—exhausted the European powers between 1914 and 1945, it cannot be concluded from that that Europe is finished. So long as intellectual and moral energy radiates from Europe, its preeminence is not over; and the evidence today is that Europe's dynamism, far from lost, is in fact intensifying.

European thoughts are not American thoughts. European assumptions, imaginings, and ambitions are not American. European beliefs about elite education and responsibility, classes and races and their relations, the defects of democracy as well as its virtues, the alternatives to democracy (unimaginable to Americans), the qualities of heroism, conquest, endurance—of pride, caste, sanctity: all these remain deeply un-American. That this is so, and has always been so, lies at the source of the American uneasiness with Europe that has marked both societies from the seventeenth to the twentieth centuries (nearly to the twenty-first); but since 1945 this has resolutely been ignored on both sides.

American ideas about Europe have often been complacent ones. The repudiation of Europe as a politically corrupt and dangerous civilization was at the source of the American Revolution, and a notion of Europe as a used-up civilization is at the intellectual and emotional roots of American political consciousness today. We rejected "dynastic Europe" in the eighteenth century, "imperialist

Europe" in the nineteenth century, and the Europe of "power politics" in the twentieth, at the time of Woodrow Wilson. Each time Europe nonetheless continued to dominate international affairs, and to generate the determining ideas of contemporary civilization—to our discomfiture, and sometimes to our sorrow.

After 1945, Americans felt confident that Europe had finally finished itself off. Since then, Americans have taken the West Europeans as intellectually and morally our followers. (After their experiences of 1914–18 and 1939–45, they were, for the most part, content to be so taken.) Western Europe was made our protectorate. Louis Heren, a former editor of *The Times* of London, has written of this period: "The United States became more than the first among equals. Generally speaking, it saw the European allies as so many Germanic tribes guarding the eastern glacis of the American empire. Levies were confidently expected to be sent to fight elsewhere, in Korea and even Vietnam . . . For almost a generation [the Americans] had grown accustomed to political as well as economic and military power, and they tended to regard Europeans as once Indians and Africans were regarded by their European colonial masters." We scarcely thought seriously about Central and Eastern Europe, where so much trouble has originated in modern times. Responsibility for that region was consigned to the Soviet Union—as we made plain at the time of the Hungarian Revolution in 1956, the building of the Berlin Wall in 1961, and the Czechoslovak Spring of 1968.

A fundamental difference between the United States and Western Europe arises from a different understanding of democracy. Americans really are democrats, however badly democracy is practiced; the national imagination does not run to any alternative. We obey the dictation of numbers, to the despair of American artists and intellectuals, who always lose to the masses, even when the mass market takes them up (or most of all when it does so). The Europeans are not levelers. They believe in elites, even if from time to time they rise up and murder them. There has been a European taste for abstract truths in disregard of practical consequences, while Americans like ideas for their practical use, and will even supply the ideas—as we often do in foreign policy—to justify what we have already decided that we want to do. Europeans believe in democracy—or, at least, in republican government—but they have considered the alternatives, and continue to do so, and that scandalizes Americans.

Europe is dangerous. If the United States goes wrong, we have, we think, a fairly clear idea of how we expect it to do so—apocalyptically, as befits the scale of the country, and no doubt democratically, carrying the national logic to the bitter end. The European possibilities are more subtle, and European history suggests that they would be more original. Americans should worry about Europe, and consider what the American relationship with Europe may become as the existing alliance weakens and change takes place in the relations of East to West inside Europe. The Europeans, whether we like it or not, count the most for the future security of the United States. They count because of their strategic position. They count because of their economic power, their population, their military potential, and their proven capacity for intellectual, scientific, and social innovation—for good and for bad. They count because Europe is the source of American civilization. They certainly count, in the long run, for more than Russia, even if something like a miracle takes place to transform the blocked and sterile Russian society of today. Indeed, Europe in the future may count for more than the United States. It has the more formidable historical record.

Europe is today possessed of quite exceptional strength, and a political as well as economic potentiality still ill-appreciated in the United States. Individually the West European countries are major economic powers, but collectively they are an industrial giant on a scale with the United States, more than two times the economic size of Japan, much larger than Japan combined with the rest of newly industrializing Asia. Potentially, in coalition, they make a military power of the first rank. The fortunes of this Europe have been uneven since the Coal and Steel Community Treaty—the origin of today's European Community—was signed in 1951. The oil shock of 1973 hit Europe hard, producing a lasting period of slow growth and high unemployment, both, however, diminishing as the 1980s advanced. This is not a book on economics and can scarcely attempt to deal with arguments over the relative quality and strengths of the European economies today, as compared with the American. However, most academic economists would have been likely to concede the argument made by Raymond Barre, former French prime minister and himself a university economist, that the European recovery after 1973 was a great deal more soundly based, albeit slower, than the American. There was more intelligent attention to the investment and technological base of sustained development than in the United States. European business decisions have not generally been driven by considerations of short-term stock-market return, as have those of American corporations. The work force in Europe generally possesses higher levels of education and skill than the American. Europe suffers ghettos of the immigrant poor, but by and large these are the working and ambitious poor, rather than a subproletariat that has fallen out of the job market (not to speak of the community itself), as is often the case in the United States. In most of the West European countries, and in the European Community institutions, there continue to be high levels of state support for basic research, unrelated or only indirectly related to military research, while American federal funding has mainly gone to military projects whose commercial interest is not always evident.

The Community's loss of political as well as economic momentum in the 1970s produced a period marked by what press and politicians called "Europessimism," but this changed with the decision taken by the Community nations in 1985 to eliminate all trade, tariff, and financial barriers within the Community by 1992. The boldness and ambition of this plan had an accelerating effect in the years that followed, and by the start of the 1990s had become probably the single most important factor in the political and economic decisions being made in the twelve Community states. Out of it came a series of new world-scale industrial groups, produced by merger under pressure of the competitive challenge of the 1992 deadline, some of them aggressively active on U.S. financial and commercial markets. The principle of a common European central bank as well as of a common currency, was generally accepted by 1988 (Britain's Margaret Thatcher the notable dissenter), implying an eventual convergence of social as well as fiscal priorities, and a rising level of political cooperation in the Community. It is important to note, moreover, that the Economic Community has demonstrated that it can function perfectly well as a loose political coalition (as well as within a loose security consensus). There does not have to be a "united states" of Europe, a federal government, for a powerful "Europe" to exist. What actually is happening is an organic political development driven by interest and need, more than by plan, whose final outcome is unpredictable. One of the chief reasons it is unpredictable is that the Community still is only a portion of Europe. Eastern Europe is equally Europe—starved for forty years of economic progress and consumer satisfactions, an immense market that also possesses a well-educated and technically sophisticated work force, whose addition to the West European Community could produce economic consequences far more explosive than anything that can reasonably be expected of the Pacific Basin, at least in the twentieth century.

Western Europe in 1989 is in a curious situation, and perhaps a very significant one. Passionate political controversy takes place over matters that usually amount to very little. Economics dominates the scene, and in the end the argument concerns how certain generally agreed-upon goals can best be achieved. It is really an argument for specialists. The nature of the society sought is not in serious question. There is surprisingly little difference among the major Continental parties on fundamental economic policy. The limits of nationalized enterprise are generally conceded, but it is still taken for granted that governments must be held responsible for employment and for public welfare. It is expected that health, employment, and retirement will be insured at levels that many Americans still find scarcely credible. The European governments have admitted the economic rigidities such policies produce and the Community has attempted to reduce them in the Single European Market. In countries such as Greece, Portugal, or Spain, where not all of these measures of social protection were feasible in the 1980s, they were nonetheless the accepted aim. Businessmen in the big corporations of Continental Europe tend not to see themselves as enemies of this consensus or as its victims; they defend their profits as the necessary index of efficiency for organizations whose raison d'être is the production of goods and employment for the common good. The entrepreneur is defended as neither less nor more than the supplier of a necessary commodity—risk capital. Virtually nowhere in 1980s Western Europe, with the qualified exception of Britain under Mrs. Thatcher, was there a major political party, even a businessmen's party, whose views on the economy, distribution of income, social insurance and welfare, and planning were not to the left of the Democratic Party in the United States.

For most of this century, what has set Europe off from the United States has been that both the constitutional foundations of European states and the goals of European societies have seemed provisional, open to challenge or even violent overthrow. From the downfall of the monarchies to the present day, Continental Europe has seemed in flux, in recurrent upheaval. There has been violence, revolutionary struggle, the recurrence of autocratic or dictatorial governments. There were nineteenth-century efforts by the middle classes to establish themselves against aristocratic and oligarchic power, and then a working-class struggle, articulated and led by socialists and Communists. Whatever social and economic turmoil Americans went through, our political system never seemed in doubt. Even the South justified its attempt to secede on constitutional grounds, saying that the sovereign rights of the states contracting to the original Union had been usurped by the federal authority. This difference in our histories is at the heart of a largely unconsidered but absolutely basic American perception of Continental Europe as entirely different from us—and as insecure, unstable, and somehow dangerous. It is not just the fact that we were drawn by Europe into two world wars that lies behind this perception. The whole political evolution of Europe over the last two hundred years contrasts with our own national experience.

But, of course, the European experience during these two centuries has been immensely creative and fruitful, and not simply violent. Americans have been in debt to this experience in deeper ways than we may recognize. The internal struggles of Europe, animated by revolutionary politics, defined modern expectations about what a political society and an economy could and should become. We Americans created our own version of egalitarian prosperity and an open society in our own way, making use of the advantages provided by an open frontier, great natural wealth, and an immigrant population possessing a necessary commitment to optimism and the possibility of progress. Perhaps our way was also Canada's, but it has been unreproducible outside North America. Even Australia and New Zealand, which enjoy similar social and geographical conditions, and are perhaps the most egalitarian societies on earth—and in that sense are much more "American" than America—became what they are by means of labor movements and parties patterned fundamentally on West European models. We Americans really seem to be the only truly nonsocialist society on earth.

It makes a fundamental difference between European society and that of the United States that Europe, in crucial ways that have nothing to do with managing the liberal economy, is hostile to the marketplace. Americans conscientiously submit a remarkable measure of public and even private life to the proposition that the market must arbitrate, and that it is impartial. Americans will usually claim that free enterprise and free political institutions are mutually indispensable. This would not only be rejected by virtually all on the European left, many of whom are likely to argue that the two are mutually hostile, but by European conservatives and much of the right as well. The American neoconservative intellectual groups that celebrated the Reagan administration for what they held to be its liberating marketplace liberalism are specifically and incommunicably American; they express a lasting factor in the alienation of the United States from Continental Europe—and, indeed, from nearly all of the rest of the world.

The American uneasiness with Europe as a whole has always had a moral component, in which the outlook of the two societies upon class and hierarchies is central. The American experience, accelerated since the 1950s, has been of dismantled hierarchies. The United States has never been a country of fixed classes, in the European sense, but there were nonetheless hierarchies that outlasted the first century and a half of national existence. The most ignoble was racial, but another was of values, in which a certain system prevailed, of Protestant religious origin and British legal and social origins. The United States was a Protestant, Puritan nation—entrepreneurial, unintellectual, middle class in outlook. Those who did not belong to the white Protestant ascendancy but wanted to succeed made themselves as much like it as they could—Booker T. Washingtons of every race.

In our time, the Protestant establishment has lost its authority. The Bush presidency was "Eastern" and "establishment" by virtue of the geographical and social origins of many of its members, but it represented no specific moral or intellectual authority or tradition that the rest of us acknowledge. The old establishment had included the national political elite, which dominated public affairs (although not politics) as late as the Second World War, when its members oversaw the development of an internationalist and interventionist foreign policy and the creation of the modern American institutions of foreign policy management. Since the war in Vietnam, which destroyed the confidence and predominant influence of this elite, the governing American apparatus of international policy has no longer possessed a recognizable class character. This circumstance is the most visible development in a national mutation that conservatives have described (quoting Robert Nisbet of Columbia University) as a "loss of confidence in political institutions . . . matched by the erosion of traditional authority in kinship, locality, culture, language, school, and other elements of the social fabric." Certainly we find ourselves in a situation we could not have expected even in the 1950s, when American life and government were still dominated by a Protestant gentry certain of its values.

The problem of elites is an old one for which Americans have found no solid answer. A generation ago, a Harvard or Yale president or a private-school head might well have been willing to defend the idea that hereditary service to society justified hereditary privilege. We have, after all, been proud of our Adamses, Jameses, Roosevelts. The American educator might have been willing to say much the same thing as a former head of France's Ecole Normale Supérieure: "Democracy needs an elite, to represent the only superiority it recognizes, that of the mind. It is up to us to recruit this elite." These sentiments are not likely to be heard today in the United States, and yet it is difficult to imagine what else can be said with conviction. An American elite exists: the people who possess power are, de facto, our elite. In an aristocratic system, or in a meritocracy assimilated to an aristocracy, as in the British case, or in the closed and formal French system of *grandes écoles* and *grands corps*, those who possess power are also aware of a corporate identification and obligation. Both in that respect are undemocratic elites, hostile to the values of the marketplace. This in the past was true of the American military, the closest to a corporate elite that has existed in the United States. George Marshall was its product, and his biographer notes his refusal of a million-dollar offer for his memoirs after the Second World War, motivated by his belief that one does not enrich oneself from public service. The contrast with what public life in Washington has since become needs no emphasis. The problem with a spontaneous, unstructured, and democratic elite, such as the American, in a time of fractured structures and a mutation of values, is that obligation and duty are at best professional. The criterion for membership in the elite is mere success in the climb, money-making, the morally neutral ability to perform. This is perhaps one reason that American government in recent years has not been entirely a success.

Tocqueville noted that "liberty is not the chief and constant object of their [the Americans'] desires; equality is their idol." Equality is not the European idol. It is not the idol even of European socialists. President Mitterrand in Paris, an intellectual of measured speech, product of an elite school, was not an egalitarian. Anthony Benn in Britain, born to become Viscount Stansgate, sometime left-wing challenger for the leadership of the Labour Party, claims to be an egalitarian. While it is possible to doubt that he really is one, it is also beside the point to do so, since his form of egalitarianism, like that of France, land of *égalité*, is doctrinal and normative, related to Marxism, and has nothing to do with mass man and mass values, and least of all with the dictates of the marketplace.

Americans are the egalitarians and levelers. We are so because we had compelling historical reasons to renounce national philosophical and religious dogmas and any fixed hierarchy of values. Our assumption is that—for practical purposes, at least—numbers make truth. Our national optimism permits this. "Americans . . . should be born with fins, and perhaps they were—perhaps money was a form of fin," Scott Fitzgerald wrote. "In England property begot a strong place sense, but Americans, restless and with shallow roots, needed fins and wings. There was even a recurrent idea in America about an education that would leave out history and the past, that should be a sort of equipment for aerial adventure." (This seems today to have been largely achieved.) Our optimism is the national vanity, the conviction that we can fly. It makes tolerable the costs of that undoubted and unstinted popular democracy that justifies our national existence.

Europeans, by contrast, are inclined to see in such airy optimism a submission, a failure of passion and of will, an abdication. Their faith in democracy is more qualified. An antidemocratic intelligentsia, making a principled case for inequality and authoritarian rule, existed in Europe long before a democratic intelligentsia, and survives into our democratic age, whereas in the United States it has been virtually unknown since Puritan theocratic days, or at least since Southerners ceased feeling compelled to rationalize slavery. Between the two world wars, there were probably more enemies, or critics, of democracy in Western Europe as a whole than there were defenders of it, for the system then seemed, even in Britain and France, politically and intellectually exhausted, and perhaps hopelessly corrupt as well—a system that "enriches only speculators, and leaves the destitute to stew in their destitution," Georges Bernanos wrote in 1941. It was, he added, "monstrous squandering of a huge productive achievement" of our civilization. Hence not only the defections to Communism of bright young men and women everywhere in Europe, from Cambridge to Budapest, before the war (and after), but equally the defections to Fascism—which were more numerous than it was convenient to remember after 1945.

The critique of capitalism made in Europe today is not actually very different from that which was made before the war, even though democracy and capitalism are now in incomparably better condition than they were during the 1920s and 1930s. The critique is neither the ideological nor the instrumental one—that these institutions do not work well enough—or it is that only as an afterthought. The critique is moral. The moral spectacle of capitalism still offends, as does American capitalism's implacable insistence that the market determine value even in the political, intellectual, and artistic spheres. The Europeans resist the fatalism of the market, which in its way is as monstrous a fatalism as that of racism. They regard the objectivity of the market as a disguise for an abdication of values and of intellectual independence. It is the same criticism that was made more than a century ago by Baudelaire, when he wrote in his notebooks that the ruin of republics follows from "the degradation of the human heart," which is the result of the "pitiless wisdom which condemns everything except money."

There was a debate in France in 1981 on the question of whether the French are inherently Fascist. A foreigner might think this is a frivolous charge to bring against a people commonly held to be turbulent and revolutionary, and who had that year—against the international tide—just voted in a socialist government. The author of the accusation, Bernard-Henri Lévy, was in fact saying that there is a definite tradition in France of "national revolution" based upon the belief in an "organic" society that is agrarian and hierarchical, hostile to individualism, cosmopolitanism, liberalism, and capitalism. He calls this Fascism—which is wrong. These ideas inspired France's Vichy government and provided theoretical justification for Francoism in Spain and the Salazar government in Portugal, certainly, but they were also the ideas of the left-wing poet and "saint" Charles Péguy, killed in the First World War; of a good many socially progressive Catholic intellectuals of the interwar years; and of others on the non-Marxist left. They may actually be described as conservative ideas, whereas Fascism proper is radical, not conservative, and is certainly not religious.

A related European criticism of democracy is aesthetic in origin (or motivated by class), expressing a fastidiousness about the claims of politics—or of those of the mass of men. This was the Bloomsbury attitude, summarized in E. M. Forster's remark that he hoped he would betray his country before he betrayed a friend. The sympathy for the right shown by Yeats, Lawrence, Pound, and some others in the interwar English (or London American-Anglo-Irish) literary scene stemmed from an essentially aesthetic revulsion against democracy and capitalism. Stephen Spender wrote years later that the politics of these men of the right "were projections of their hatred of fragmented modern civilization and the idea of 'progress.'" They were, in fact, reactionaries rather than Fascists, as the critic John R. Harrison has noted, and they falsely credited Fascism with being linked in some (concededly vulgar) way to the reconstruction of the "integral" civilization of the European past. They did not recognize Fascism as a radical and modern phenomenon. Their political ideas, Spender says, were attempts to

rationalize in a political way their aesthetic intuitions—"irresponsi-
ble attempts to be politically responsible." But virtually the same
thing could be said of the literary left—the Blunts, Spenders, Corn-
fords, and Day Lewises, Audens, and other intellectual Communists, both in England and on the Continent, during the same
period. They all, on left and right, also believed in heroism, in the
possibility of extreme change through intervention by what Rex
Warner called the "great leader," C. Day Lewis the "new healer,"
Auden "Him."

Bourgeois capitalism, in either case, was the enemy. Louis
MacNeice wrote with satisfaction in 1938 of an end to

> Conferences, adjournments, ultimatums,
> Flights in the air, castles in the air.
> The autopsy of treaties, dynamite under the bridges.
> The end of laissez faire.

Hostile as Americans always have been in principle to the existence
of formal or inherited class, it is only recently that the United States
has really discovered what it is to be a society without a recognizable governing class, and thus without that consensus on political
values which is implicit in the existence of such a class. This may be
of more lasting consequence to the country, as a political entity,
than the drastic recent changes in racial and ethnic makeup and
loss of linguistic uniformity. We have entered unmapped territory.
Democracy is deceptive; Britain and France, democracies certainly, societies Americans think most like our own, nonetheless
possess enduring structures of political class at the center of their
national lives.

This seemed most obvious in the case of Britain in the 1980s.
When Margaret Thatcher formed her first cabinet, in 1979, all but
one (besides Mrs. Thatcher herself) of twenty-one members were
the products of private boarding schools. Seventeen were educated

at Oxford or Cambridge, while three others had gone straight from "public school" into the Army or Royal Navy. There were in the cabinet five former members of the Brigade of Guards and two former officers of fashionable cavalry regiments. There were six Old Etonians, two Wykehamists, one Old Harrovian, one Rugby man. Five were barristers, two of them Queen's Counsel. There were three peers of the realm and three knights in the cabinet. Including appointments to the second rank of Mrs. Thatcher's government, there were, in all, fifteen peers. An editor of the Tory *Sunday Telegraph*, Peregrine Worsthorne, wrote that the Thatcher cabinet was "encouragingly full of hereditary peers, self-made and hereditary millionaires, wealthy landowners," and he also declared, "It is quite marvelously well-heeled. Most of its members have either made, married, or inherited splendid fortunes. Some are even the proud owners of great ancestral country estates. . . . Tory rhetoric in recent years tended to suggest that Socialism and egalitarianism had destroyed the old order beyond repair. . . . This is not quite the picture presented by the new Government." In fact, this cabinet was not so very different from the cabinet of Edward Heath, Mrs. Thatcher's predecessor as Tory prime minister, from 1970 to 1974. That, too, was a cabinet of barristers, stockbrokers, and bankers, ex-Guards officers and public-school men—although the incidence of inherited privilege was not as large as in the cabinet of Mrs. Thatcher.

One might object that this was at the start of Mrs. Thatcher's three terms or before; and that times have changed, as they have. Nonetheless, in August 1988 the conservative London *Sunday Times* could still remark on "the unpalatable fact . . . that the upper tiers of [Mrs. Thatcher's] government are stuffed with the products of educational privilege, quite unrepresentative of Tory voters at large or the country as a whole. The Conservative party may no longer be dominated, as it was 30 years ago, by a network of old landed families, but Tory position and influence are still too easily achieved on the playing fields of England's public schools. . . . Too many members of Britain's permanently ruling classes are still drawn from the overlapping circles of aristocracy, public schools and Oxbridge. Their outlook is out of keeping with the age in which we live and their values continue to ignore the vast forces at work in the world around them. They may not seem like magic circles to those within them. But they remain a row of zeros for those with talent but no inside track. Who can doubt that the old Establishment is still there, broodingly potent if no longer all-powerful? Examples abound in politics, the professions and business."

The survival in British politics and power of an upper-class elite is a phenomenon setting Britain apart from both America and Continental Europe. During the last two hundred years this elite has only occasionally yielded power, always able to return, assimilating to itself talent from outside and below—as with Mrs. Thatcher and Mr. Heath, both of lower-middle-class origins—compromising with the times and with change so as to give up what has to be ceded in order to save the essential. It has been an elite of honorable service as well as of privilege, willing to lead and die in Britain's wars, ambitious for the country and doing well for it, on the whole, but also doing well from it and, by its hereditary character and claim to privilege, serving as a cause of bitterness and alienation—perpetuating Britain's divisions, limiting its possibilities. This has been the most enduring elite in Europe, strong because it is, properly speaking, a meritocratic governing class assimilated to a hereditary aristocracy and to the values of that aristocracy. Those values are essentially agricultural, anti-industrial, anticapitalist; the social ideal is the landowning gentleman.

The ethos is profoundly seductive, and not least to Americans. Its seductive power comes in part from a style acquired over decades, when survival was connected to lack of sentimentality. The novelist Simon Raven has spoken of "the steely self-sufficiency, the boundless ability to overlook the feelings or welfare of others, that is perhaps the purest characteristic of the upper class." That puts it cruelly; but there is no cant in these circles, and that is a factor in their attraction for Americans. In a puritan democracy, ruthlessness is usually cloaked in sentiment and cant. For Americans, intimately involved with British civilization yet always separate, the antipathy to capitalism of British aristocrats is also an unexpected attraction. It is an ethos opposed in significant ways to modern times, about which Americans perhaps know too much. This upper class deserves to be called brilliantly modern, having not only survived but triumphed over every democratic threat to its existence. Its survival, though, comes from an instinctive manipulation of powerful and traditional national images of landscape, succession, family, hierarchy, and ritual. The effect on British life has been to perpetuate an Arcadian illusion, and to mask necessary choices, by sustaining for the British what Julian Moynahan calls "an idea of themselves as indeed a people with immemorial rural roots and of a spiritual disposition that is at home among tall trees, clear streams, hunting fields and sheepfolds, ricks, roses, and hedgerows." This in the country that invented the dark satanic mill.

But the meaning of class in Britain is dangerous ground for an American, and one should simply insist upon the evident minimum: that there is an identifiable upper class in Britain with an aristocratic ethos and a hereditary base, although open to talent, not closed; that this class perpetuates itself through certain institutions, of which primogeniture and the public school are the most important; and that this class has proved itself to be of lasting political importance, with durable links to power and money. It is an intelligent and able upper class. Its aristocratic French, Italian, and German equivalents have lost power because they were incompetent, stupid, or possibly unlucky. To be a marquis in France or a baron in Germany today arranges marriages, affords invitations to parties with others bearing titles, provides the odd business introduction or invitation to earn fees decorating someone's board of directors; it may imply inherited wealth, but it provides no serious and sustained link to political power. A French nobleman's social card carries his title; his business card does not. Industrial and economic power in Continental Europe is held by a business class that survives on merit. In politics, a West German, French, or Italian cabinet composed mainly of aristocrats, bankers, former officers of fashionable regiments, and graduates of a small group of socially exclusive secondary schools is simply inconceivable today. It is as absurd an idea as an American presidential cabinet made up of graduates of Groton and St. Mark's, ex-Knickerbocker Greys, members of the *Social Register.* But the analogies fail. The United States does not have institutions equivalent to the British public school and the good regiment. Harvard and Yale will not do. Perhaps seventy-five years ago there could have been a comparison, a limited one.

This is not, of course, the only British elite. The Labour Party includes public-school men in its leadership, but, like the mainstream parties of Continental Europe and the political parties in the United States, it also finds its leaders in local government, the trade unions, the universities and middle-class intelligentsia, business, law. Neil Kinnock is a product of the Welsh middle class. Harold Wilson was an Oxford don before entering politics, but his origins are in the provincial professional classes as well. James Callaghan's father was a petty officer in the Royal Navy who died when Callaghan was nine. While Clement Attlee, the first postwar Labour Prime Minister, was a public-school man, a barrister, and the son of a solicitor, the Labour government that preceded his, before the war—Britain's first Labour government—was led by Ramsay MacDonald, who was the illegitimate child of a farm housekeeper and a head plowman, and was educated in a Scottish village school and in the trade unions.

It thus would be false to argue that Britain is dominated by a certain class. There is no lack of mobility or economic openness in the society as a whole or in the parties. In business, in intellectual life and the schools, in the professions and the press, things are much as they are in all the other modern industrial societies. The

Tory Party itself is a middle-class party, resembling the center-right parties elsewhere in Europe, and the policies it defends are wholly in the West European mainstream. What is unique in this party is its attachment to the rural, aristocratic ethos and its alliance with a hereditary social class. Here is the problem. Since a hereditary class and the Tory Party are allied, the Tories' turns in national leadership tend to divide rather than reconcile. There is a sizable part of the British public that simply refuses to concede legitimacy to a leadership linked to a hereditary elite. It is inherent in the existence and nature of this class to divide. Its essential claim—to be apart, different from the others—rests historically and morally upon the belief in an inherited hierarchy of duty and privilege that democratic Britain has formally renounced. But, then, that puts it too strongly. The hereditary peerage in 1989 still has a constitutional role in British government, however attenuated. The peculiar symbolic force of the honors system is to associate with the hereditary nobility those commoners who have earned the state's gratitude, thereby reinforcing the position of the former.

The English elite's success in maintaining its link to domestic power was accompanied by, possibly even connected with, a willingness—a need, it has even seemed—to yield Britain's external power position to the United States in the first place, and to its former colonies. While the French have battled to reclaim a global political and strategic standing lost during the war (so that today they are the world's third-ranking nuclear and naval power), have kept their Pacific possessions, and have remained the principal non-African political presence in Africa, Britain not only yielded its imperial position with precipitation—destructively so in the case of India's summary partition, and in East Africa—but has insisted on giving priority to a transatlantic link that even now keeps it isolated within the European Community. This is paradoxical, for polls indicate a far closer commitment to Europe among the British public than conservative governments have been willing to concede. Indeed, Britain in 1945 could have had the leadership of Europe for the asking. Its government did not want it. Not only had the British incarnated the cause of war against Nazism from the start, but (as the historian John Lukacs writes) no one, "the exile governments in London, the resistance groups across the Continent, indeed, no one who opposed Hitler, doubted that Britain would be a great power after the defeat of Germany, that she would play a great role in the affairs of Europe. . . . Even Stalin believed this." The British, or perhaps it was the governing elite of Britain, were the ones who did not believe in such a destiny. This fact has been heavy with consequence.

There was, to be sure, an obvious economic factor in Britain's post-1945 political retreat. It was not that something drastically changed in its national performance; growth after 1945 was somewhat quicker than between the two world wars. Other European countries simply moved faster and accomplished more, and this made an eventual difference, so that Britain fell from being the leading European economic power to a middle rank, surpassed by West Germany, France, and probably by Italy (there is a question about the size of Italy's underground economy). During this period the other West Europeans all dealt with equal or worse material challenges than Britain's, so that it seems to follow that the British rejection of the leadership offered it by postwar Europe represented a political or moral faltering, a crisis of will, even now unmastered.

Britain's policy since the 1940s has been to ally that nation to the United States at virtually any cost. As early as 1940 Lord Lothian, wartime ambassador to the United States, was speaking of the need "to yield up the sceptre to America." British interests repeatedly have been subordinated to American when the two conflicted. This had undoubted justifications in the Second World War, but the impulse to abdicate to the United States seems to have antedated not only the 1940s but even the First World War. It is a curious affair, whose consequences for Britain, for the United States, and for all of Europe remain inadequately appreciated. Elie Halévy, in his *History of the English People in the Nineteenth Century*, argues that it came as a result of the Spanish-American War's impact on British popular feeling. The government and the Tory Party were hostile to the United States' attack upon Spanish power in Cuba and the Philippines, as were the Continental European great powers. But popular opinion in Britain, and especially nonconformist Protestant opinion, enthusiastically backed the United States in what was seen as a crusade by a Protestant and progressive power against supposed Spanish obscurantism and papist oppression. Popular feeling compelled Britain to align itself with the United States, against the Continental nations, and afterward, says Halévy, the British government and press never "departed from the attitude, now definitely adopted, of deliberately courting the friendship of the American government and people."

Yet one looks for something more subtle than a mobilization of Protestant bigotry as reason for this change. Consider, as evidence, that when the young Cecil Rhodes, already wealthy from the South African diamond fields, wrote his first will in 1877, he wanted a secret society established to bring the United States back under the British Crown. His object (according to the 1911 edition of the *Encyclopaedia Britannica*) was "nothing less than the governance of the world by the British race." Two decades later, in his last will, establishing the Rhodes Scholarships, he wrote that he sought to promote understanding among the great powers so as to "render war impossible," and thus he offered Oxford scholarships to Germans. Americans were offered the scholarships so they might acquire "an attachment to the country from which they have sprung, but without, I hope, withdrawing them or their sympathies from the land of their adoption or birth." Thus the archimperialist.

What was happening during the quarter-century between 1875 and 1900 to account for Rhodes's change of heart? The Boer War was in progress from 1899 to 1902, dividing opinion in Britain in a way not unlike the division Americans experienced over Vietnam. Kitchener's victory at Omdurman and the subsequent extension of Anglo-Egyptian control to the Sudan took place in 1898. Nonetheless, imperialism had passed its historical peak, and with it the unquestioned conviction that the British race was destined by God to rule the better part of the world in the world's own best interests. Max Beloff, in his history of the "liberal Empire," identifies this as the period of the "weary titan." But there is suggestive evidence of another kind of fatigue—or doubt—at the end of the century. Raffles, "the gentleman cracksman," was a figure of the popular fiction of the time; the first volume of the stories appeared in 1899. Contrary to what most people today assume, Raffles was a traitor to his social and moral origins, who deliberately had given up the role of "gentleman" for crime. A public-school man, he became a thief, betraying the confidences of friends and of his social class, not for ideological reasons or out of political motivations, not to right injustices or give to the poor, but because he liked excitement, money, and leisure. The author, E. W. Hornung, makes no bones about this. Raffles might be called the Philby or Blunt of his day, yet his adventures were immensely popular.

It is difficult to adduce a satisfactory explanation or even provide comprehensive evidence for this kind of change. One must simply state what seems to be true: that Britain's elite, for whatever reason or reasons, passed a certain peak of self-confidence and self-assurance during the late nineteenth century. Moral subversives, such as Raffles, were admitted and admired. The old imperial confidence was undermined. People stopped believing in a British right to dominate and educate others. T. E. Lawrence, a few years later, in wartime Arabia, was not an imperial romantic but a modern one. He was helping the Arabs make their "own" revolution, and he tortured himself afterward that British and French political interests had subverted the outcome and that what was to have been an independent Hashemite kingdom was divided into mandates under British and French rule.

In 1914, the start of the First World War, a sense of passage, of loss, existed in Britain that was only to be confirmed by the calamitous social and human losses that the war began to inflict upon the whole of European civilization. D. H. Lawrence, no Tory romantic to mourn the loss of rural England or of Empire, nonetheless wrote: "When I drive across this country, with autumn falling and rustling to pieces, I am so sad, for my country, for this great wave of civilization, 2,000 years, which is now collapsing, that it is hard to live. So much beauty and pathos of old things passing away and no new things coming: this house—it is England—my God, it breaks my soul—their England." There is something anomalous about this sense of a disintegrating civilization and a lost generation, as if the war were really gratifying what had for a long time been anticipated. T. C. Worsley, the critic, writes of a seeming death wish evident in Rupert Brooke, who said in a letter shortly before he died: "I really think that large numbers of people don't want to die . . . which is odd . . . I've never been quite so happy in my life." Worsley argues that this impulse was at the source of that exaltation in Brooke's poems which made him a national hero, thanking the God who had "matched them with this hour."

The explanation of the lost generation of 1914–18 can even today be heard as an explanation for Britain's European retreat and its need to depend upon "young" America. Yet Britain did not lose a generation. In the First World War, Britain suffered approximately one million killed and missing, the equivalent of 2.4 percent of the population. That was undoubtedly a ghastly shock to the society. But Germany suffered more than two and a half million men killed, dead of disease, or missing in the war. That was nearly 5 percent of the German population. What is more, the Germans were defeated, and saw the Wilhelmine state and economy collapse. France suffered fatalities amounting to 3.4 percent of the population, and the worst of the war was fought on French soil. It was calculated that in the first year of the war a French soldier had one chance in three of being killed and virtually no chance at all of escaping without a wound. Russia lost about twice as many men as Britain in the period between 1914 and the peace arranged at Brest-Litovsk in March 1918. All these nations were traumatized by their losses. France spent the 1930s in a coma, the 1940s broken and shamed, but, having touched bottom, recovered dynamism and confidence in the 1950s and 1960s. The Russian and German reactions after 1918 were politically frenzied, leading up to the Second World War, in which those two nations again lost most.

It would seem reasonable to think that the First World War was so traumatic for Britain's leadership because so many of the casualties were young men of education and promise from the elite itself. The first year of the war was a catastrophe for the landed, titled, and professional families of the country, whose sons rushed from public schools to the front in an intoxication of patriotism. For a time it seemed that all of them were being wounded or killed. Britain did not impose conscription until 1916, and a consequence of this was that the ardent went first. The national memory was of all the best shockingly and suddenly gone. Those who survived, or who followed, felt guilty for being alive. Even as sensible a man as George Orwell, who was fifteen and at Eton the year the First World War ended, said afterward that his "generation must be marked for ever by the humiliation of not having taken part." The experience of the war was eloquently articulated by the survivors, Siegfried Sassoon, Robert Graves, Henry Williamson, and David Jones, as well as by the nonsurvivors—among them Brooke, Wilfred Owen, Isaac Rosenberg. The Armistice, wrote Graves, "sent me out walking alone along the dyke above the marshes of Rhuddlan . . . cursing and sobbing and thinking of the dead."

A quarter-century later, British strategy and generalship in the Second World War displayed the most extreme caution about casualties—a hoarding of manpower and an avoidance, as far as was possible, of really large-scale battle. There were to be no more Sommes, no more Passchendaeles. To bring the United States into the war and build up an overwhelming superiority against the Germans before any counterattack upon the European continent was Churchill's fundamental policy from the start. That policy was rational, inevitable. But the question to be asked is whether the price that was paid, in subordination to U.S. leadership, was not, in the end, too much. Britain's fatalities in the Second World War were only 360,000. Yet afterward it was Britain itself that was commonly understood to be the national casualty.

The comparison with France is illuminating, because the ruling elites there have a different origin, and their conduct of national policy contrasts sharply with Britain's in the postwar era. Until the eighteenth century the French historical inheritance was much more narrowly monarchical, absolutist, and aristocratic than the British. The revolution of 1789 ended a regime and the power of the aristocracy, but important institutions and characteristics of the *ancien régime* survived, and continue to survive, under new names. France today, under its Fifth Republic, even governed by the left, can be said to remain in crucial respects an authoritarian, quasi-monarchical government, its aristocracy laicized, and its authoritarianism subordinated to elections, law, and the ultimate sanction of revolution. Government is dominated by a civil service that is sure of itself and aristocratic in its assumptions of both duty and privilege. Theodore Zeldin, in his Oxford history of modern France, speaks of "benevolent despotism, modernized by meritocracy, democratized by the public-opinion poll and a broadened social conscience, but remaining firmly seated in the old traditions of centralization and bureaucracy." France's lay aristocracy, formed in a group of special schools—the *grandes écoles*—manages the major private as well as state enterprises and holds a leading position in the country's political parties as well as its intellectual life.

Since Napoleon, the French government has been dominated by certain *grands corps* of the civil service: inspectors of finance, counselors of the Cour des Comptes (inspectors-general of the government's accounts and functioning) and of the Conseil d'Etat (its highest legal officers), and members of the diplomatic service. The power of these *grands corps* has not, however, come simply from their institutional functions. Detached from duty within the corps, their members have over the years colonized the rest of the civil service, acquiring quasi-formal control over major agencies and functions throughout the government. Together with the important engineering and scientific corps, they run most of the things worth running in French government. They lead ministers' cabinets, control key departments within ministries, advise the prime minister and the president. Since 1945, they have run the nationalized companies—energy, aerospace, transportation, communications, major manufacturing groups. They often leave the state service for high appointments in private industry, keeping up informal but effective links with the government's managers and planners. The French state and economy are dominated by this elite, and the advent of the left in 1981, and its subsequent return to power, did little to change this.

Nearly all of France's important younger politicians are members of this elite, products of a single, formal, meritocratic system of education and state service. President François Mitterrand was a graduate of the Institut d'Etudes Politiques (known as "Sciences Po"). His first prime minister, in 1981, Pierre Mauroy, was of working-class origins, but nearly all of the other main members of that and subsequent socialist cabinets were educated at the *grandes écoles*. The prime minister named by President Mitterrand in 1988, Michel Rocard, attended the Ecole Nationale d'Administration (E.N.A.) and Sciences Po, as did his conservative predecessor, Jacques Chirac. The prime minister before Chirac, Laurent Fabius, who was in office from 1984 to 1986, was the product of not one but three *grandes écoles*. Although there have been individual Communists in what has come to be sardonically described as the *énarchie,* the Communist intelligentsia as a whole tends to be drawn from the universities, such as the Sorbonne, which since the Second World War have played only a secondary role in French higher education. Of the other leaders of the governments that preceded Mitterrand's presidency, former president Valéry Giscard d'Estaing attended the Ecole Polytechnique (founded in the eighteenth century) and E.N.A., and former prime minister Raymond Barre was a graduate of Sciences Po and later a member of its economics faculty.

Ambitious young men or women in France thus have a straight course before them—if they know how to pass examinations. The national school system prepares students for the nationally administered *baccalauréat* examinations. The entrance examinations for the *grandes écoles* follow. (There is, practically speaking, open admission to the universities for those with their "bac.") Success in a *grande école* leads to a place in one of the *grands corps* of the civil service and a life's career in the governing elite of France. It is systematic, logical, inevitable. It is, in principle, egalitarian, although it is not democratic. Those who succeed must be talented in taking formal written and oral examinations. These usually are young people from cultivated backgrounds, with parents willing to inspire and sustain the kind of study needed. Special measures by the Mitterrand government to favor admission to E.N.A. of older candidates with civil service, local government, and union backgrounds changed little that is essential. The Ecole Polytechnique, with its emphasis on engineering and mathematics, tends to be more democratic. Money always is a help, since private preparatory courses have sprung up to give people with their *baccalauréat* an extra year or two's polish for the *grande école* examination, but it is not decisive. A prosperous family, ambitious parents interested in education, residence in Paris, where the best *lycées* are—all these are advantages. But in practice as well as in principle the system is open to the ambitious child of peasants or workers. More important, it is generally believed to be open. Education in France is free (or even salaried, at its higher reaches) from nursery school to graduation from E.N.A.—for the student who can make it to the end. Neither poverty nor lack of social standing is, in principle, an obstacle to success.

This provides the key to understanding the position of France's elite. Max Gallo, writer and socialist politician, sometime official spokesman for the Mitterrand government, argued in 1979 that the system of examinations is crucial to the elite because it is this which confers upon them their legitimacy: "The elite is in fact recruited on merit, at the end of a series of major competitions that assume symbolic value. These constitute both implacable rites of initiation (preparation demands endurance and a true asceticism) and signs of equality of opportunity—in which the best succeed. An elite so recruited is perceived to be legitimate and indeed believes itself legitimate. Its self-image is positive. Its members have been tested and proved. The responsibilities they exercise are in the name of the state and the service of the public. This elite knows itself to be, and wants itself to be, incorruptible. . . . It considers itself indispensable. . . . And the fact that many in the political opposition come from the *grands corps* enhances the legitimacy of the elite in the eyes of the majority."

Legitimacy is the crucial element. With legitimacy, the French elite, unlike the British, unifies rather than divides. Clearly, it is resented and criticized; but it is not, in itself, of a specific political character, and its enemies do not attack it as automatically representative of one element in French society in conflict with another. The ordinary Frenchman does not see himself reflected in the elite, in the way an American might see the civil service in Washington as broadly representative of American society, but he does not see it as a body of the left or the right. This elite has placed itself outside, or beyond, that categorization. The criticism justifiably made of this elite, other than pride—its failures, from Indochina to the Concorde, have consistently been the result of pride—is that it is an exclusive and closed system. Gallo sarcastically calls its members "the immortals." What if they really were not competent, not useful, he asked in that 1979 article. "Who can pose such questions when from one end of the political horizon to the other the only people to testify are members of the same club?"

There is another class, another elite, that comes to mind when one is considering the modern French ruling class. It was described by Ford Madox Ford when he wrote of certain pre-1914 Englishmen who governed not only an empire but much more: "If they saw policemen misbehave, railway porters lack civility, an insufficiency of street lamps, defects in public services or in foreign countries, they saw to it, either with nonchalant Balliol voices, or with letters to *The Times,* asking in regretful indignation: 'Has the British This or That come to this!' Or they wrote, in the serious reviews of which so many still survived, articles taking under their care, manners, the Arts, diplomacy, inter-Imperial trade, or the personal reputations of deceased statesmen and men of letters." This was a group quite distinct from the aristocracy. It, too, was a civil service, or an imperial service, drawn mainly from the gentry, the middle classes, but with a certainty of its right to govern, a confidence in its ability to govern, comparable to that which the French elite today possesses. These people had much the same reason for confidence. They were certain of their education, their ability, their integrity and disinterestedness.

There still is, of course, an imposing civil service in Britain, but the role of the class Ford describes has shrunk, politically and morally, in the years since the First World War, while the equivalent group in France has, by virtue of reform in its selection and training, and the extension of state power in the economy, greatly expanded. The social class in France that is the equivalent of the British aristocracy has meanwhile, since the nineteenth century, been effectively cut off from corporate political power. The comparison of these situations is inevitably invidious. It is meant to illuminate how certain fundamental problems in two traditionally hierarchical European societies have been met. France has recreated an aristocracy on the severe basis of meritocratic selection. There certainly are costs, but the result is congenial to the French and is socially and politically unifying. In British political life, the class issue persists.

The fact that the French elite is a popular rather than a class elite reflects French convictions about the centrality of French culture itself to the development of Western civilization, and about the creative radiation of French language and culture to the non-Western world. This is a form of nationalism (or internationalism) that has aroused hostility among the Americans and British, and others as well, since the time of France's real political and cultural primacy in Europe, in the eighteenth century. If contemporary Britain has been obsessed by a need to abdicate unwanted or unsustainable responsibilities, France with an equal obsession has claimed a place in world affairs that neither the United States nor France's fellow Europeans have been prepared to concede as really deserved. The American suspicion of France has roots in the American rejection of eighteenth-century monarchy, but also in national rivalry. American resistance to General Charles de Gaulle as France's wartime leader in the 1940s derived from the conviction that he represented a discredited conservative and nationalist past; his vocabulary of French tradition and glory grated upon Americans, who thought it could not be serious. Franklin Roosevelt thought him simply a reactionary émigré politician, or an adventurer. Americans embraced Jean Monnet after the war because he offered to create a "united states" in Europe, on the American precedent. De Gaulle remained an "archaic" figure to the American press and to American policymakers until the day of his death, stubbornly held by Americans to be a man of the past. It is persistently the French who are the irritants in European-American relations. Throughout the postwar years, American relations with Europe have been qualified or challenged by what might be called the French dissent.

The British conceded American leadership long before 1945. For defeated Germany and the smaller countries of Northern Europe, American primacy was fairly easily accepted, inevitably for the former, a form of insurance for the latter. Relations were eased by the fact that American society and culture are predominantly the product of Protestant Europe. With the Catholic Europeans, on the other hand, and most of all with the French, there has always been tension. For Americans, as for the Protestant Northern Europeans, Latin civilization has undeniably been seductive, but it has also been disturbing, containing alternative values and affirming certain aspects of life that we have chosen to repress. There is a tension that is an accompaniment to the attraction felt toward this alternative way of life—"that yearning," as Kenneth

Clark puts it in his autobiography, "for the long tradition of Mediterranean life, unbroken, in spite of disasters, for over two thousand years, that has fascinated Northern man since Goethe." One way by which we Americans, as well as the British, have been able to reassure ourselves as to the validity of our own values and way of life, as these have seemed challenged by the sensuality and continuity of the South, has been to regard the virtues of Latin civilization as paid for by political and technological failure or backwardness. Latin Europe is considered politically incompetent, plagued by dictators, divided by class struggle, simply not very good at practical and modern things. Much of the region remains agricultural. Only in the Latin part of Western Europe were there postwar Communist parties with important followings and a real effect upon national life. If these people were genuinely democratic and politically competent, Americans have been inclined to argue, the Communist parties would never have taken root. We are willing to concede a warmth of human relations in the South, an acceptance of sensuality denied the Protestant and ex-Protestant North, and a powerful aesthetic and artistic tradition, but we reassure ourselves that the Latins pay for this by backwardness in important things that define modern life. It would be too much if they were to possess an acceptance of sensuality and progressive technology, too.

This, of course, is another reason the French have been a challenge. They are a major, innovative, technological power. Their economy is rich. They are a successful democracy. An Englishwoman in Nancy Mitford's 1960 novel *Don't Tell Alfred* says of France: "Have you noticed it's just those very things the English pride themselves on most which are better here? Trains: more punctual; tweeds: more pretty; football: the French always win. Doctors: can't be compared, nobody ever dies here until they are a hundred. . . . The post, the roads, the police—France is far better administered." The British ambassador's wife replies, "It isn't fair. You've got these things all ready to trot out, and I suppose facts and figures to bolster them up if I begin to query them. Before I see you next I shall do a bit of prep, but for the moment my mind is a blank."

This is exactly the Anglo-American problem with the French. They implacably refuse to be backward, "Latin," or patronized. They practice a defiantly individual form of politics, whether Gaullist or socialist. They insistently go their own way, competently, being rude about it, evoking impatience, scorn, and sometimes fury from Americans—and from most other Europeans, who do not love the French at all, and to whom French intransigence has often seemed selfishly destructive of European cooperation. The French have never been popular, however admired they may be for their intelligence, their style of life, their painting and writing, their good food, the celebrated chic and beauty of their women. "Happy as God in France" was a German expression of the nineteenth century, but that did not mean that the Germans much liked the French. They are not an altogether likable people. They themselves hardly notice this, since they do not notice a great deal of what goes on outside France.

The French (the polls of recent years suggest) have a low opinion of American political competence and of "the American way of life." That is nothing new among Europeans. It does not mean a condemnation of American society as a whole—which, in fact, has deeply affected the French, from the American Revolution, which antedated their own (with Tom Paine and Benjamin Franklin lionized in Paris), to the present day, when American intellectual life and popular culture continue to exercise a powerful influence upon the French imagination. They nonetheless insist upon seeing American culture and civilization as distinct and alternative to their own. While other Europeans since the Second World War mostly have been content to accept America at the evaluation Americans themselves are inclined to set—as the "postmodern" society, model for the world, or social laboratory for mankind—the French insist upon the relevance and validity of their own model, their own definition of what the future will be.

Here, of course, is the real source of tension between us. One civilization that has been expanding, and confident of its missionary significance to the world, confronts another that insists upon its moral and intellectual self-sufficiency. A civilization for which optimism has been a historical necessity confronts a civilization of quite remarkable pessimism. But this can be deeply misleading. The pessimism of the French is deliberately cultivated, a precautionary device that actually conceals a passionate sense of national destiny. The public pessimism of French life and the gloom with which the French discuss their affairs and prospects have remarkably little effect on the decisions taken in professional and public life. The French do not act as if things will go badly; they act as if things must be made to go well, even while they declare to the world that things will turn out badly. This is an aspect of the "realism" of the French. Anyone who does not say that he expects the worst risks being thought a victim of illusion, innocent of experience.

The optimism of Americans has always disturbed the French. It bothers them, but it also attracts them. They feel an envy of it even while they mock and distrust it. They have also secretly wondered whether this American optimism might not, after all, be justified. American society has somehow appeared to be exempt from the restrictions that are the fate of other societies. To the French, the material evidence seems impressive. French shopkeepers and housewives of an age to remember will still tell Americans what it was like when our army arrived, profligate with equipment and amenities. Americans are optimists, they say, because with such riches to squander, what bad could happen to America? France in 1944 was still more agricultural than industrial; and after years of occupation, war, rationing, and substitutions it undoubtedly seemed even poorer than it really was. And there were all those rosy-cheeked, milk-drinking G.I.'s, trucking hot showers, orange juice, movies, unlimited chocolate and cigarettes, Betty Grable and Marlene Dietrich, along with them as they swept across the country. To the French, as to most other Europeans who saw them, they seemed a force of nature—a new kind of man, from a new kind of country, from a new world, or possibly not from this world at all.

What was not evident to Europeans in such a meeting with a mechanized America was the darkness in Americans' own self-perception, our vulnerability to a sense of national incompleteness as we constantly change our lives, our lack of inner security when our optimism begins to seem unfounded or betrayed. Our optimism is perhaps a necessary compensation for a pervasive insecurity, which derives from the physical and economic origins of American society—first on the frontier and then in immigrant life in cities. Hardly suspected in Europe is the profound and sometimes anarchic pessimism that this insecurity can inspire in us.

Europeans, and particularly the French, have never been troubled by this peculiarly American kind of doubt. The French have admired American power, confidence, and even, perhaps grudgingly, American world leadership. But they have always believed that in important respects they live better lives than we do. They believe that as a civilization they count in the world—more than we do. They really believe in what a former minister, Alain Peyrefitte, has called their "strange vocation to be exemplary." The confidence of the French in the power and importance of their own high culture has never been shaken. Unlike the British—and certainly unlike the Germans, still haunted by the barbarism that erupted within their culture—the French have since the war felt no fundamental doubts about their manner of thought and of life. However divided they have been by politics and ideology, or by the experiences of 1940 and Vichy, they have not doubted the ends to which their social institutions are devoted. They are intensely critical of their national behavior but not of their values. There is no hesitation over the relentless emphasis in French schools upon mathematics and clarity of expression, the severe demands made upon children. The French would say that the realism of their culture is expressed exactly in an unhesitating acknowledgment of a hierarchy of intelligence and ability as well as of accomplishment. In his famous study *Village in the Vaucluse*, Laurence Wylie of Harvard noted: "It took time for me to become accustomed to the honest, objective manner in which parents openly appraised the intelligence of their children. They recognize the fact that some people are more intelligent than others, and since it is a fact it must be recognized, faced and accepted like all other facts. They see no point in hiding it, or denying it, or even in minimizing it. One cannot hide what is perfectly evident to everyone, and little purpose would be served in minimizing it. It is better to accept such facts as they exist and to try to make the most of them. Consequently, parents, teachers and children discuss differences in intelligence with relative frankness. When a parent says, 'My child is not so intelligent as yours,' he is not fishing for a compliment; he is stating a fact." To most Americans, an intensely selective school system, whose examinations can settle the fate of a child at an early age, may seem both ruthless and reactionary. To the French, the American hostility to anything that formally acknowledges or ratifies a hierarchy of natural intelligence or talent seems a matter of absurd sentimentality and unwillingness to face facts. The difference in national outlook is basic.

But Americans are different from everyone else in the world—except the Canadians, and Americans are more different from the Canadians than they often think. The whole point of being American is to be unique. This, however, is exactly what the French think about themselves. Americans look upon their differences from the rest of the world as progressive and normative—at the leading edge of a development in liberty, where others must follow. The French see themselves as exclusive, a fixed civilization, a unity, always apart from the rest—but also exemplary. The tension between the two societies has only superficially to do with political matters. It is a moral rivalry.

The conviction held by the British and the French about the importance of their nations as civilizations contrasts with a German insecurity, related to the disastrous failure of German nationalism. French and British national confidence is cultural in origin, and hierarchy within the society rests on certainty about national accomplishment. An equivalent confidence is undermined in West Germany by the disasters of German political history between unification in 1871 and the partition of 1945. The uncertainty of Germans about the identity and "purpose" of Germany has been a cause of European unrest and war since the time of Napoleon. For the French and the British, as for Americans, questioning the "purpose" of France or Britain or the United States is all but incomprehensible. "Purpose" is thought either irrelevant or self-evident. Each of these is a mature, achieved nation. Germany is not, and will not be, such a nation even when reunited. The German Reichs and republics that have existed since 1871 have been unions of some or most of the hundreds of separate German political entities that existed at the beginning of the nineteenth century, legatees of the collapse of the Holy Roman Empire. The Hapsburgs, last holders of the Roman imperial title, renounced it only in 1806. Modern Germany was the political creation of Bismarck, and it lasted in approximately the form he gave it for less than seventy-five years.

Austria, and even the German-speaking cantons of Switzerland, are as logically part of "Germany" as Saxony or Brandenburg, the historical entities that made up the German Democratic Republic. The problem of the political form that a German nation should take has been the most explosive and destructive single issue in world politics since 1806. It was responsible for the Franco-Prussian War, for both world wars, and for drawing Soviet Russia into Central Europe, to assume the "imperial" role that the Hapsburgs and Ottomans had earlier been unable to sustain.

The "German Question" was responsible for the continuing presence in Continental Europe, a half-century after the close of the Second World War, of American, British, and Canadian military forces. That it is an unresolved question was constantly recalled by the polite but insistent reference to German unity in the political discourse of the West German parties and the policy of the West German government before unification. A German nation (or nations) has still to be defined, and it is possible to think that this will not happen without yet more suffering for the Germans, and perhaps for their neighbors.

Because of the lack of a specific and coherent *national* tradition, Germany has consistently looked for justification in causes larger than mere national aggrandizement. From the time of the Teutonic Knights and their crusades against pagan Balts and Slavs, Germans have believed in a destiny of European consequence—a historical mission. The *Drang nach Osten* of the Middle Ages was the mission of the German Knights to Christianize the pagan East. German nationality was universalizing, being "Roman," and the conquered and converted could acquire it. Even the Prussians originally were Balts, colonized by the Teutonic Order. The obligation to Christianize the East was solemnly assumed by the emperors, who were "Augmenters of the Reich." It was after Napoleon destroyed the old Reich, in 1806, that, as George Bailey has said in his indispensable book *Germans: The Biography of an Obsession,* "the European dimensions of the German problem began to emerge."

The destruction of the Reich had the effect of leaving the Germans without a fatherland. As late as the Congress of Vienna, Metternich said that "the German people" and "Germany" were abstract concepts. Meanwhile, France, in contrast to Germany, had become the first modern nation—a coherent community under strong central rule. Germany at the start of the nineteenth century remained a loose confederation—"impregnable in defense and incapable of aggression," as a contemporary observer said. What we know as Germany consisted then of 1,789 separate and independent political units, held together by obligations to the old feudal empire. The least of the German princes and dukes was equal to the greatest in his relationship to the Holy Roman Emperor. In order to maintain themselves, many had been forced to look for support outside the Reich. Few had major resources or an army. Many of the smaller principalities had been under French subsidy for generations. The eighteenth-century German whole was thus considerably less than the sum of its parts. It existed because of the feudal relationships of the princes to the emperor and to the Pope, and it expressed political universality modeled upon the unity and universality of Christianity—qualities that in fact had long been undermined in the Church itself by the Renaissance and the Reformation. The Empire had formally survived a century and a half after its effective demise, to be ended by Napoleon's creation of the Confederation of the Rhine in 1806, and the abdication by the Hapsburgs (who remained Austrian emperors) of the Roman imperial title.

Napoleon divided the Reich, and thereby accelerated the rise of Prussia and inadvertently set the stage for Germany's nineteenth-century unification, which took place at France's eventual cost. The Germany unified under Prussian rule, the Second Reich, attempted to emulate the modern French state that had destroyed the original Reich. Although this Germany's unification had been accomplished through war, and revenge was taken upon France in 1870, it nonetheless looked for a larger meaning, its justificatory mission, this time in intellectual and artistic matters—a romantic notion of Germany as the "harvest of all time." Someone has made the cynical observation that in the nineteenth century, "on account of bad weather, the German revolution took place in music." Fritz Stern, of Columbia University, in *The Failure of Illiberalism,* says of the nineteenth century that "German nationalism, inflamed by Napoleon's triumphs, turned against the political ideals and achievements of the French Revolution. What was exalted by German nationalism was the cultural achievement and destiny of the Germans, their peculiar gifts for poetry, truth, and music. Consequently German nationalism was less concerned with the political destiny of the Germans, with their practical rights and liberties as citizens." In this period of romanticism, the German regard for artists as demoniac evokers of universal powers (Doctors Faustus) reached a strength that was to affect our own times. Even the Nazi leaders wanted to be considered artists: Hitler was an aspiring architect and a painter; Goebbels published a novel; Göring was a patron of the arts. They sought to be universal figures, transcenders. The German historian Ludwig Dehio said after the war: "We were the last, and the most daemonic, power to exercise hegemony over the declining old continent of Europe." The Germans had finally been successful in summoning demons: the demons came.

The Second—Wilhelmine—Reich was destroyed physically and morally in the First World War, the dreadful losses of which began with the *Kindermord,* at the first Battle of Ypres, in the fall of 1914, when German boys fresh from school marched in waves into the rifle fire of British regulars. Begun in exultation, the war ended, for the Germans, in troop mutinies and revolution. The kaiser abdicated. The Weimar Republic that succeeded him was asked the old question of what its universal mission was. The Weimar Republic had none. It was merely a democracy; that was not enough. It had to be destroyed. It was unsuitable for a German people entrusted with a historic destiny—temporarily unspecified. It was thus supplanted, in 1933, by a movement whose commitment proved to be to death—administering it to others and eventually being claimed by it. But this, too, was something for which a word in German already existed, *Todessüchtigheit:* thirst for death. As Bailey remarks, Germans do not fear death as others do. Suicide is a "reasonable recourse." The Austrian historian Friedrich Heer writes of Pelagian freedom: man so free and exposed that he can assert himself only through mastery of the material world "and—terrifying thought—its human material."

The year 1945 was the Year Zero, the Germans said, when "Germany" began again. This was taken for granted in West Germany, even if the nature of the new society, in 1989 in its Year 44, remained incompletely known. Germany's resolution of its interior unrest, its need to justify its national existence, has in modern West Germany been satisfied in ways that now are coming to an end. Though West Germany's strategic dependence upon the United States has persisted, and will do so as long as the United States government interests itself directly in the balance of power in Central Europe, the German moral dependence upon the United States has ended. It had to end, even if there should be trauma in the ending.

In a book called *The German Catastrophe,* published in 1946, the late Friedrich Meinecke, a distinguished historian, argued that West Germany must recover its culture and its poetry, and might hope eventually to resemble those other once combative and now pacific states—Holland, Sweden, and Switzerland. There "all the moral forces and energies of man find room for expression," he said. "Let us resolve to follow their example." The actual solution was the opposite—to turn outward, toward the Atlantic and America. It proved a feasible solution, because in the course of its military occupation, the United States discovered affective, as well as political and strategic, motives to make West Germany into a protectorate and then an ally. The American army had not much liked France or the French (just as our government looked upon General de Gaulle as a reactionary and disruptive figure and was never to understand him); but the army respected Germany and the Germans. The Germans, it found, were amenable to American leadership and also had an American approach to practical problems. They simply looked familiar, like Americans, and their voices had an American pitch. The United States Army even adopted a green uniform in the style of the Wehrmacht—an uncalculated tribute of some significance. It gave up olive drab and khaki—which derived from horsemen's garb and tropical service—and the influence of British military tailoring for Central European green and gold, high-peaked German caps, and black leather in place of brown. It is usually the defeated who emulate the conqueror, or smaller nations their larger allies. The wartime United States Army officer's uniform—olive-drab tunic and "pink" (taupe) slacks—survives today in the Dutch army.

Political events also compelled the United States to turn what had been an enemy nation into an ally. A degree of cooperative work was necessary to secure West Germany from the perceived threat of the Soviet Union. This cooperation, which was accomplished with characteristic American pragmatism and goodwill, and was all the easier because the United States had not really suffered very much at German hands, eventually resulted in a relationship in which considerable respect and good feeling existed on both sides.

The West German adherence to the United States rested originally, however, on a lie. The United States casually, even thoughtlessly, pledged itself to reunion of the two Germanys. The lie was not calculated; most of the Americans involved in making policy on Germany and Central Europe during the early Cold War believed that Germany had to be reunited. Yet the reunion of Germany was not in America's national interest or in that of Germany's West European allies. Quite the opposite. Those who had had to fight a united Germany had a logical interest in Germany's remaining divided, and therefore unlikely to threaten them again. The United States pledged the reunification of Germany because this seemed an appropriate way to combat the Soviet Union, occupier of East Germany. The commitment reached its rhetorical apogee with President Kennedy's cry in West Berlin, in 1963, that he was a Berliner. But, of course, he was not, and could not be. His essential interests, and those of his country, diverged from those of Berliners, just as American interests diverged from those of Western Europe in general. The emergence of these differences after the exceptional period of wartime and Cold War Atlantic cooperation was one of the chief political themes of the 1980s. It was an inevitable one—with, however, serious consequences for West Germany.

For West Germans in the 1950s, the American link was a step in the solution of their national problems. They gained the respect and support of their conqueror. The former enemy became their guarantor and sponsor. The next step in their rehabilitation was to come to terms with their Western European neighbors. This was accomplished in the cooperative institutions of the European Coal and Steel Community, which led to the Treaty of Rome and the European Community. Germany was reconciled with France—a reconciliation solemnly ratified by President de Gaulle and Chancellor Konrad Adenauer when the two met in the Cathedral of Reims in July 1962. "Whoever wishes to be a German must see to it that he becomes a European while there is still time. We must have patriotism in an entirely new understanding of the word," said Franz Josef Strauss, who was ordinarily thought of as a German nationalist.

The West Germans renounced unlimited sovereignty in favor of "Europe," by doing so reacquiring a conception of themselves and of their purpose as something more than merely national. To create Europe was an appropriate task for Germans. Yet over time, the attractions of the European Community diminished for the Germans, because of its lack of moral purpose, the fact that it remains largely a mercantile arrangement, a customs union, a matter for what de Gaulle used to call contemptuously "the commissariat," and one that an older generation of Germans, too, would have despised. The elder Helmuth von Moltke, first Chief of the Great German General Staff, spoke for the governing class of his generation when he said, in 1880, that the noblest virtues of man were developed by war: "Without war, the world would sink into materialism."

So it has, and that it is a mercantile arrangement is a valid criticism of what Europe is today, and what it seems to be becoming. Yet materialism is not a bad thing for a country, or a continent, whose modern history has been as packed with crime and tragedy as Germany's and Europe's. The tensions—of values, of national consciousness and ambition—that continue to exist in Germany are factors in a national mutation. It is no longer a nation remotely like what it was made into by Bismarck, but it is still posing to itself perplexing questions about what it *ought* to do, about what justifies its national life.

The foreign observer must ask why German society must have a mission, an identified national destiny, in order to accept itself. The English, French, and Italian senses of national identity have always had a great deal more to do with civilization as such—the national culture—than with state or political programs. Even when Italian nationalism flourished most strongly, in Mussolini's first years of power, no one agonized over unanswered questions of national meaning and purpose. It was perfectly evident. Mussolini often boasted that Italians had three times given civilization to a barbarian world and now were going to do it again. It is troubling today to find that liberal Germans still cannot wholly accept a national identity of Germany expressed in the language, literature, music, philosophy, and technological and economic accomplishments of the country.

Germany's dependence upon the United States, which in the 1950s made possible the Federal Republic's moral as well as economic recovery, went on long enough for the American influence to become to many Germans a form of oppression, albeit benevolent. The nation's moral burden, Nazism, for which the association with America and the commitment to NATO and to European unification were answers for the generations of the 1950s and 1960s, for a younger generation found a new, if provisional, resolution in the peace movement. If the peace movement's premises were correct—if all war is criminal, nuclear war the most criminal of all—then the war of 1939–45 and the regime responsible for it were merely particular instances of a general evil against which the Germans of the peace-movement generation led the struggle. No essential distinction had to be made between the Nazis who launched the Second World War and the Americans who were willing to plan to fight another war. The guilty were those who did not demonstrate against missiles and war. The dangerous ones were those who only skeptically responded to Mikhail Gorbachev's disarmament proposals. Having provided the world with a model of evil in the past, these Germans now imagined themselves providing a necessary model of good, again in a millenarian spirit. There was an urgency here that is in the German tradition. For Luther, too, the end of the world was close; conversion was urgent.

The importance of unachieved nationalism as a force in West German politics, including its peace-movement politics, was taken for granted by the West Germans themselves in the 1980s. It was recognized with concern elsewhere in Europe, and especially in France, which had obvious reason to pay attention to what was happening in West Germany. The French reaction was to attempt to remedy the consequences of German opinion's estrangement from a defense system dominated by the United States by supplying a plan for a new one, predominantly if not entirely European. President Mitterrand launched programs for expanded French military cooperation with West Germany in the early 1980s, proposing "an alliance within the alliance"—between France and West Germany. The French Army created a five-division Rapid Action Force (of airborne, airmobile, light-armored, and Alpine units) able to reinforce the French Army corps already stationed in southern Germany (three armored divisions) or to intervene elsewhere in a German battle. A Franco-German brigade was formed, under joint command. Planning for French participation in a NATO battle in Germany went so far as effectively to terminate that independent (militarily nonintegrated) role in NATO which France inherited from General de Gaulle.

The extension of a Franco-British nuclear guarantee to West Germany was also discussed, in more or less explicit terms, in France, and was proposed to Britain. The French strategist General Pierre Gallois noted that on current programs, by 1995 at the latest, France and Britain together would acquire the nuclear capacity to destroy two thousand targets in the Soviet Union, and France alone would by 1992 be in a position "to paralyze the military apparatus of the Soviet Union by precise attacks, without—initially, at least—attacking Soviet cities." From this he concluded that "one can therefore envisage a substitute for the American guarantee provided by France and, a fortiori, Great Britain." The West Germans, however, were not disposed to rest their security upon France, or even upon France and Britain in combination. A joint Franco-British nuclear force was unlikely for another reason. There was in Britain little serious interest in such an arrangement, and it seemed all but certain that a proposal for one would be refused by any British government. The ancient maritime bias of British strategy and the country's instinctive distrust of the Continent—based on a history of war with the European powers and of threats from Europe—together with the deliberate Atlantic commitment of British foreign policy in this century, suggested that a Continental Europe estranged from the United States would more likely drive Britain closer to the United States. The divergence between the West Europeans and Britain was considerably larger than was generally appreciated in the United States. This is significant to the American understanding of Continental Europe, which for reasons of language and cultural kinship passes substantially by way of Britain, filtered through British perceptions and the British press—themselves influenced by American assumptions. Shared errors are reinforced. Europe is still too often considered an undifferentiated unity.

In a part of West German opinion, a process of rejection of the United States began in the 1970s, a process that, needless to say, deeply disturbed that German majority which still found its security in the American alliance. The process is not confined to Germany alone. In the 1980s there was a significant shift in how the West European link to the United States was perceived, and some doubts about the utility of that link. Relatively few people in West Germany, or in Europe, were eager to see the United States remove its troops and terminate its guarantee of European security; but there was no longer a conviction that this guarantee could or would function. There was anxiety that the conduct of the United States was itself a source of risk of major war, for which Europe would provide the battleground. A measure of the older sense of solidarity with the United States had been worn away by America's involvements in Vietnam, Cambodia, Iran, and Central America, and by the fairly ruthless self-interest of American economic policies. The vacillations of Jimmy Carter and the erratic course of Ronald Reagan produced a belief that the United States was no longer in competent hands. As the scholar and political commentator Raymond Aron said just before his death in 1983, the

United States had become "no longer comprehensible to either its enemies or its friends."

The development within the United States of an important current of opinion in favor of a policy of no first use of nuclear weapons reinforced the uncertainty of the American nuclear guarantee and the implausibility of a NATO strategy that rested on a presumption that an early recourse to nuclear weapons was possible. Unwilling to spend what was necessary for a conventional defense (or deterrent), the West European powers took refuge in this threat of an American nuclear response to a Soviet conventional attack—a threat they were not really prepared to see carried out, because of the obvious probability that they themselves would be the immediate victims of a Soviet nuclear counterattack. The only form in which they could really contemplate nuclear war was a strategic nuclear exchange between the United States and the Soviet Union that would spare Europe. Europe has been defended— or, at least, Europeans had imagined themselves defended, without articulating the contradiction they knew to exist—by means of a threat of general destruction. The psychology was that of the doomsday machine.

A troubled situation resulted. West German, Dutch, British, and other West European peace movements were one consequence. West German distress at the fact that the only nuclear missiles left in Europe were those of a range to strike only Germany was another. This merely followed, though, the divergence that developed in how the West European and American publics saw the future. Polls comparing public attitudes in the United States with those in West European countries in the past found Americans more afraid of war, more anxious about Soviet influence, more concerned about neutralism and pacifism, more worried that their country was not strong enough, and more anxious to gain and keep nuclear superiority over the U.S.S.R. than any of the allies. Later, Americans were found to be more trusting of Mikhail Gorbachev than many Europeans, more willing to promote cooperation with him, rekindling in Europe old fears of a superpower settlement that could leave Western Europe alone to cope with the Soviet Union and with the unresolved problem of Eastern Europe.

The center holds; passion falls away. That is what has happened ideologically in Western Europe over recent years. Admittedly, one must choose one's words carefully. The difference between the Europe of 1940—or 1950—and that of the present day is not that ideology now is dead. It is not. But it no longer resonates among the people at large. It no longer dominates voting. It does not produce great popular movements. In 1940, both Fascism and Communism could motivate people to passionate struggles. Political ideologies had the power that religion once possessed—the power to send great masses of people out to sacrifice themselves, convinced that they served truth and could bring about a redemption of society. Even just after the war, the Communists of Western Europe still could command something like that mass allegiance; their parties were tightly organized political forces whose members believed in the possibility of a transformed humanity, a totally new society. Today, the belief in a revolutionary transformation of society—and perhaps the belief in the need for such a transformation—survives chiefly among a fraction of the political intelligentsia.

Albert Camus said in the 1950s that his work, and that of his fellow intellectuals, should be "to clarify definitions in order to disintoxicate minds and to calm fanaticisms, even when this is against the current tendency." Before 1945, Europeans had pursued ideas into the void, in the midst of a political culture half ruined by what it had already done to itself between 1914 and 1918, in the pits and tunnels of Verdun, at Ypres, amid the Masurian Lakes. The third quarter of the century saw a retreat from all that. The European generation that followed the First World War, and described itself as feeling like the last link in a broken chain, had by 1940 turned desperately to ideological politics. Fascism offered strength, mastery, the triumph of the will. Communism purported to be a science of history able to bring to power a classless class, ending human exploitation. Both ideologies fed on hatred as well as idealism. Hatred was an inheritance of that generation, for its members had in their own lives confronted the consequences of that political corruption which had caused the sacrifice of the generation of 1914. The British novelist Nicholas Mosley has said that the war in 1914 conformed, in its way, to evolutionary theory: Europe, "having grown sick, and having felt itself sick, not through failure, but through the successful completion of some cycle . . . was now seeing to its own breaking-up with a view perhaps to some possible rearrangement." Among the characteristics of the time was "the ability to get pleasure from what was inevitable—inevitability being terrible, but often ridiculous."

Today in Europe hardly anyone remains who can seriously believe in the old ideological doctrines. Revolutionary rhetoric persists, a conventional language, just as globalist and Wilsonian rhetoric is the conventional language of official American discourse on world affairs. But even among the Europeans who use the revolutionary vocabulary—Communist Party activists, surviving members of the movements of the New Left, anarchists and latter-day Trotskyites—all have private reservations, like Catholics since Vatican II.

Revolution once meant something desperate and dangerous, action taken because the conditions of life were no longer humanly tolerable. That is not the situation today. There are no longer such conditions in Western Europe. The problems of Europe today are "good" problems, which is to say constructive problems. Life is good, and political action starts in that reality. Most people in the major countries of Western Europe are better off by material standards than they have been at any time in the past. They undoubtedly are made anxious by this new condition of life—"consumerist," materialistic, possessions-oriented, in important respects cut off from the custom and discipline of the past. In the 1980s there was still an anxiety born of that generation's own historical memory—the fear that peace and security could not last, that inflation would resume, that unemployment would endure and increase, that there might be a new economic slump. Yet the general political tendency must be described as one of radical moderation. The obvious trend has not been rightist, leftist, or even properly centrist. It has, between 1945 and 1989, been toward safety. People have voted for the center, to the extent that the politicians would let them, and this was not so much because the policies of the center were so attractive as because the center seemed safe. What Europe clearly has wanted ever since the war's gunfire lifted and it became possible to put stone upon stone again is security and peace.

Nonetheless, the European nations have less in common with the United States than forty years of slogans about the free world and Atlantic civilization suggest. There are crucial values held in common, but one must challenge the general and largely unanalyzed assumption made since the Second World War that all are societies going in the same direction, toward the same goal, led by the United States. It has been taken for granted that no alternative has existed to intimate transatlantic political and military relationship, such as we have known since the 1940s. But alternatives have existed, and they exist today. We did not inevitably arrive where we are. It is, in fact, odd that we have done so, given the American past. Before the Atlantic Alliance began and NATO was conceived, no one expected American troops to remain in Europe more than a few months after the end of the war. "A year or two at most," John J. McCloy remarked, recalling his conversations about postwar European security with Franklin Roosevelt before the war's end and with Harry Truman in the sober months of the early Cold War. No one then imagined that American soldiers would still be in Europe a half-century later.

The Atlantic Treaty relationship began in a simple U.S. military guarantee to Europe and formal, although qualified, agreement among the North Atlantic nations to stand together against a Soviet attack. This modest degree of association was soon expanded. Its original military dimensions were given an extremely ambitious political framework, in which some people even envisaged transatlantic political federation. Europe itself was certainly urged to become a federal union on the American model, acting as a single power, expected to see things as America sees them, intimately aligned with the United States. Customary rhetoric held that since the Atlantic nations were united by values and culture, a political union existed *in potentia.*

This was a great error. There is much that the Atlantic nations have in common, but there is much that they do not, and the differences have grown larger. All have representative and democratic governments. All are related in their historical culture. The Europeans have a political history in common, and much of it is blood-soaked. Those things which the Europeans possess in common have not spared them constant tension and a history of pillage and war. The last two apocalyptic exercises in European internal warfare, and the consequent postwar vulnerability of Europeans to the non-European powers, changed a great deal. But they did not turn ordinary Englishmen into Frenchmen, or Frenchmen into Germans. What those wars did accomplish was to cause Europeans to look at their common civilization with a new appreciation of its vulnerability as well as of its power, and to dismiss for the present, perhaps for good, the recourse to war as an instrument of policy in dealing with one another.

The biggest mistake I made in the first edition of this book was my argument in this chapter that Germany would not be reunited. It seemed contrary to the national interests of all of Germany's neighbors, as well as to those of Russia and the United States. I underestimated both the capacity of Mikhail Gorbachev to rise above an elementary *Realpolitik* and the lack of that same quality in American policymaking. Once Mr. Gorbachev and George Bush agreed that Germany should be reunited, the hostility of Margaret Thatcher and François Mitterrand of France became irrelevant, and Germany became one state. This restored German confidence, and in some real sense closed the door on the past.

The Berlin Republic will not be the Germany we knew during the first forty years after the Second World War. Germany's unification provided a final reconciliation of the other Europeans with Germany. The criticism sometimes made—that Europe thereby was subordinated to Germany, and that Germany peacefully gained the continental domination it had failed to achieve by war in 1914–18 and 1940–45—is simply untrue. Germany does not have the material means to dominate Europe, and it certainly does not have the will to try to do so.

The "German Question" nonetheless remains unsettled. What new form will a protean German civilization now assume? The Berlin Republic still is not an achieved nation. There still is a question of its "purpose," although the Germans have perhaps heard enough from foreigners about their supposed need for a universal mission, and are weary of apologizing for a past for which they have no personal responsibility.

The political nature of the class issue in Britain changed decisively during the decade after this book was first written. The Labour government of Prime Minister Tony Blair has ended hereditary membership in the House of Lords, a quality of that body which was intellectually indefensible yet made a pragmatic claim to have leavened parliamentary deliberation over the years with disinterested interventions.

The leading political parties have changed. A cabinet such as Mrs. Thatcher's first government has become politically impossible. The Tory Party rejected its grandees, Old Etonians, and Guardees during the 1980s and 1990s, in part (although not entirely) because they were cosmopolitan and open to "Europe," while Margaret Thatcher and her successors were stubbornly hostile to the European Union and to European influence. The issue of British membership in the E.U. and in its single currency obsessed the Conservative Party during the years following Mrs. Thatcher's destitution and undermined its political relevance, which by 2000 had yet to be reestablished.

No recognizable governing "class," either of right or left, exists in post-Thatcher Britain (although class consciousness has not gone away). Mrs. Thatcher expelled from power the upper-class "one-nation" Tories with their paternalistic social conscience. Tony Blair has established a Scottish parliament and Welsh assembly, stoutly pursued Northern Ireland settlement (as the Conservative John Major had done before him), cut the power of trade unions in the Labour Party, declared the class war over. He presided over the mutation of New Labour into a New Establishment. New Labour is a party of the liberal middle classes, with the emulated Bill Clinton's commitment to the cultivation of image and to "communication" as a method of government. In this it could not be more different from old Labour, an alliance of working-class trade unionists with middle-class reformers, which destroyed itself through its stubbornly unpragmatic commitment to ideals which time had transformed into sectarian ideas.

Some in Britain, including survivors of the Thatcher governments and Mrs. Thatcher herself, would like to see a still closer British attachment to the United States, even British membership in the North American Free Trade Area, as alternative to the connection with Europe. A former editor of *The Spectator*, Alexander Chancellor, has observed that this would effectively make Britain the fifty-first state, which undoubtedly is the subliminal and psychologically unavowable ambition of many who are sympathetic to the project. Not taken into account is whether Americans would really want to add Britain's problems to their own. The Blair government, on the other hand, has taken the lead in constructing a European defense "identity," which has disconcerted Washington.

There are British revisionist historians who take a different view of ties to the United States. They blame Washington for Britain's loss of empire and influence. They challenge the conventional argument that Britain's wartime alliance with the United States was inevitable or even desirable. These writers include the academic historian John Charmley and the late Alan Clark. Lord Clark (son of the art historian), a military historian and minister in the first Thatcher government, said that Britain's entry into the European war was itself a mistake, arguing that Germany and the Soviet Union, left alone, would have fought one another to exhaustion, leaving Britain, its Empire intact, as arbiter.

Charmley writes that under Winston Churchill's leadership (his mother was, of course, an American), Britain willfully abandoned its imperial interests to appease the United States. He argues that Churchill possessed a romantic vision of eventual union of the English-speaking peoples (his final books were a history of those peoples), and this caused him to see the wartime British-American alliance as a step in the fulfillment of Britain's destiny. The United States, which did not share this view, pursued its interests at British expense. (One reason the U.S. Navy resisted Franklin Roosevelt's decision to give the war in Europe priority over the Pacific war was that the Navy Department traditionally had held that American and Britain Empire interests could never coincide.) Charmley says the Empire could have been saved. Certainly it would have been possible to preserve an alliance of what then was called the "White Commonwealth" of Canada, Australia, New Zealand, and South Africa—all of whom postwar Britain treated with perverse indifference.

A French writer, Philippe Grasset, has listed what he sees as wartime and postwar American betrayals of Britain, meekly accepted, which include Washington's appropriation of what originally was a joint nuclear program, cutting the British out of postwar cooperation in American nuclear projects even though early British research had made the atom bomb possible, and its takeover of Britain's pioneer radar developments and invention of the jet engine (the first postwar American jet fighters had engines of British design). He writes that while the American logistical contribution to the war against Germany was enormous and decisive, the technological advantage was all British: Lend-Lease aircraft deliveries to Britain were generally second-rate (the P-40 fighter, the Lockheed "Boston" bomber), while Britain gave the U.S. the Spitfire and Hurricane's Rolls-Royce engine, which, fitted to the North American P-51 long-range fighter, "saved the American strategic bombing offensive from disaster."

France, since I wrote in 1988, has seen a noteworthy but as yet unsuccessful rebellion against rule by *"énarchie"*—as the nation's domination by graduates of the Ecole Nationale d'Administration is called. What had been regarded as an able and legitimate leadership corps, responsible for what the French now call the *trentes glorieuses* (thirty glorious postwar years of growth and social progress), came under attack for its alleged arrogance, corporatism, and isolation from public opinion, and because it embodied Colbertian ideas of centralized, interventionist government, as against the doctrines of deregulation and market solutions which have made their way in France, even within governments of the left, although not without difficulty. (The French nonetheless have found that a residual Colbertism has not been an obstacle to economic performance superior to that of Germany.)

Less often criticized is the link that continues to be made in France between educational certification and career. Success in rigorous *grandes écoles* examinations continues to decide entry into the higher reaches of government and society, although industry has become more open to what the French call "le self-made man."

Is the dynamism of the European Union really intensifying? The single market of 1992 was followed by the European Central Bank and the single currency, adopted by eleven of the fifteen E.U. nations in January 1999. The war with Serbia over Kosovo greatly increased pressure for a single European security policy to provide greater independence from the United States. Industrial and financial consolidation continues, and the European Union's collective industrial, financial, and trading power and potential is immense, greater than that of the United States. Yet in the absence of a common economic authority capable of setting priorities and imposing structural reform, international opinion justifiably continues to form its judgments of "Europe" in terms of the performances of its most powerful members, Germany and France. European growth, overall, improved over the decade, rising notably in 2000, when high rates of unemployment in Germany, France, Italy, and Spain began to drop. By mid-2000 some were predicting that Europe had entered a new period of high growth that would rival that of the postwar period, and that it was finding its own version of the American "new economy." A writer in the usually pro-American *Economist* magazine, Michael Prowse, has ventured the argument that the twenty-first century will belong to Western Europe, with a living standard and quality of life superior to the American.

Elsewhere in Europe, Poland has enjoyed a dynamic revival, as to a considerably lesser extent have Hungary and the Czech Republic. The other ex-Communist countries, except for Slovenia, still founder economically and remain politically insecure. The European Union made the fateful choice, reiterated in 1999, against early admission for any of them. (The year 2003 would seem the earliest possible date for enlargement, even though the enlargement process was redefined in 1999 on the "regatta" principle of individual admission as soon as "realistically" qualified.) This was politically inevitable, given the E.U.'s commitment to a "federal" (meaning highly integrated) union: the others do not fit into such a Europe, with all of its "acquired benefits" and institutionalized sectorial subsidies. Extending the E.U.'s common agricultural policy to Central and Eastern Europe would alone destroy the E.U.'s budget, and radical reform of the CAP has thus far proven a political impossibility. No effort has yet been made to create forms of junior or adjunct E.U. membership that could have begun the formal integration of the former Communist states and bound them to the E.U. As a result, the "Europe" that Central and Eastern European dissidents longed—dreamed—to join at the beginning of the 1990s now is regarded with disappointment and some bitterness.

U.S.-led NATO, on the other hand, welcomed those countries as members or auxiliaries, offering a way station, the "Partnership for Peace," for those not ready for full membership or whose full membership would have been politically awkward (the case for the Baltic states). A new division thus opened between the E.U. and the Central and Eastern Europeans, and a new line of insecurity drawn between the new NATO members and those left outside the alliance: the Baltic states, Romania, and Bulgaria. A momentous opportunity was lost by the European Union, damaging to itself as well as to those others whose new attachment to the United States must in the nature of things prove an eventual disappointment. Whatever Washington may say or the East Europeans wish, the United States is not a European power. The American public certainly knows otherwise. For the Central and East Europeans, NATO membership cannot take the place of political and economic integration into that larger Europe where geography and history have installed them.

A common European foreign and security policy was mandated by the Amsterdam Treaty but has yet to be formulated, although someone was selected to conduct it—Javier Solana, formerly NATO's secretary-general. One may reasonably doubt that he will have much of a political policy to conduct, other than on anodyne matters of the second rank. The European record of agreement on matters of foreign policy substance is a discouraging one. Europe's performance throughout the successive episodes of the Yugoslav crisis of the 1990s, from Germany's recognition of Croatia and Slovenia in 1991 to the bombing campaign against Serbia in 1999, was well intentioned, courageous, but incoherent and largely ineffectual. European forces in the U.N. Protection Force stoically endured significant casualties during the Bosnian war, but left the people of Srebrenica to be murdered. European diplomacy contributed little to the eventual solution (such as it was) of the Bosnian problem. American initiatives, when they came, were criticized in Europe, and Washington's predilection for military action deplored, but those measures resolved (for the moment) both the Bosnian and Kosovar crises—for better or for worse. The British and French influenced the outcome, but there never was a fully united European Union position.

The conduct of the war over Kosovo reemphasized to the Europeans how completely dominated they are by the United States in security matters. It revealed that NATO, which they had assumed to be a well-prepared and efficient military machine, had in reality become an incoherent military bureaucracy. Jane Perlez of *The New York Times* quoted an official of the alliance as saying of the Kosovo campaign, "NATO got in way over its head, stumbled through, didn't know how to get out, was scared to death by what was happening." It won through brute force, not professional competence—and thanks to Russian diplomacy's abandonment of Serbia. The American-imposed technological mode of war, with its inordinate concern to protect Allied forces at the price of failing to protect the Kosovar victims of the war, compromised the moral stance of the allies, and in some European military circles was regarded as dishonorable. NATO was damaged by the affair, not strengthened.

The Europeans' realization that their security, and in major respects their capacity to conduct serious military operations, depended, via NATO, all but totally upon Washington, inspired declarations of determination to end all that, which on British initiative have taken on real substance. A sixty-thousand-man intervention force with air and naval support is promised and may even be achieved. The United States has looked upon this with annoyance, since it takes place outside NATO, under European Union command. In a poll conducted in eight European countries soon after the Kosovo intervention which asked if the respondents favored an "independent European defense," 63 percent said yes. Only in Britain and Greece was there less than majority support (49 percent in Britain in favor, 47 percent in Greece).

The great obstacle to a common European foreign and security policy is the divergence in the European countries' national and historical interests and attitudes. Former empires with experience of great-power roles in world affairs do not easily find a common policy with small states accustomed to neutrality, or those whose perceived national interest is to stay out of great power quarrels. The enthusiastic Atlanticism of states like Norway and the Netherlands owes much to the fact that a powerful but distant American friend counterbalances the influence of less powerful but inconveniently exigent next-door neighbors. The historical threats to Dutch and Norwegian independence came from Spain, France, Germany, and from Sweden and Denmark, not from across the Atlantic.

The second half of the twentieth century actually constituted an exceptional period in America's historical relationship with the Europe it had repudiated with its founding claim to independence. During the first century and a half of America's existence, lasting into the 1940s, Europe and its empires were seen as hostile to American interests. This was true even during the Second World War. American policy under Franklin Roosevelt was not only to defeat the Axis powers but also to dismantle the European empires. When NATO was created in 1949, it was meant not only to keep the Russians out of Western Europe but to control Germany. The impulse behind Washington's early sponsorship of European unification was to neutralize potential threats from Europe by promoting an American federalist model of union that would bind Europe to the United States through NATO, safely subordinating that continent from which, in American eyes, disorder flowed. This, in substance, largely unrecognized even by those who practice it, remains American policy today.

It is a normal American geopolitical interest that Continental Europe not be dominated by, or become, a united rival power. The world wars and the Cold War posed the threat of Europe's unification under German or Russian domination. Today the rival power that dominates Western Europe is the European Union. The United States has yet to come to explicit terms with this reality. It is a reality already perceived in Western Europe.

European-American political hostility would provide a deplorable climax to a half-century (and more) of American support for Europe's unification: underwriting Jean Monnet's early efforts, constantly supporting Monnet's ambition to see European federal union against the Gaullist vision of a European union of autonomous nations, rival to the United States. However, American efforts to increase or consolidate its global political and military dominance could in the new century provoke Europe, finally, to make the Gaullist choice.

The European-American strategic relationship, structured as a military alliance dominated by the United States, lost its raison d'être when it lost its Cold War strategic rationale. Neither side wishes to see change because it would be destabilizing and possibly dangerous, but there are several important categories of conflict. One is trade and finance, concerning the future role to be played by the single European currency, the euro, as well as the difficulties posed by trade disputes, including Europe's refusal to accept certain categories of American agricultural exports, regarded by the European public as dangerous. Important commercial difficulties also arise from disagreement over issues of cultural identity and the protection of intellectual property and artistic works.

The most significant conflict is undoubtedly that which arises from transatlantic competition in strategic, high-technology industries that both sides consider essential to economic sovereignty and national security. In industry, the "normal" evolution of competition would be toward transatlantic mergers. In industries of strategic importance this is politically unacceptable when it results in the loss of national control over the producer of strategic goods. This is true in both Europe and the United States.

It is a characteristic mistake in American discussion of competition with Europe to describe these threats in military terms, as "Fortress Europe," or by suggesting (as the economist Martin Feldstein did in 1997, in a notorious article in *Foreign Affairs*) that Europe's adoption of a single currency could lead to war between Europe and the United States. War is not the issue, but rather an intense economic and industrial competition that neither side is likely to "win," but whose political consequences could end the American-European relationship that has existed since the close of the Cold War.

Rivalry between European and American industry has until recently been a creative rivalry, conforming to the English economist David Ricardo's model, proposed two centuries ago, of mutual progress achieved through free trade and the exploitation of national advantage. Most on both sides of the Atlantic today seem to expect this to continue, notwithstanding disputes over trade practices, industrial subsidies, cultural and other exceptions to trade harmonization, Washington's (perhaps waning) enthusiasm for secondary boycotts and legislating extraterritorially, and potential competition between the euro and the dollar.

The eleven members of the single currency (twelve, as Greece joins) have made a major political commitment to the euro's success. The single currency is typical of the ambitious and sometimes rash economic initiatives by which "Europe" has thus far been constructed. From the time of the original Coal and Steel Community of 1951, from which the E.U. evolved, to the Single Market of 1992, and now to the single currency, Europe has progressed by ambitious leaps forward in economic integration, which have brought in their train new and sometimes unforeseen forms of political integration, some of which might have seemed unacceptable had they been independently proposed.

The new European currency proved less strong than expected during its first year and a half of trading (to the advantage of European exporters, benefiting from what in another day, in relation to another currency, the dollar, Americans called benign neglect). The euro's drop to dollar parity was actually a return to where it started, in that the euro's original value was that of the European Currency Unit, or Ecu, precursor to the single currency, which was created in 1979, at parity to the dollar, as a basket of European currencies. It was meant to determine intra-European exchange rates, promote monetary stability, and facilitate pan-European business. The fall of the euro to below dollar parity in April 2000 was attributed to the extraordinary vigor of the U.S. economy in 1999 and 2000, and also to maladroit management of the European Central Bank, but structural problems in the flows of international investment were also thought to be behind the problem. In any case, inflation in Europe between the time of the euro's creation and mid-2000 was lower than in the United States (whose inflation rate was itself low). The eleven members of the euro zone have been protected from imported inflation by the fact that two-thirds of their imports come from the euro zone itself. Most of the European economies have improved in performance since the euro was adopted, and the single currency has banished intra-European currency instabilities. It has created a much larger euro bond market than anticipated, which has provided the credit for expansion and consolidations and facilitated an unprecedented rate of cross-border mergers and acquisitions activity. There seems no reason why the euro should not prove in the long term a strong and stable currency and rival for the dollar, as generally is recognized. It could attract funds now invested in U.S. securities and funding the U.S. deficit. It could be a rival for denominating international trade products, including aircraft, oil, and other raw materials. So long as these remain priced in dollars, the United States benefits. The United States' ability to set the pace of the world economy through control of U.S. interest rates will eventually be weakened. The European Central Bank now independently sets rates for a currency bloc as large as the United States.

The challenge of transatlantic industrial competition is rather more serious. The natural tendency of a free market is to produce monopolies, and globalization has brought a concentration of strategic industries, resulting in intense transatlantic competition in several areas of high technology. Before the European Airbus consortium was formed, there were three major commercial aircraft manufacturers in the United States and several lesser ones in Western Europe. Since the Boeing–McDonnell Douglas merger, subsidized by the U.S. government, and Lockheed's abandonment of the commercial market, there are only two in the world.

The European Airbus consortium ended 1999 having won orders for 476 new aircraft, 85 more than were ordered from Boeing during 1999. This gave Airbus a back-order book almost as large as Boeing's, and that was before an engineers' strike and manufacturing problems in 2000 worsened Boeing's competitive situation. The European consortium has now reconstituted itself as a conventional company and expects by the end of 2000 to launch a program to produce a super-jumbo commercial transport, larger and more advanced than the Boeing 747 series that has given the Seattle company a profitable monopoly in very large commercial aircraft.

The French-led European space consortium ended 1999 holding half the world market for commercial satellite launches, and has put in service a new large version of its Ariane launcher, more advanced than anything in the American commercial inventory. In military aerospace a similar competitive challenge is developing. European manufacturers now offer three fighter or fighter-bomber aircraft of later design than the one advanced American aircraft actually available for export, a version of the F-16. The very advanced Lockheed F-22 project is in difficulty with congressional critics who question the need for the aircraft, and the so-called Joint Strike Fighter, supposed to become the dominant, new-generation combat aircraft of the twenty-first century (and incidentally, according to the trade journal *Aviation Week and Space Technology*, "destroy" Europe's military aeronautics industry), does not yet exist even in agreed prototype. Neither the U.S. Navy nor the U.S. Air Force seems ready to fight for it in the bureaucracy and in Congress, each preferring its own service solution (for the Air Force, the F-22). However, as *Aviation Week* has noted, the future both of Lockheed and of Boeing's military division (and ancillary industry producers) is now so dependent on the JSF that it "is more a national industrial strategy than a fighter program."

The Pentagon-demanded merger of the major American military producers had the unanticipated effect of creating three semimonopoly producers (Boeing, Lockheed Martin, and Raytheon Hughes) less interested in competitive innovation than in producing stockholder value. The transatlantic mergers which the Pentagon also promoted, expecting them to make European manufacturers effectively the subsidiaries of American companies, were rejected for just that reason; instead, two big European companies have been created. One, now known as BAe Systems, comprises the biggest British military producers; the other is a merger of France's Aerospatiale Matra with DASA, the aerospace division of German-controlled DaimlerChrysler, together with smaller Spanish and Italian producers, which together now form what now is known as EADS, the European Aeronautic, Defense, and Space Company (which also owns most of Airbus). EADS is now the third largest military aerospace firm in the world, behind Boeing and Lockheed, and has been lobbying Washington for greater access to U.S. military markets—which it is unlikely to obtain. Rainer Hertrich, head of DASA, who has been active in the effort, has remarked to *The Wall Street Journal* that there have been "frank acknowledgments by high-ranking officials in the Pentagon that there is more of a 'fortress U.S.' problem" than the "fortress Europe" frequently deplored in Congress and by U.S. government officials. However, the integration of Europe's military and civil aerospace, rocket, electronics, and other strategic industries will lead almost inevitably to some form of European preference in procurement, which will be seen in the United States as a hostile development.

America's political primacy in the transatlantic relationship has always been tolerated, if not always welcomed, by West Europeans (because, as the German commentator Josef Joffe has said, the United States "irks and domineers, but it does not conquer"). However, political relations are a complex and shifting matter of cooperation as well as leadership, and of interacting mutual and national interests. In industrial mergers the transfers of power, resource, and sovereignty are unambiguous. They place one or the other side in control and determine who gives orders to whom, who controls the resources of whom, who determines what is done, and who profits. In the strategic high-technology industries they determine whether a nation, or integrated block of nations, possesses the industrial and military guarantees of sovereignty.

The idea of a European challenge to the United States seems, in political terms, highly implausible. However, one must qualify that judgment where issues of European economic and technological sovereignty are concerned. There is an overriding common European interest in the prosperity of its currency, the independence of its industry, the security of its investments, the dynamism and success of its technology, and the expansion of its trade. The single market and the single currency guarantee that in these vital matters there will be a common stand vis-à-vis the external world, and certainly vis-à-vis the United States, Europe's largest trading partner, but also its most formidable competitor. The European Commission has already forcefully intervened in matters of European-American economic relations and commerce, and will increasingly do so in the future.*

Economy and politics within Europe are integrally related, so that further political unification in Europe probably will in part be provoked, or necessitated, by resistance to American industrial and economic competition. Efforts to divide the Europeans, a common practice in American trade diplomacy, will eventually push the Europeans closer together, since even the most Atlanticist European governments recognize that their primordial interest today lies in solidarity with their European neighbors. If the United States forces the issue, that is the choice they will have to make.

---

*In October 1999 Germany let it be known that it had made an unprecedented demand that the United States withdraw three CIA agents (undeclared in Germany, contrary to agreements between the two countries) who had been engaged in technological and commercial espionage. A similar episode occurred two years earlier in France when CIA agents were seized in the act of attempting to suborn a French civil servant in order to obtain trade intelligence. There is increasing criti-

The European Union's fifteen nations today do not want to make a political challenge to the United States. France is the only nation whose government believes that European political affirmation vis-à-vis the United States is a strategic necessity. It is interest, not volition, that will alter and deepen the rivalry between the United States and Europe. To the extent that European industrial and technological sovereignty seems threatened, European political sovereignty—the most fundamental of interests—will be seen as under threat. That will have consequences.

cism in Continental Europe (and in the European Parliament) of the large American communications intercept installations in Germany and Britain, which are suspected of being used against European commercial and economic interests; the United States denies this. However, R. James Woolsey, a former director of the CIA, wrote in *The Wall Street Journal Europe* on March 22, 2000, "Yes, my Continental friends, we have spied on you." He explained that this was not to steal technology, since "most European technology is just not worth our stealing," but because some European companies bribe customers, which gives them an unfair advantage over American companies. He concluded, "Get serious, Europeans. Stop blaming us and reform your own statist economic policies. Then your companies can become more efficient and innovative, and they won't need to resort to bribery to compete. And then we won't need to spy on you." This intervention, needless to say, did not improve matters.

# CENTRAL EUROPE                                          3

Central Europe is where the Cold War began. It is why the Cold War began. Control of Central Europe was the issue—above all, the control of Germany. Germany was a wounded and exhausted nation between 1944 and 1948, but it had come within reasonable distance of defeating both Russia and the Western Allies, and in the late 1940s it was thought capable of trying to do so again. In geopolitical terms, Central Europe remains the most important arena of conflict. It is where United States and Soviet forces were in direct contact for more than forty years, deployed for war. Nothing suggests that the Soviet Union looked upon any other front as more important to its own security than the Central European one, or that it regarded any threat as more preoccupying than that of disruptive events in Eastern Europe and eastern Germany. Nothing is settled if the Central European problem is not settled.

The future of Central and Eastern Europe is inseparable from its past. The region is made up of very old and culturally autonomous societies, which thus far have successfully resisted every effort, however catastrophic, to subdue them to some grand or sinister uniformity. There is no reason to think that this will not continue to be the case, barring their nuclear obliteration. The independent national societies and cultures of Central and Eastern Europe will certainly survive their present submission to Soviet power. The events of the years after 1945 represented, as the Czech novelist Milan Kundera has said, "a drama of the West—a West that, kidnapped, displaced, and brainwashed, nevertheless insists on defending its identity." The fears of the 1940s and 1950s that in totalitarian political techniques men had found a way of permanently altering the quality of a society—of eliminating from human consciousness the very conceptions of truth and justice—proved to be wrong. The consequences of Hitler's totalitarianism and war obviously changed the political geography of Europe, but Hitlerism—Nazism—proved so ephemeral that we now can scarcely imagine how such a man and such a doctrine could have evoked the enthusiastic support and intellectual justifications they enjoyed in the 1930s and 1940s. It all seems as remote from us now as the Pharaohs. The Soviet Union, despite Stalin's worst—Gulag, purge, terror—can now be clearly seen to have descended directly, in social norms, in political habits, and in foreign policy, from czarist Russia. Even that component of messianism which expressed itself in the export of Marxist revolution has its czarist antecedents.

To speak of Central and Eastern Europe in this way is to consider the long term, in which, it is true, we will all be dead. But in the long term is where those who follow us will have to confront the results of present-day decisions. There is only one eventual outcome imaginable here, given the endurance and power of European civilization and the inevitable transience of Communism, one of that civilization's incidental phenomena. It is that in one way or another (and there are ways in which this could certainly prove extremely unpleasant) Soviet power will eventually be withdrawn or expelled from Eastern and Central Europe. It may be withdrawn as a consequence of its own atrophy and of the cultural autonomy and resilience of the East European states. Or it may be violently ejected. There will also, in time, be a withdrawal of American forces from Western Europe. This may come about in an orderly or a disorderly manner; it may be intelligently planned or not. But the present situation cannot last indefinitely. A constructive policy would look for a way in which these eventualities could come about in a reasonable fashion, causing as little trouble and insecurity as possible, avoiding violence—or as much of it as can be avoided. Without such a policy, we are left not only with deterioration and stress in the Western alliance but also with the certainty of crisis in the Eastern bloc.

A.J.P. Taylor, the English historian, has written that the twentieth of August 1939 was "a milestone in world history, it marked the moment when Soviet Russia returned to Europe as a great power." The occasion was the signing of the Nazi-Soviet nonaggression pact. The Soviet "return" was by way of the secret protocol to that agreement, which divided Poland between Soviet and German spheres of domination. Modern Poland then had existed for just twenty years, brought into being at the end of the First World War, after more than a century of partition among Russia, Austria, and Prussia. The Nazi-Soviet pact reimposed partition, after Poland's army was crushed in a three-week German military campaign. Its eastern districts were at once occupied by the Red Army, which, in the common phrase, stabbed Poland in the back.

"Since my awakening I had felt something preventing me from bending back my head, and I now groped for it with my hand. My friends, who had grown somewhat calmer, had just shouted, 'Be careful, don't hurt yourself,' when my hand closed behind my head on the hilt of a sword. My friends came closer, examined me, led me back to the mirror in my room, and stripped me to the waist. A large, ancient knight's sword with a cross-shaped handle was buried to the hilt in my back, but the blade had been driven with such incredible precision between my skin and flesh that it had caused no injury. Nor was there a wound at the spot on my neck where the sword had penetrated, my friends assured me that there was an opening large enough to admit the blade, but dry and showing no trace of blood. And when my friends now stood on chairs and slowly, inch by inch, drew out the sword, I did not bleed, and the opening on my neck closed until no mark was left save a scarcely discernible slit."

This dream of Franz Kafka's was described in his diary for January 1915. It is the dream of a Czech whose country's wounds, unlike Poland's, have hardly bled, although, since its creation out of the old Austro-Hungarian Empire in 1918, it has faced approximately the same events and choices Poland has faced, choosing differently. These choices by small countries are vital for them, but may be more momentous than commonly understood for others as well, including the major powers, who presumptuously believe that they are in control of events. Czechoslovakia's choice in 1938 was a demonstration. The Czechs did not have to submit passively to dismemberment by Nazi Germany, as occurred as a result of the Munich agreement among Germany, France, and Britain. They could have fought, and had they fought, it is arguable that the Second World War could have been prevented. The Czechs, betrayed by their Western allies, owed nothing except to themselves. They had not even been asked to take part in the Munich conference, where Britain and France agreed to the German occupation of a part of Czechoslovakia, the Sudetenland. They could have refused to accept the Munich settlement. The Sudetenland, which contained the German ethnic minority in Czechoslovakia, also included the system of Czechoslovak defensive fortifications, modeled upon the Maginot Line and installed in difficult and mountainous terrain. There is reason to argue that the Czechoslovak Army might have stopped a German invasion, and certainly that it could have made it very costly.

Czechoslovakia possessed a modern industrial plant, incorporating what, at the time, was the second-largest armaments industry in the world. Its army was large and well equipped, in many respects better equipped than the German Army of 1938. Germany was not yet prepared for a two-front war. When the German Army did enter Czechoslovakia, it could spare only five first-class and seven reserve divisions to cover the Western Front, facing France. Evidence was adduced at Nuremberg that Czech resistance, certainly had it been followed by an Allied move in the West, could have provoked a German generals' attempt to depose Hitler. One of those generals was the Chief of the General Staff, Ludwig Beck, who was to resign because of his opposition to the invasion of Czechoslovakia. Earlier he had written: "History will burden these leaders with blood-guilt. . . . Their military obedience has a limit, when their knowledge, their conscience, and their sense of responsibility forbid the execution of a command."

But the Czechs capitulated. They had been abandoned by France, which, like Russia, had been committed to Czechoslovakia's defense, and by Britain. Czechoslovakia's Inspector-General, Jan Syrovy, said at the time to some British colleagues: "In this affair, messieurs, we have been willing to fight on the side of the angels, and now we shall hunt with the wolves." The Czech authorities forthwith collaborated, handing over anti-Nazis whom Germany had wanted arrested. Theirs even seemed a successfully expedient decision at first. The Czechs suffered lightly in the war that followed. Afterward, a free Czechoslovak republic was reestablished and briefly survived, until it became an inconvenience to the Soviet Union.

The Poles, on the other hand, in 1939 did fight. Having refused help to the Czechs in their time of trial, and even having helped the Germans dismember Czechoslovakia, the Poles, in turn, were attacked by Germany. They fought ferociously but vainly. But by doing so, they, too, made a difference. Germany's invasion of Poland compelled the British and French, against their will, to go to war. Even Hitler was surprised that they really did it. At first, he ordered that there be no offensive action in the West and told his entourage that "the whole business will evaporate" once Poland was overrun. He did not take the prospect of general war seriously until Churchill was made First Lord of the Admiralty on September 5, four days after Poland's invasion. Then he said to Albert Speer: "Churchill in the Cabinet. That means that the war is really on. Now we shall have war with England." His attack on Poland, and victory, although he could not know it, was actually the beginning of the end for Nazi Germany.

France and Britain had given guarantees to Czechoslovakia that they would not honor. After that, they felt compelled to give new assurances to Warsaw, this time guarantees they could not effectively honor but which they did honor, exactly because they had previously defaulted. These committed them to war. But Poland's frontiers were indefensible. Its regular army was unprepared for modern war. The Germans seized frontier railheads before the Polish reserve divisions could be mobilized and deployed. The Wehrmacht had had another year in which to continue its rearmament. By this time, Hitler, repeatedly successful, had intimidated the General Staff, and the officers opposed to him had been removed. With the attack on Poland, Poland was doomed, but a general European war followed.

Thirty years later, in 1968, when the Soviet Union invaded Czechoslovakia, following the Prague Spring of ideological ferment and political reforms, the Czechs once again did not fight. Again, they might have done so, no doubt hopelessly, but perhaps, again, to historical effect. However, they submitted to the proposition, implicitly conceded by the United States government of the time, that the Soviet Union possessed the privilege of intervening in a neighboring country to enforce "socialism."

When, at the end of the Second World War, Stalin had ordained that Poland's frontiers be moved westward so as to yield to Russia territory in the east, while extending Poland into formerly German territories in the west, up to the Oder and Neisse rivers, he believed that he was solving the fundamental problem of Soviet national security. He remarked cynically to General de Gaulle in 1944 that he would make Polish-German reconciliation permanently impossible. "Poland has always served as a corridor for the Germans to attack Russia," he said. "This corridor must be closed off, and closed off by Poland itself." The objective was valid. The means chosen by Stalin proved a failure. A bitter reconciliation between Poland and West Germany has, in fact, taken place. Stalin could not have imagined Willy Brandt in tears in the Warsaw Ghetto. He made a moral error in thinking that hatred could be fixed forever between Poles and Germans by a mere boundary-shifting. After the murder by Germans of six million Poles, including virtually all of Poland's Jews, and the Nazi attempt to exterminate the culture of Poland, what could a border change add to the total of hatred? The reasons for Poles to hate the Nazis were so immense that Poles had nothing they could do about them except to try to forgive the Germans.

The second error Stalin made was political. By imposing his own government upon not only Poland but all the East European nations that had been overrun by the Soviet Army at the end of the war, he meant to create a permanent security zone protecting the Soviet Union against attack from the West. Germany was partitioned, and the eastern half of it was stripped. Its industries were dismantled and shipped to Russia. The states under Soviet military domination between Germany and the Soviet border—Romania, Czechoslovakia, Hungary, and Poland—were forced to become political and military satellites of the Soviet Union. This did not, however, make the Soviet Union secure. It did the opposite. It created a condition of permanent insecurity for the Soviet state. The subordination of these states increased the international tension that Soviet policy was meant to counter. Poland's fate provided the first big dispute between the Western Allies and Stalin, the crack in the wartime alliance. The Allies wanted a free postwar government in Poland. Stalin wanted, and got, rule by the Lublin Committee, a Soviet creation dispatched to Warsaw in the baggage of the Red Army. Throughout the war, the Polish government-in-exile in London had commanded the underground home army and the exile army. But in 1945 this government-in-exile was abandoned by the principal Allied powers. Franklin Roosevelt said, "The Russians had the power in Eastern Europe. . . . The only practicable course was to use what influence we had to ameliorate the situation." Churchill and de Gaulle were more severe, but nothing was done to impede the Russians.

There was, in any case, a certain complaisance. It was Poland's misfortune to be in the wrong place, between two large and expansionist nations, and the Poles themselves had in the past played their hand to unhappy effect. Brave they undoubtedly were, but they were also uncompromising, romantic, and, in American eyes (of the 1940s), illiberal. As the Cold War developed, between 1945 and 1948, there were American tears for Czechoslovakia, a liberal, constitutional state created by a sometime American resident, Tomas Masaryk, under the patronage of Woodrow Wilson, but there were few for Poland. The Czechoslovak coup d'état in 1948 reiterated for Washington the lesson of Munich—that dictators were never content with what they had, and that only a firm stand could prevent an eventual world war. It was a lesson that was to determine American policy until the withdrawal from Vietnam, twenty-five years later.

What Stalin did in Eastern Europe failed to provide Russia with security, then or later. It deepened the actual insecurity of the Soviet state by inspiring the hostility of the United States, which alone was capable of seriously threatening the Soviet Union. It created in Eastern Europe a system of repression, hostile to those nationalisms of the region that not many years earlier had contributed to the destruction of the Austro-Hungarian Empire. It placed Soviet Russia in the historical role of a latter-day Austria, as counterrevolutionary policeman of Central and Eastern Europe. The Central and East European nations placed under Soviet control lacked even that representation in their governance that the Austro-Hungarian system had granted its member nations.

The cost of this policy to the Soviet Union mounted. The Soviet Union in 1989 was less secure on its western approaches than it was in 1945. Certainly it was less secure than it was in 1947, when Stalin had consolidated the bloc, or in 1952, after the Rajk and Slánský trials—the last of the great purges. That was the eve of Stalin's own death, and of what came to be known as the Thaw. Afterward, there were repeated rebellions and threats of revolution—the East Berlin uprising in 1953, the Hungarian revolt in 1956 (accompanied by the first of the Polish insurrections against Soviet domination), Czechoslovakia's Prague Spring in 1968, the renewed Polish movement of dissidence at the beginning of the 1980s, all involving some risk of war. The danger to the Soviet Union was also political. The lies necessary to justify Soviet domination of the East European states convinced no one in the region. The "blank spots" in this history, as Mikhail Gorbachev himself called them, tended to undermine Soviet doctrine itself and, with it, the East European socialist system.

The essential fact about the events in this region during the four postwar decades is that a cultural struggle was lost by the Soviet Union. Milan Kundera wrote a celebrated essay on the Central European consciousness in 1984 in which he said that, in each of the anti-Soviet rebellions from the 1950s to the 1980s, "the collective cultural memory and the contemporary creative effort assumed roles so great and so decisive—far greater and far more decisive than they have been in any other European mass revolt" because culture itself became "the living value around which all people rally." Whatever the political morale or expectations of the people of this region, they have not the slightest doubt who they are and to what civilization and political tradition they adhere. In the early years after the Second World War that was not always true. There was an influential notion that Soviet Communism perhaps did stand for the future—that one might hope in it, or detest it, but that it represented the future, and it was useless to stand against it: that Europe as it had existed before was now, as a civilization, terminated.

Afterward, the Soviet Union remained militarily dominant in the region and Communist parties ruled. This changed nothing fundamental because the Soviet Union failed to display the cultural authority, the élan or magnetism, the quality of apparent inevitability, able to evoke mimesis (to use Toynbee's term)—able to persuade the East Europeans that they wanted the Soviet Union as a model, wanted to follow it, would accept its values, saw in it their future.

It was otherwise in successful empires. Those conquered by Rome wanted to become Roman citizens. Elites in colonial India and Africa in the nineteenth and early twentieth centuries wanted to study at Oxford or in Paris. The notion that a young Pole or Hungarian of the forty postwar years would have longed to go to Moscow to study and make a career, to find a place among its painters and poets, to bring its civilization back to his own country, is ludicrous. His grandfather or father had wanted to go to Vienna, Berlin, Paris, New York—and so did he. Nothing in the postwar half-century produced conversion to the values or ideas of the Soviet Union. The opposite was true. The prestige the Soviet Union possessed in intellectual and working-class circles before the Second World War, as a revolutionary society, the workers' fatherland, became discredited. Pro-Western and pro-American sentiments intensified in socialist Europe, often unreasonably so. The idealism of prewar Communist cadres, of the Comintern and the wartime Communist underground, the people who established the first postwar governments and were willing to justify brutality and expedience as necessary to the redemptive transformation of society ("What vileness would you not commit to exterminate vileness," Bertolt Brecht wrote in 1931, "embrace the butcher, but change the world!"), was replaced by cynicism or careerism. Nothing was accomplished to give ordinary people any reason to want to stay in the "socialist camp."

The Communists' attempt to create a vast, integrated, socially progressive economic bloc proved a fiasco in practical terms. These countries, more or less developed European nations before the war, fifty years later suffered systematic shortages of food and basic consumer goods. "Why should we live like this? What have we done? We work so hard . . ." That was spoken by a young East German who, exceptionally, was allowed to visit family in German Switzerland. Why should East Germany, the old industrial center of imperial and Nazi Germany, have lagged hopelessly behind West Germany in industrial productivity and sophistication, and in its standard of living? Why should there have been chronic food shortages in Romania—formerly a major agricultural exporter—and rationed electric power in that country, which is a major oil producer? Czechoslovakia was the industrial core of the Austro-Hungarian Empire. Before the Second World War it was one of the world's principal arms and heavy-industrial exporters. Its industry by 1989 was hopelessly uncompetitive on international markets.

People in Eastern Europe knew that they lived under an economic and social system that, while it originally was put forward as a progressive idea, proved to be a failure in economic terms, robbed people of freedoms universally enjoyed in the rest of Europe, and even deprived people of the privacies, the amenities, the luxuries, to which their work would easily entitle them in Western Europe or North America. Why should they not have the structures of social protection taken for granted in nonsocialist Europe? Why should Polish workers not have had a real union? They had one under the prewar right-wing dictatorship. Why should the serious literature, drama, and art of Czechoslovakia, Romania, East Germany, and Bulgaria be suppressed, condemned to underground existence, samizdat publication, or furtive performance and showing? Why should Romanian peasants of Hungarian or German ethnic origin suffer suppression of their traditional cultures and a grotesque regrouping of rural population into high-rise apartments, with the expropriation and destruction of whole villages? Why should the historical center of Bucharest, a charming and elegant city, have been destroyed because "socialism" bestowed upon Romania a dictator, Nicolae Ceaușescu, who despite his Neronian delusions enjoyed the de facto endorsement and putative military backing of the Soviet Union? This writer, in Ceaușescu's Romania, heard an official remark, apropos the "contradictions" history produces, that "we should have set out to build Fascism."

Central Europe's political and cultural connection to Western Europe has been a fact for more than a thousand years, and that of Southeastern Europe goes back to antiquity. Romania was a Roman province, as were what now is Yugoslavia, much of Hungary, Bulgaria, and Turkey—where the Eastern Roman Empire was to have its capital. Rome's frontiers in Europe, under Augustus, were the Rhine and the Danube. Central Europe was the center of the Holy Roman Empire, which succeeded Rome in the West.

Slavic Bohemia's first dynasty, in the tenth century, adhered to the Empire, and in the fourteenth century Bohemia was the seat of that Empire. Later, the Bohemian religious reformer Jan Hus anticipated the Reformation, and Bohemia, together with eastern Germany, became a center of Protestantism. The Thirty Years' War, settling the character of Central Europe into modern times, began in Bohemia, between the Roman and Protestant versions of Western Christianity.

Bulgaria and Romania both were part of the Eastern Roman Empire, then of the Ottoman Empire, subsequently falling under Russian influence, and their Christianity (like that of Greece and Serbia) is the Eastern Christianity of Cyril and Methodius. Even then, Romania insisted on its Latin culture and Roman origins. (Romanian is a language accessible to anyone who reads Italian or French.) Romania occupies more or less the former Roman province of Dacia and emerged as a modern nation in the mid-nineteenth century, taking a German prince, a Hohenzollern, as its monarch. His successor, another German, married a granddaughter of Queen Victoria—Marie of Romania, who lived until 1938, an intelligent and energetic woman who wrote books and for the press, organized charitable enterprises, and interfered in Romanian politics, being considerably more capable than her husband. She became an international celebrity, toured America in 1926, lectured and was lionized—even adopted into the Sioux Nation.

Bulgaria emerged from Ottoman control, with Russian support, at roughly the same time as Romania, and also acquired a German monarch (a Battenberg, to be followed by a Saxe-Coburg-Gotha). Its independent national existence began in considerable tension with Serbia, Greece, and later with post-Ottoman Turkey, over the possession of Macedonia (in 1989 part of Yugoslavia). The two Balkan Wars (1912 and 1913) resulted, ending with Bulgaria's defeat and loss of further territory. Bulgaria entered the First World War on the Central Powers' side chiefly because of its claim on Macedonia, and in the event lost further territory to Greece and Yugoslavia. It fought on the German side again in the Second

World War, until the Red Army reached its frontiers. In the post-war settlement it was given South Dubruja, a contested region to its northeast, taken from Romania. Romania was deprived of Bessarabia, now Moldova. Since 1945 neither has challenged its territorial loss, nor has Hungary officially contested Romania's rule of disputed Transylvania (although relations between the two countries reached the point where the writer István Csurka, speaking at an officially encouraged rally in Budapest in June 1988, said, "Formally, Romania is our ally—in practice it is our enemy"). The Romanian as well as Bulgarian Communist governments "sold" their ethnic German citizens to West Germany, a trade about which there was little publicity, while Bulgaria was engaged in a campaign to suppress the language and culture of its Turkish minority (160,000 Bulgarians of Turkish culture were simply expelled in 1951–52).

The Hungarians are an Asian people of obscure origins and were dominated by the Ottomans for a century and a half (1526–1699) during the Ottoman Empire's farthest penetration of Europe. But their connection with the West, and especially with France, began soon after their stabilization as a nation in the tenth century. The Hungarian nobles compelled the king to grant the "Golden Bull," a concession of power to the nobility, described as the Hungarian Magna Carta, in 1222, seven years after Runnymede. Under the Jagiellon monarchs, Poland developed a quasi-parliamentary system at the same time, earlier than in Britain, and there was a form of habeas corpus in Poland before this emerged in English law. It was a Hungarian journalist who telexed the world in the final moments of the Hungarian Revolution of 1956 to say: "We are going to die for Hungary and for Europe"—a phrase with which Kundera began his 1984 essay, adding that for Hungarians, Czechs, and Poles, "the word 'Europe' does not represent a phenomenon of geography but a spiritual notion synonymous with the word 'West.' The moment Hungary is no longer European—that is, no longer Western—it is driven from its own destiny, beyond its own history: it loses the essence of its identity." The concern for Central

European civilization by such exiles as Kundera often expressed a nostalgia for the multinational Hapsburg system, which so many of its citizens—Czechs first among them—were eager to destroy in 1918, in favor of romantic national causes.

Adam Zamoyski observes in his history *The Polish Way* that "throughout the last three centuries, the Poles have been at pains to stress that they belong to the West, to Christendom and to Rome. There are strong ideological reasons for this claim, since they have absorbed so much of the moral and cultural heritage of Rome, and this constitutes the greatest distinction between them and their Slav brothers to the East. Their zeal, however, is the zeal of the convert, for they were not conceived by Rome or born in Christianity." By the time medieval Christianity reached Poland, there was already a nation-state in existence, a Slavic state that had emerged around the ninth century under a pagan monarchy, that of the Piast dynasty, as a substantial obstacle to the eastward expansion of the Holy Roman Empire. From the tenth century, when the Polish monarch was baptized a Roman Catholic, together with his court, Poland was primarily concerned with its relationship with that Empire, to which it was never annexed; with the expansionist and aggressive order of Teutonic Knights in what subsequently was Prussia; with neighboring Bohemia, the other major East-Central European power; and with Lithuania, with which Poland imprudently united itself in the fourteenth century. Polish intellectual life was in steady interaction with Italy, in particular, but also with France and Britain.

By the late Middle Ages Jagiellon Poland incorporated much of what now is Hungary, Romania, Czechoslovakia, Croatia, Belorussia, and Ukraine, as well as Lithuania, ruling a region extending from the Baltic Sea to the Adriatic and the Black seas, and from Vienna nearly to Moscow. The extent and power of the medieval Polish commonwealth is usually forgotten because of Poland's virtual disappearance from the map in modern times. Its

eighteenth-century partitions among Russia, Austria, and Prussia—
in part the result of its own "democracy," the system in which each
of the noble members of the Seym, or parliament, possessed a virtual veto over national policy—were not ended until 1918. The
nation again disappeared under Nazi rule in 1939, and after 1945
was under Soviet domination. The result is a profound experience
of survival as nation and culture despite foreign control. The transfer of the crucial elements in national education to "flying universities" and other unofficial schools, which occurred after the 1940s,
the flourishing underground publishing and cultural life, the rallying around the Church as guarantor of national culture, all
reflected what had to be learned when Poland had no formal existence as a state.

Following the emergence of Mikhail Gorbachev in the U.S.S.R.
there was a profound misunderstanding between the Soviets and
the East Europeans on their definitions of reform. Gorbachev and
his colleagues called for a return to Leninism. This meant to them
a return to the idealism of the Revolution and, they contended, to
the "democratic" institutions destroyed by Stalin. They looked to a
restored Leninism to provide moral as well as political legitimacy to
the rule of the Communist Party. For the East Europeans a return
to Leninism meant a return to repression, ideological dictatorship,
and the "revolutionary discipline" invoked by Stalin and his apolo-
gists to justify the terror of the 1950s.

The attempt to reform Marxism-Leninism and its economic
and political institutions met a fundamentally different situation in
Eastern Europe and East Germany from that in the Soviet Union.
Reform in the U.S.S.R.—perestroika, glasnost, "new thought"—
took the form of an acknowledgment of long-denied truths about
the failures and crimes of the Soviet system and modern Soviet history, with an attempt to change the Soviet Union within the terms
of the inherited Leninist system. For the Soviet leadership there
was no evident alternative to Leninism. To discard it would be to

discard the leaders' own right to lead—the basis of their legitimacy. In Eastern Europe, rejection of the Marxist-Leninist system was not only thinkable, but generally assumed, in all but the most reactionary party circles, to be the only real solution to the problems with which these countries, and the elites themselves, found themselves confronted.

Unlike the Soviet leadership, which lacked an alternative example of what Russian society might become, other than Leninist, or czarist, the East Europeans had obvious models of change, not only in their own histories but in the contemporary West, to which they believed themselves in any case to belong. They wanted some version of the pluralist political system of the West, and some form, usually conceived as social-democratic, of the open economy that has given the West its prosperity. If in 1989 one talked with economists, journalists, members of the scientific institutes, and even some officials in Poland and Hungary—all of them people engaged in running their countries, not the dissidents—they generally were perfectly open about this. They said that if it were not for Soviet domination of the region and the ideological/military division of Europe as a whole, they would quickly abandon a discredited economic, political, and social system for that of Western Europe, which demonstrably works.

In Czechoslovakia, East Germany, Bulgaria, and Romania, people were more circumspect because the authorities in those countries were, in the late 1980s, highly unsure of themselves in the face of the Soviet Union's reforms. Nevertheless, such people as Valtr Komarek, the director of the Czechoslovak Academy of Sciences' Institute for Forecasting, were willing to say to Western correspondents (as Komarek did, to *The New York Times* in late 1987) that the events of preceding years "led to suppressing the creative possibilities of the people. This has brought socialism to a deep contradiction with modern science, technology and modern economic and social forces." Socialism "is on the threshold of crisis. If there is not a total reform the crisis is inevitable." Some three hundred thousand Czechoslovaks signed a petition in 1988 for complete religious freedom; the "Charter 77" human rights group, begun in 1977, continued to be active despite official persecution; and the East German Lutheran Church provided "free space" in which East German social and political dissidence was able to function. Some Gorbachev speeches were censored in Czechoslovakia and East Germany, as were some press accounts of developments in Moscow. *Pravda*, as well as the main Soviet organs of reform—*Moscow News, Ogonyok*—were sold out almost as soon as they arrived in East Berlin, since they provided information the East Germans could not obtain from their own press.

The westward anchorage was economic as well as moral and intellectual. The East European countries all had important economic links to Western Europe until the cataclysm set off by Hitler. Czechoslovakia, a part of the Hapsburg system until 1918, was the second industrial power of the region (Germany, of course, the first). West Germany reassumed prewar Germany's position as principal trading partner for the entire East European (Comecon) group and as principal supplier of foreign capital. The pattern of this trade became roughly that of before the war, when Eastern Europe supplied raw materials and agricultural products to the more sophisticated German economy. West Germany bought fuels, raw materials, and semimanufactures from the East. German chemical companies bought large quantities of bulk chemicals from East Germany, Czechoslovakia, and Hungary, which went into the fine chemicals and chemical products West Germany exported elsewhere. *The Financial Times* wrote in 1988 that "no other Western country provides anything like this enormous market for the East's low added value products."

It was a deliberate West German political policy to maintain trade with East Germany at no less than 10 percent of East Germany's total foreign trade (although this constituted only some 2 percent of total West German trade). This was not easy to do, since the G.D.R., like the other countries of the socialist bloc, had difficulty producing anything that could compete on world markets other than raw materials and semimanufactures. Thus West Germany even sent crude oil to East Germany for refining, taking it back at three times the price at which it was sold, despite much unused refining capacity in the Federal Republic.

The intra-German relationship was so close that East Germany was sometimes referred to in Europe as the thirteenth member of the Common Market. The West German government defended its subsidies, real and virtual, to the East German economy (which included "buying" political prisoners) as a humanitarian obligation to the fellow Germans who continued to pay for Hitler's war while West Germans enjoyed prosperity and world respect, but it was also a policy intended to make East Germany dependent upon the West.

Similarly, West German loans to Hungary (which had the highest level of debt in the socialist bloc, and in 1987 was saved from bankruptcy by the West Germans) were provided in exchange for political concessions: the continuance of liberal reforms in the Hungarian economy, plus such specific improvements in Hungarian–West German relations as the opening of a West German cultural center in Budapest. Even with West German help, the Hungarian situation continued in 1989 to be dramatic, with high inflation, overall loss of buying power, rising unemployment, and a flight from currency into real estate—the cost of which, in Budapest, rose by 30 to 50 percent during the twelve months prior to May 1988. Hungary then had a non-Communist president (a largely ceremonial post), Bruno Straub, and its first non-Communist, nonpolitical union since just after the war, an association of scientific workers. In January 1989 the National Assembly made independent political parties and associations legal. The Hungarians and their neighbors, the Austrians, proposed a joint Austro-Hungarian World's Fair in Vienna and Budapest in 1995, with free movement between the two cities.

West Germany was also Poland's largest creditor and trade

partner. Economic reform proposals meant to improve Poland's chaotic economic condition were in late 1987 the subject of the first wholly free election held in Eastern Europe since the aftermath of the war—and the government lost. Its loss followed from the fact that it had set a quixotic standard for success: a majority of all eligible voters. It won the referendum in terms of votes actually cast, but about a third of the electorate abstained. The Jaruzelski government acknowledged the legitimacy of a "socialist opposition," which had been proposed in the Soviet Union as well. The Polish military government's self-justification was that military rule was necessary to prevent popular dissidence from provoking Soviet intervention, with consequent catastrophe for Poland. The Solidarity movement's supporters conceded the geopolitical constraints that weighed on Poland but insisted that pluralism offered the only way out of the crisis. Poland's prime minister, Mieczyslaw Rakowski, told *Time* in October 1988 that "politically, the decades-long monopoly of the Party is over" and that opposition representatives could be expected in the Polish parliament in 1989. It was extremely significant that Poland should have fallen under military government—unprecedented in the Soviet bloc (and contrary to Leninist political norms). It came to power because the civilian Communist government of Poland simply collapsed under popular pressures at the end of the 1970s. The crisis of Communism was more advanced in Poland than anywhere else, the military regime really a post-Communist custodial government—negotiating its succession, awaiting developments.

The Soviet Union remained, in 1989, deeply uncertain about what to do in Eastern Europe. Its proposals, made to the Western powers, on conventional force reductions in Europe, lacked political context, even though reduction of the Soviet troop deployment was a potentially explosive affair. Gorbachev expressed the intention, speaking to the Hungarians in 1988, to remove Soviet forces from Hungary, even as a unilateral action, without waiting for Western concessions. In Hungary and elsewhere in the bloc the message was passed—or was understood to be passed—that the Brezhnev Doctrine was finished. (If there ever was a Brezhnev Doctrine, beyond an ex post facto rationalization for invading Czechoslovakia in 1968.) Gorbachev repeatedly told the East European parties that they must solve their own problems and that the U.S.S.R. had no answers for them. He even told the Hungarians that the Soviet Union itself must learn from Hungary's reforms.

This was all very well, but left the question of what would happen if the Soviet Union found its security zone in Eastern and Central Europe crumbling. It was an urgent problem, at least in the short term. One had the impression in 1989 that the Soviet leaders had not seriously thought the matter through, or possibly shrank from thinking it through, because the possibilities seemed so painful and contradictory. They ostensibly wanted troop reductions, eased relations with both Western and Eastern Europe, political and economic reform in the bloc, but they could not bring themselves to acknowledge that the only effective reforms would involve disjunctive change in the nature of their relationship with the East European countries, the latter's effective abandonment of the Soviet model of development, and a fundamental change in the security situation in Europe as a whole.

A Soviet security zone in Eastern Europe, respected and even guaranteed by the West European powers and the United States, possessing a solid political base in the free consent of the East European peoples, was a perfectly realistic idea. This already existed on the Soviet Union's northern border, in Finland. It was what the Polish opposition attempted to offer Leonid Brezhnev at the time of the initial crisis over the Solidarity movement, in 1981. It could have provided the Soviet Union with far more solid long-term security assurances than the existing system, which repeatedly had broken down, requiring military interventions, deepening the alienation and embitterment of the East European populations, and poisoning relations with the West. A changed security system required, however, freedom for the East European peoples to choose the commitment to Soviet security voluntarily, doing so as a function of their free choice of institutional evolution toward West European norms—on Finland's precedent.

Although the Russo-Finnish border was in 1989 the frontier upon which the Soviet Union was most secure, Finland had been a source of political and military tension and threat for the first thirty years of revolutionary Russia's existence. Finland had been a part of Sweden until 1809, when it became a grand duchy under Russian suzerainty. During the Bolshevik Revolution, the Finns declared their independence—initially with Bolshevik approval. They subsequently had to fight, however, as the new Russian government supported Finland's Communists in an attempt to seize control of the country. With German help, Finland's Whites succeeded in establishing an independent state, electing a German prince as king of Finland. He renounced the Crown, however, when Germany lost the First World War. A second Soviet-Finnish struggle, over Finland's eastern boundary, was finally settled by negotiations in 1920 and 1922. In 1939, Nazi Germany and the Soviet Union made their nonaggression pact, with its secret provision giving Russia a free hand in the north. Moscow made new demands upon Finland for territorial concessions, which the Finns refused. The Soviets attacked, with a puppet government waiting on the border to be conveyed to Helsinki by the Soviet Army. But Finland held, counterattacked, and threw the Soviet forces back into Russia during the Winter War of 1939–40. The Finns then gave limited concessions, and the Soviet Union dropped its efforts to replace Finland's government.

When Germany invaded Russia, in June 1941, the Finns attacked to recover what had been lost the year before. After the German forces began their retreat on the central front, the Soviets counterattacked Finland, but again the four million Finns resisted. Moscow eventually agreed to negotiate. Finland had to cede territory to Russia, resettling 10 percent of its population from the lost land, but Finland remained a parliamentary democracy. Max Jakobson, Finland's former representative to the United Nations, has said that "besides Great Britain and the U.S.S.R., Finland was the only one of all the European countries involved in World War Two which was not occupied; the only one to maintain the continuity of her Constitution and political institutions; the only one to make the transition from war to peace without an internal rupture—without a single execution." Finland's policy after 1945 was directed to allaying Soviet anxiety about security on this sensitive frontier, less than a hundred miles from Leningrad. The Soviet government had to be convinced that its essential strategic interests could be reconciled with the existence of an independent and democratic Finland. This was accomplished.

After the war, Norway and Denmark joined NATO, but Sweden, concerned with maintaining a "northern balance," agreed to stay out of the Atlantic Alliance as part of a tacit arrangement to moderate Soviet pressure on Finland. Russia was thus given additional reassurance on the northern front. It had gained what Stalin had wanted from Poland: a potential corridor of attack effectively closed. In this instance it was done by the free actions of the two peoples involved. The Soviet government later reduced what it had asked of Finland. The important Porkkala military base was handed back in 1955. That was the same year the Soviet Union, with Stalin dead and Khrushchev and Bulganin in power, signed the Austrian State Treaty, restoring Austrian sovereignty, and withdrew Soviet troops from eastern Austria. The Soviet leaders went to Yugoslavia that year and accepted responsibility for the 1948 break between Stalin and Tito. They conceded that more than one road to socialism could exist. The momentous 20th Soviet Party Congress, where Khrushchev delivered his secret speech on Stalin's crimes, took place in February 1956. Many political prisoners were freed.

It was a time of unseized opportunities. Proposals were being made in the East as well as the West for basic change—and liberalization—in the Central European situation. Polish foreign minister Adam Rapacki proposed a nuclear-free zone in Central Europe. The American diplomat and scholar George Kennan put forward a plan for military disengagement in Central Europe. In Britain, Winston Churchill, Anthony Eden, Denis Healey, and Field Marshal Montgomery all gave support to one or another version of disengagement and neutralization in the region. But Washington was against it, and the Soviet position was never seriously tested, so nothing was done.

The manner by which Finland preserved its security, and that of Russia at the same time, was turned into a subject of wrongheaded, indeed ignorant, American foreign policy dispute during the late 1970s, when it was said that the European countries were becoming "Finlandized"—defined in this case as a process by which an independent country is compelled, by military intimidation, effectively to surrender its freedom. This was a completely false interpretation of what actually happened to Finland, where a policy of prudence was the means by which the country saved its freedom when, by reason of war, geographical position, past actions, and lack of foreign support, its freedom was in extreme jeopardy. "Finlandization" actually imposed a check upon Soviet expansion, so that the Soviet Union in 1989 had less influence over Finland's affairs than it had at the end of the war. It might have dominated Finland, but the Finns made the price too high. The American debate about the alleged "Finlandization" of Western Europe distorted not only the truth about what happened to Finland but also the real significance of the Finnish example, which was for Eastern Europe.

The crucial fact about the Finland settlement is that, in Finland, Soviet security was willingly guaranteed by the Finnish people themselves. In Eastern Europe, Soviet security rested upon governments without popular consent, maintained in power by the presence of Soviet military forces. Their neighbors, the West European powers, were allied with the United States against the Soviet Union. If war came, the Russians could have no confidence that their own reluctant allies might not turn on them, causing the Soviet Union to face an uprising or mutiny of Romanians and Hungarians, as well as of the embittered Poles. The interest of these nations was not to defend Russia, or to defend a zone of neutrality, but to recover their independence.

This situation endangered the survival of the Soviet Union. It was in the Soviet Union's own interest that a security system that rested upon compulsion be exchanged for one that was voluntary. A system of military constraints and confrontation needed to be supplanted by political arrangements acknowledging the fact that no one involved had anything to gain from a war. Whatever American and Soviet confrontation or competition might have implied in the Middle East or in Central America, the strategic status quo had been accepted and ratified in Europe, and there was no evidence that either side envisaged its violent change. While forty years of sterile polemics between the blocs made this difficult for the Soviet Union to understand, the Western nations had long since conceded the legitimacy of the Soviet security interest in Eastern Europe. The historical grounds for the Soviet fear of an invasion across the Polish plain were widely appreciated in the West. The Soviet desire to have friendly states on its border was accepted as a reasonable one. The principal Western objection to the existing system was that it unnaturally, cruelly, and in the end unrealistically and unsustainably, suppressed the national feelings and political autonomy of the East European states. It was objectionable because it was unstable, repeatedly had produced crises, and risked war. The interest of the Western governments was that this system be reformed in a way that would gratify the national feelings and desire for autonomy of the East Europeans, while meeting legitimate Soviet security needs.

The particular military threat to the Soviet Union that the East European system was meant to prevent was, in the 1980s and after, a fantasy based on obsolete military and geopolitical assumptions. No sane Western military man would imagine launching a conventional land assault upon the Soviet Union across Poland or through Czechoslovakia, Romania, Hungary—into those limitless Russian spaces that destroyed Napoleon and Nazi Germany. Napoleon's and Hitler's invasions, in their day, had some strategic rationality, a promise of decisive success by seizing Moscow, against the resistance of what was believed to be a weak Russian state. No one in 1989 argued that NATO could march on Moscow and win. In any case, win what?

War remained conceivable, if highly implausible, between the Soviet Union and the Western powers, or between the U.S.S.R. and the United States, but it would have been a strategic nuclear war, or, if not that, a war in some third zone of indirect strategic interest. No imaginable scenario of Western land attack upon Russia offered anything to the United States and the NATO states except the certainty of tragedy. Europe was ripe—forty years after the war—for a political settlement that recognized this reality, which ameliorated the strains under which the East European states lived, and by doing so gave to them positive and popular motives to provide a guarantee of Soviet security, substituting for an alliance of compulsion one of mutual interest among states, in essential respects again independent nations. The general framework of such an arrangement presumably would have included mutual Soviet and American military withdrawals, joint guarantees of existing frontiers, and of the political integrity of the European states. Washington's argument against military disengagement in the 1950s was that Soviet forces would fall back a few hundred miles on good railroads and highways, while the American army would go back across an ocean. In a day of long-range deployment and prepositioned equipment, this was no longer a decisive objection in 1989. The argument was also made that American troops were necessary as hostages to European nuclear security. In fact, the European powers were already capable of providing themselves with a convincing nuclear deterrent force. If the presence of American hostages contributed to deterrence, such hostages did not need to be numerous. An American color guard in Berlin might serve. The conventional defense of Western Europe was entirely within the industrial, economic, and demographic capacity of Western Europe.°

The principal obstacle in the past to a settlement followed from the belief on both sides that Germany would have to be reunited and "neutralized"—a prospect that seemed unrealistic even then. Germany is too important and dynamic, in too important a place, to be made a neuter. Today it seems clear that the only settlement seriously imaginable must ratify some form of the division of Germany, possibly in the context of a larger "European" political framework. The division of Germany suits everyone except some—by no means all—of the Germans themselves. Historically, the "normal" condition of Germany has been division. Unity was a matter of less than a century, and was filled with disaster—two world wars and the moral abomination of Nazism. It was no success, least of all for the Germans. A unified Germany deeply unsettled Europe, because it was too big. The basic problem of Europe from 1871 onward was how to deal with this unified, disproportionately powerful Germany. The answer finally was found in 1945, at great cost. It was to redivide Germany. This, almost certainly, will prove an irreversible verdict, as far as the future can be foreseen. The many German states that existed before Bismarck, and the four that can be said to exist today—the Federal Republic, the German Democratic Republic, Austria, and the German cantons of Switzerland—could, can, and do live at peace with one another and with their neighbors. The problem of disproportion is solved. West Germany is not notably more powerful than France. East Germany is an industrial power on the order of Poland or Czechoslovakia. Europe, for the first time in a century, enjoys an equilibrium of forces, and it is in the interest of everyone that this continue. The truth, usually unspoken, is that every country in Western and Eastern Europe, as well as the Soviet Union and the United States, has a fundamental interest in the continued division of Germany. To

---

°The rest of this chapter appears as it did in 1989, without the amendments of tense made in the text of the previous pages.

acknowledge this in a European political settlement would do no more than acknowledge, finally, the true geopolitical meaning and consequence of the Second World War.

Within such a revised international framework, which substitutes political measures of security in Central Europe for the military means that have been relied upon since 1945, the hardest problem is posed by Germany, and after that by how the changes in the East European states can be made to enhance rather than jeopardize Soviet security. Possibly these nations would remain formally socialist, with Communist parties continuing to play leading roles; but these parties could no longer be guaranteed a monopoly over political activity or determination of national policy. The object of the necessary changes would be to obtain popular consent for government and for the security policies pursued. Popular consent, after what has happened in the last half-century, would inevitably be given only guardedly, to prudent governments, or to expedient ones. But there is a vital difference between a freely chosen prudence, on the Finnish model, and the imposed version. The Soviet Union can be truly secure only when the Polish, Czechoslovak, and Hungarian governments are secure, enjoying popular consent. A Poland that willingly acknowledges an obligation to defend Soviet security, and has that obligation formally acknowledged by the Western powers, solves the problem Stalin posed in 1944. A turbulent Poland, with a rebellious population, worsens that problem. All this, of course, runs against the Soviet Union's political and ideological investment in things-as-they-are. Yet Moscow has in the past shown itself capable of sudden acts of realism, and Mikhail Gorbachev has demonstrated a clear grasp of the scale of his problems, if not always of their solution. Moscow has proved itself less bound by sentiment, and even, on great occasions, by ideology, than the United States. It has cut losses and seized opportunities. It did so in 1955, leaving Austria. Today, intelligent men in the Soviet diplomatic and political services must see that the present course of events in Europe undermines not only the eventual security of their country but its domestic tranquillity. They recognized the

threat to the Soviet Union in prolonging an unprofitable intervention in Afghanistan, and they decided to cut their losses and leave.
In Central and Eastern Europe the Soviet leadership faces problems resembling those of Austria-Hungary's rulers before 1914. To
suppress the aroused national feeling of such great historical states
as Poland, Bohemia, and Hungary is, in the end, an unrealistic and
unsustainable policy. But Soviet Russia is not a country that looks
into history to learn things, least of all into the history of a Hapsburg Empire that failed.

The leaders of the Soviet Union are disturbed by the argument that
the East European countries belong to Western Europe and Western civilization, and that a distinct Middle European civilization
exists—as are Soviet intellectuals, and indeed all Russian intellectuals, who see in this an implied exclusion of Russia from Europe.
At a literary conference in Lisbon in early 1988, Soviet writers in
attendance were angry to be told that the Soviet Union is seen in
the part of Europe the Red Army freed from the Nazis as a repressive rather than liberating force. The exiled Russian poet Joseph
Brodsky, who lives in New York, defended them, saying to those
who spoke of a Middle European consciousness that "the concept
of Central Europe is not known to Soviet citizens."° Soviet writers
are prepared to talk about a socialist consciousness, but not a Central European one, whereas for everyone else the notion of a distinct socialist consciousness is an ideological relic of the 1930s.

There also are people in Western Europe who find the idea of
a distinctive Middle Europe disquieting, arguing that its political
realization might take the form of a neutralized Central Europe
(although it must be asked in what respect Central Europe would
be neutral; its military neutralization, as with Austria or Finland, is
not automatically a bad idea). There are those who prefer what an
American policymaker once called a "more organic" Soviet–East
European relationship—perpetuating Soviet control—because

°Joseph Brodsky died in 1996.

they fear that greater political autonomy in the region would invite new unrest in an area of many unresolved conflicts. They prefer present arrangements to an unpredictable future. This case would be more easily defended if change had not already gone so far, and if the Soviet Union's own crisis was not a primary instigator of the changes under way. Middle Europe exists, whether or not these people, or Joseph Brodsky, or the Soviet intelligentsia, like it, and the political and national issues of Central and Eastern Europe and the Balkans will inevitably, eventually, have to be faced—the "German Question" among them. Consideration of this has been all but absent from the Western policy debate.

Bureaucrats and policy planners talk of "getting ahead of the curve," an expression for anticipating the inevitable and making creative use of it—which is what used to be known as statesmanship. Certain developments are inevitable. It is inevitable that the Soviet Union will leave Eastern Europe. It is inevitable that American troops will one day be withdrawn from Western Europe. It would, one must think, be useful in the settlement of Europe's affairs to gain something valuable in exchange for an American withdrawal. It is inevitable that West European and American security perceptions and policies will diverge even more than they have already done. To reformulate the European-American relationship as a means to constructive reform in Central and Eastern Europe would be to get ahead of the curve. Leonid Brezhnev said to Czechoslovakia's Alexander Dubček after the Soviet invasion of that country in 1968: "Your western frontier is not merely yours alone, it is that of the socialist camp. It is a result of the Second World War for which the U.S.S.R. paid a high cost. The Soviet Politburo does not have the right to place in jeopardy the results of that war." That is a comprehensible position, but it is not, in the long run, a sustainable one. To alter the Soviet–East European relationship in a way that actually strengthened both Soviet and European security would be an act of statesmanship.

Old Russia's fear, in its consciousness of weakness and backwardness, was of encirclement. Enemies seemed to press in from

India, to threaten Russia through Central and Eastern Europe, to dispatch their agents through Finland, across the Caspian, into Mongolia. Stalin's policy followed from that learned fear, reinforced by his own experience of Western interventions in the Russian civil war. It was not a complicated policy. It was to control as far as you can reach, strike ruthlessly when you must strike, and not think too much about the future. It accounts for the Soviet Union's murder of Polish officers in the Katyn Forest in 1940, and the Soviet Army's halt on the Vistula in 1944 to allow the Nazis time to suppress the Warsaw uprising and destroy the independent Polish resistance. Stalin did not expect to pay a price for those things in his lifetime. His manipulation of the Polish border in 1945 expressed his confidence in revenge as a political force. Better possibilities exist.

Revenge has not provided the answer to Russia's security problem. There is nothing further that revenge can accomplish for Russia—or for Poland, or the other East European nations—except to jeopardize their survival. Modern Polish thought has made much of the idea of Poland as the advance guard, in the East, of Western civilization, and of irreconcilable Russian and Western influences. This idea/belief reflects a persistent messianism and catastrophism in Polish thought since the period of the partitions, a belief that only a great upheaval will produce a redemptive change in the nation's situation. The relationship between this and the messianism in the Russian tradition is obvious and dangerous. In fact, a third way has been demonstrated in Poland, and elsewhere in Eastern Europe, by prudent and strenuous actions defending the autonomous and "Western" elements in the moral life, literature, and civilization of these countries, and successfully reestablishing a measure of popular influence in the governance of society. The problem is to ratify, legitimate, and advance this accomplishment, which—if the Soviet government can bring itself to recognize it— shows a way out of what has become a dead end for the Soviet Union itself, in which risks are growing, not diminishing.

It has been the policy of the Soviet Union, defensively, to

attempt to break the Western Alliance link and separate the European powers from the United States, leaving its own strategic and political investments in Eastern Europe untouched. Mikhail Gorbachev's talk of the "common European house" is widely thought, in Western Europe, to express a reformulation of that policy. It is an obvious way for the Soviet Union to attempt to reduce the apparent threat to itself. Russia's sense of threat derives from its history of being invaded, and particularly from the suffering inflicted within living memory by Nazi Germany. This fear has appeared to be validated by the system of alliances that rings the Soviet state: the existence of a huge and hostile China on one side, and NATO Europe on the other, both sustained (Europe directly, China indirectly) by the immense power of the United States. How can the Soviets loosen their grip on Poland and Eastern Europe, forming their defensive glacis on the west, so long as this risk continues? The rationale for American security policy in Europe, on the other hand, has been the fear that Russia will come to dominate Germany and the rest of Europe, and the larger belief that the Soviet Union is ideologically committed to world conquest.

The Soviet national economy, unbrilliant to begin with, is crippled by the presumed need to support both a huge standing army designed to defeat an invasion analogous to Hitler's and a strategic nuclear force to rival that of the United States. During 1988, Mikhail Gorbachev finally addressed the fact that the colossally expensive military confrontation in Europe relates to the past, not the present. The West is defending itself against Stalin, and the Soviets have been defending themselves against Hitler—and, beyond that, against history itself, which has never been kind to Russia.

In 1904, a writer in the German satirical magazine *Simplicissimus* said of the Prussian soldier that "at the top of the uniform is situated the head, to inform the soldier of the height to which his salute should be brought." There is something of this logic in our present condition. We arm to meet the level of threat we perceive in our enemy's having armed to deal with what he conceives to be the threat we present to him. All wring their hands at the danger, but resist attempts to go to the political sources of the conflict. The security arrangements that now exist in Europe have served their original purpose. They have kept the peace in Europe for more than four decades. That they can continue to prevent violence is by no means clear.

The Soviet position in Eastern Europe is steadily worsening. The United States was compelled to acquiesce in Soviet control of the East European states during the 1950s because the alternative seemed to be war. This arrangement is now itself the principal cause of instability in Europe. The West has a positive interest, as does the Soviet Union, in replacing this system, which can no longer be relied upon, with an agreement that would substitute political for military guarantees of security to both sides in Europe. Past efforts to modify the Cold War have often deliberately avoided the political dimension. The arms-control effort has expressed the engineer's (or the scientist's) approach, not without success. It arose in scientific circles, rather than among politicians or diplomats, and has looked for objective and technically workable reductions in mutually identifiable risks—avoiding "extraneous" considerations, such as why the risks exist at all. The apocalyptic approach of the disarmament and antinuclear movements, emphasizing the unprecedented nature of nuclear war, has called, without success, for the reinvention of politics—the abolition of conflict—another way of begging the question.

A new attempt to find a political settlement in Europe would be time-consuming and complicated to negotiate and would possess a real cost in destabilizing the existing security arrangements. It presumes a minimal openness and genuine "new thinking" on the part of the Soviet government, but under President Gorbachev there is reason to think that these exist. It would also represent an opportunity to capitalize intelligently upon the Soviet Union's waning power to dominate Eastern Europe, and the approaching end to America's guardianship of Western Europe—and thus to turn to constructive use what cannot be avoided. On the other hand, the destructive forces now at work, left unchanneled, threaten to bring about an American withdrawal from Europe on terms of acrimony, leaving disorder behind, with nothing gained from the Soviet Union in exchange, and Europe left in greater danger.

The matter is dangerous in ways that are not immediately evident. The disputed nationalisms and separatisms of Central Europe and the Balkans are not problems over which the great powers are again going to go to war; there are no Sarajevos on our horizon (even though Serbian nationalism made an explosive return to the news during 1988). Germany is an issue. But the real problem is what will become of Russia. This engagement in Europe, to the Elbe, has been an internal as well as an external solution for the Soviet Union—a solution to ambition and to the force of political messianism in Russia. Leninism's formal ambition was to lead human society itself to a new level of civilization. After 1948 it could be claimed in Moscow that half of Europe was on its way, under Russia's direction. During the Khrushchev and Brezhnev years the challenge was pushed out into the non-Western world. Nikita Khrushchev in 1961 undoubtedly did believe that physical labor could be banished and that the Soviet Union could "overtake and surpass" the West by the 1980s, reaching "full Communism" by 1990. He could believe that the "national liberation struggles" in Asia and Africa would find their natural culmination in union with the U.S.S.R. All that is over. Mikhail Gorbachev has liquidated the Soviet Union's military investment in Afghanistan (and in its "revolution"), as in Angola, Ethiopia, the Horn of Africa, Cambodia. The Soviet deep-water fleet cruises closer to home. The Soviet economy is overtaking and surpassing no one.

Now the Soviet leadership and people must come to terms with the fact that they cannot hold Europe either. The European connection is important for Gorbachev and the reformers because they represent the Westernizing, Europeanizing, tradition of reform in their country. Against them are forces of Russian nationalism, reaction, and isolation. It would be better for the reformers if they had a socialist Eastern Europe that worked—reforming itself in effective ways, a partner in reform with the Soviet Union. That clearly is what Gorbachev wants, and asks, from the East European parties and governments. But they have nothing to give him. Their societies face in another direction. The effort in the last forty years to change them spilled much blood, sent thousands into the camps, imposed harsh conditions of life on millions—and has come to nothing. Russia is thrust back on itself. This may be the worst thing that could happen to the reformers.

Chaos, in mathematics and physics, describes a phenomenon in which a process is critically and unpredictably altered by very slight change; the usual example is torrential turbulence in a fast-flowing fluid caused by a slight change in the channel. Inertia is the force of resistance to change. There obviously are political analogues to both. It is extremely difficult to divert nations from the civilization and values that have dominated their past. When change is imposed, however brutally, the tendency is to accommodate what is new by modifying it to conform with what already was there, or to reject it as alien tissue. It is a commonplace observation that Marxism, German in intellectual origin, became a very Russian affair as was practiced in Russia. This Russification of Marxism in turn has been an obstacle to its acceptance in societies with historical grievances against Russia and a history apart from and hostile to Russian civilization. In Eastern Europe the relationship with West European civilization has been responsible for a rejection of the Soviet Union and of Soviet Communism. There is nothing surprising in this. If there is anything surprising it is that so many people, in the West as well as in the Soviet Union, could have believed in the possibility of a radical and permanent break in the continuity of these societies.

On the other hand, changes, individual but incremental, are being made in the political process of the Soviet Union itself and in its conscious relationship with its own past. It would be very rash to think that the result is predictable. It may not prove to be chaotic in either nonscientific or scientific meanings of the word, but it would be imprudent to think that what finally comes out of this will necessarily be liberalizing, democratic, benign. It may be, and one hopes that it will be, but the internal contradictions of the Soviet situation today are very serious, and the process of change is one in which a single variable can make a difference. Consider the decision of the German General Staff in 1917 to introduce the exiled Lenin into a Russian Revolution already under way. Max Hoffmann, Chief of the General Staff on the Eastern Front, afterward wrote: "At that time nobody could foresee the fatal consequences . . ." Ludendorff, Germany's war lord, said: "In sending Lenin, the Chancellor [Bethmann] promised us more rapid development of the Russian Revolution and an increase in the desire for peace. . . . Headquarters considered that in this way the defenses of the army would be weakened." It seemed a good idea at the time. The Belgian socialist Emile Vandervelde was more prescient; he commented on his own visit to revolutionary Petrograd with a phrase from Nietzsche: "There must be chaos, that out of chaos may come forth new stars; there must be chaos that new worlds may be born." The year 1917 was a beginning from which, today, other things have begun.

# 4 THE SOVIET UNION

"Starting from the magnetic core of the Eurasian heartland, the Soviet power, like the reality of the One of Neo-Platonism . . . flows outward, west into Europe, south into the Near East, east into China, already lapping the shores of the Atlantic, the Yellow and China Seas, the Mediterranean and the Persian Gulf. As the undifferentiated One, in its progression, descends through the stages of Mind, Soul, and Matter, and then through its fatal Return back to itself; so does the Soviet power, emanating from the integrally totalitarian center, proceed outwards by Absorption (the Baltics, Bessarabia, Bukovina, East Poland), Domination (Finland, the Balkans, Mongolia, North China, and, tomorrow, Germany), Orienting Influence (Italy, France, Turkey, Iran, Central and South China . . . ), until it is dissipated in *MH ON*, the outer material sphere, beyond the Eurasian boundaries, of momentary Appeasement and Infiltration (England, the United States)."

This is a passage from an article by James Burnham in the Winter 1944–45 issue of *Partisan Review*. The florid description, the analogy with spiritual forces, suggest the extent to which Stalinist totalitarianism was perceived in the forties as a force of evil itself, and no mere political phenomenon. To many, it seemed an irresistible power. Burnham's description of Soviet influence was extravagant at the time, but certainly expressed that chilled view of the future which many people legitimately held. There have been many since who, with less reason, have written and continue to write very much the same kind of thing about Soviet power—its extent, its expansion into Latin America and Africa, its supposed influence in foreign countries (including England and the United States), its assumed irresistibility. But it was not irresistible in the 1940s and 1950s, nor was it afterward.

The power of the Soviet Union was resisted by means of a Western effort that proved strenuous but well within the means—moral as well as military—of the supposedly doomed democracies. The years of resistance to Communism were the years of Europe's economic unification and of the most brilliant material development and prosperity ever known for all the democratic nations. At the same time the Soviet Union experienced political sterility, stunted social as well as economic conditions—its living standards unable to attain even East European standards, its agriculture gravely incompetent, its technology backward in all except narrow military-related areas, its intellectual life stultified, Soviet power over the East European bloc maintained only by military and police measures.

In the 1940s, however, Soviet power seemed qualitatively new, part of a new reality for which a new word had been necessary. As employed by Hannah Arendt, Waldemar Gurian, Franz Borkenau, Carleton Hayes, George Orwell, and others in the 1930s and 1940s, "totalitarianism" was an expression describing regimes that seemed to mark a radical departure from the dictatorships, despotisms, or oligarchical governments familiar before, by making a "total" claim upon a people's allegiances, against the claims not only of other political movements but of religion and family. To be a Fascist or a Communist was supposed to allow no superseding loyalty. Nazism, Italian Fascism, and Soviet Communism seemed original phenomena in this respect, and also because they were mass movements. Unlike conventional dictatorships, they rested upon mass parties and seemed to enjoy mass consent. They therefore seemed corruptions of democracy, or the dialectical antitheses of democracy. Precedents were seen in the ideological intoxication that had produced the Terror in the French Revolution and in certain mass movements of millennial religious fervor in the Middle Ages. The contemporary movements nonetheless seemed to possess unique qualities—unmistakably modern in scale and organizational technique, grandiose in their secular ambitions. Each had been carried into power, if not by majorities in their countries (never the case), nonetheless by popular movements that had to be acknowledged the most dynamic political forces of the time.

Totalitarianism was said to respond to the anomie of modern society, where the masses of people had been deprived of the structures and anchorage previously provided by class and religion, a previous social stability destroyed by industrialism and by war. The new movements provided "total" systems of belief—eschatological, quasi-religious, not merely political—which demanded of their members moral and intellectual submission in the name of historical necessity. Hannah Arendt, in *The Origins of Totalitarianism*, her unforgettable account, published in 1951, of the radical originality of these movements, called them "mass organizations of atomized, isolated individuals." She said that they demanded "total, unrestricted, unconditional, and unalterable loyalty of their individual members." This comprehensive claim, she went on, was deliberately framed to be without concrete and practical goals, so that it became a demand for belief for belief's sake. Without tangible, and therefore debatable and attainable, goals, totalitarianism's followers were invited to join in what amounted to a metaphysical quest from which they would never return. As mass organizations, the totalitarian movements were said to transform momentary, transient emotions of political commitment and enthusiasm into something permanent, "extinguishing individual identity permanently and not just for the moment of collective heroic action." They brought transcendence to their members, who by their participation abandoned the ordinary, and "thought in continents and felt in centuries."

The totalitarian regimes demonstrated a power to invent history, to make and unmake "truth," altering "facts" about the past and present to suit their own needs. Truth to them was plastic, relative to the doctrinal purposes and primacy of the party. As Stalin demonstrated, they could change the official judgment upon some event or person, past or present, and then change the encyclopedias, remove the relevant files of newspapers, eliminate offending names from books, removing the evidence that the unacceptable fact had ever existed, making it a nonfact for all that could be shown, substituting a new "fact," even—as Stalin also tried to do—imprisoning or murdering those in a position to bear witness to this fact that had been made into a nonfact. "All the confessions here are true," the implacable O'Brien says to Winston Smith in George Orwell's classic fictional account of totalitarianism, *Nineteen Eighty-four*.

A monstrous, even satanic, force seemed in the 1930s and 1940s loosed upon the world, defeated in Germany and Italy only at exhausting cost, in a world war. The war ended, it seemed to have found new strength in Stalin's Soviet Union and to be expanding, its potentialities awesome. "Never have we depended so much on political forces that cannot be trusted to follow the rules of common sense and self-interest—forces that look like sheer insanity, if judged by the standards of other centuries," Hannah Arendt wrote. This was not only a force of evil but one of perverse indifference even to its own advantage. Hitler had devoted enormous resources to the extermination of Jews, Gypsies, and Poles in the midst of the Second World War—when all these people, by any expedient judgment, should have been put to work in factories to produce for the German war effort. Stalin not only had murdered his colleagues and the leaders of factions within the Soviet Communist Party, which might have been explicable in terms of a struggle for power, but just before the war he had also murdered nearly all the higher command of his army, on manifestly false charges of treason and espionage, so that the army was decapitated when the German attack came. This inexplicable quality made totalitarianism seem a force that did not function by rules the rational mind could grasp or counter.

• • •

The predictions made for totalitarianism in the 1940s did not, however, come true. Stalin had indeed rewritten the official history of Bolshevik Russia in order to diminish or extinguish the roles of his rivals and exalt himself. It was not a success. As soon as he was gone, the truth came out; even in Russia, too many people knew what had really happened, had themselves suffered under Stalin, and were determined to vindicate themselves and make sure that no one else would get into such a position of power over them. When Nikita Khrushchev told the truth about Stalin to the 20th Congress of the Soviet Communist Party in 1956, it was a sensation because these terrible things actually were admitted: but no one protested that they were not true. To the extent that each of the listeners to Khrushchev's speech had witnessed what had gone on under Stalin, each knew very well that it was all true.

Lies continued to be told in the Soviet Union, as in every authoritarian system (not to speak of the rest). But increasingly they were simple lies, conventional, meant to cover up the increasingly unmanageable legacy of past lies—or to blacken a rival or an enemy, promote a career, advance the party's or the state's interests. Meanwhile, dissidents within the Soviet Union made phone calls abroad and talked to Western correspondents. They lectured Westerners on what the Soviet regime was really like. The Soviet government would deny what they said, harass them, put them into hospitals and jails. But not even those committed to mental hospitals and pumped full of drugs came out like Orwell's Winston Smith, abjuring Crimethink, thinking Goodthinkful thoughts, talking Newspeak, thanking their persecutors for having corrected their errors.

Communism in Russia had more than seventy years and unlimited means to turn people into the pliant, morally amputated creatures totalitarianism was supposed to create—deprived of emotions and thoughts other than those dictated by the party. Instead, the Soviet Union kept turning up Sakharovs, Solzhenitsyns, Zinovievs. It forced them into exile, jailed them, sent them into the psychiatric ward, could even have killed them—in the past did kill them—but could not eliminate them, to say nothing of converting them.

The Communist leadership in Moscow also had more than forty years of virtually unchecked power over Eastern Europe during which to remake those societies into numbed vassalages of Big Brother. The reality was Titoism in Yugoslavia, revolutionary uprising in East Berlin and East Germany in 1953, in Budapest and other cities of Hungary in 1956, near-uprising in Poland in the same year, the Czechoslovak Spring in 1968, the defection to nationalist Communism of Romania and Albania, and in Poland after 1980 a continuing, open, virtually unanimous national repudiation of the legitimacy of the Communist Party's government of that country, causing the collapse of party rule and a succession of military government. The totalitarian prophecies proved wrong. Nineteen eighty-four was just another year.

Yet what Arendt, Koestler, Orwell, Hayes, Burnham, Borkenau, Gurian, and so many others described in the 1930s and 1940s was once reality in Stalinist Russia and Nazi Germany, and something very like it existed in the China of the "Great Leap Forward" and the Cultural Revolution, and in Cambodia in the 1970s. Modern governments have existed that claimed to embody doctrines of historical truth or global destiny. They proclaimed their doctrines as successors to religion and to the outmoded values of bourgeois and liberal society, condemning to history's ash heap the political, social, and intellectual values of the past. They held themselves free to employ any measures of violence, however drastic, and to commit any crime, however immense, so as to sweep away the residue of centuries and break through to thousand-year Reichs, millennially perfected societies. Such phenomena are not to be taken lightly.

Possibly totalitarianism was something rooted in its particular time, an irreproducible consequence of the First World War. The war provoked revolution in Russia, and the revolution in Russia formed a generation of revolutionaries in Asia. Whatever Leninism otherwise might have become, in the actual conditions of

1918 it took for its social model what was before it in the West—
the war state, "totally" mobilized, with hundreds of millions of
people under arms or drafted to war production, centrally
planned, directed by governments given exceptional powers over
how citizens lived, where they worked, how they died. This was
the West that Asian revolutionaries also knew. Chou En-lai and
Ho Chi Minh were actually in France in those years, the latter a
founder of the French Communist Party in 1920. Indochinese
labor battalions served on the Western Front. Japan's participation in the First World War was the occasion for its initial attempt
to force concessions of sovereignty from China (the "Twenty-one
Demands").

In the case of Nazi Germany, the connection is again direct.
The decisive experience of Adolf Hitler and his generation of Germans had been four years of trench war followed by defeat, social
and economic collapse, preludes to revolution. Nazism used the
forms and symbolism of the war system to reconstruct the German
state and take revenge against its national enemies, while simultaneously exacting revenge upon liberalism, religion, internationalism, and socialism—all of which had been part of the prewar
European system that had led to a German catastrophe.

Those who accepted totalitarianism were in some sense retro-
actively justifying what they had been through in the world war. An
appalling sacrifice had been demanded, and had been made. The
values of the societies that enthusiastically had gone to war were
the values that the war itself contradicted or discredited. Nihilism
was thus the war's principal outcome. Why the sacrifices? Perhaps
the only practical answer was that sacrifice was justified for its own
sake. Men had abandoned the pettiness and selfishness of their
prewar lives to give themselves to their nation and to their com-
rades. They had experienced a stoic fraternity in the "storm of
steel" of which Ernst Jünger wrote. Not victory "but war in itself . . .
inspired the poet," Thomas Mann said. Hannah Arendt quotes a
German worker as saying, "It doesn't matter whether one lives a

few years longer or not. One would like to have something to show for one's life." Prewar civilization, "fake security, fake culture, and fake life," had been blown apart. What made continued existence tolerable was loyalty and sacrifice. It is not strange that the survivors accepted new political movements, first in Russia and Italy, and then in Germany, which decisively condemned the past, cut out cant and lies (it seemed), turned to the masses in place of the elites who had failed, and above all asked for subordination of the individual and for sacrifice. Prewar notions of "objective" truth, "objective" and skeptical thought of the kind that lay behind the catastrophe, all were jettisoned.

One cannot say that it will never happen again, or that it cannot happen. Current political reality, nonetheless, continues to be distorted by the thoughtless identification of existing conditions with what existed under Hitler and Stalin, or with what might have happened had their two regimes succeeded in perpetuating or reproducing themselves. The radical possibilities of political evil demonstrated in Russia from the 1930s into the 1950s, and in Germany between 1933 and 1945, need to be remembered for what they really were if we are to continue to avoid them. The nature of Soviet totalitarianism under Stalin cannot be appreciated if the U.S.S.R. of Khrushchev and Brezhnev is treated as if it were the same thing. If reactionary regimes in Chile, Greece, Argentina, or Iran—or a racialist government in South Africa—are routinely described as Fascist, then we lose a grasp of what Nazism and Fascism really were.

These distinctions are central to political and even moral choices made today. If the contemporary threat to the West were really that of the past, measures of defense would be justified that otherwise might be disproportionate. Much of the controversy over policy toward the Soviet Union that developed between West Europeans and the American government during the 1970s, and especially during the Reagan administration in the 1980s, followed from a failure to make such distinctions, a failure to define seriously the changing nature of the threat and the moral proportionality of the chosen means of defense. A defense formulated in terms of an incredible or widely unacceptable description of the threat undermines itself. A realistic statement of threat is essential to make a defense strategy credible and politically sustainable.

For a considerable time the U.S. government itself experienced difficulty in resolving its differences on what to think and do about the Soviet Union. From the death of Stalin to the inauguration of Ronald Reagan, administrations of both parties by and large gave up the totalitarian model in formulating policy toward the Soviet Union. (It was, in the 1960s, conceptually transferred to Asia; China was considered the new, unstoppably aggressive totalitarianism. Hence the war in Vietnam.) The working assumption of the American government was that the Soviet-American rivalry functioned within negotiable limits and need not lead to war. The Soviet Union was considered to have finite aims, its rhetoric notwithstanding. It was not taken to be an outlaw power. Treaties and other agreements, even secret "codes of conduct," were sought and signed by the Eisenhower, Nixon, and Ford administrations, and also by those of Presidents Kennedy, Johnson, and Carter. The Soviet Union was thus presumed to be a "normal" power, albeit a ruthless one, and to be concerned essentially with its own security and well-being. Its Leninist commitment to world revolution was regarded, in practice, as subordinated to national interest whenever conflict arose between the two.

In the Washington of the Reagan administration, this view of the Soviet Union was seriously challenged at the highest levels of government for the first time since the mid-1950s. The new administration included a significant contingent of people committed to the proposition that no negotiations with the Soviet Union on basic questions could be profitable and no agreements trusted. They believed that the difference between the two countries, a matter of fundamental values as well as of ideology, necessarily produced conflict and that it was sentimentality to think that coexistence could be anything other than a mask behind which the Soviet Union continued to aggrandize its power and attempted to undermine the West. This challenge to longstanding American policy convention echoed the orthodox Leninist and Stalinist position— that the bourgeoisie would not yield without a fight, and that armed struggle between revolutionary forces and those of entrenched capitalism and imperialism was therefore inevitable. The new American argument held that by its very nature the Soviet system rejected any true coexistence with the liberal West. If the U.S.S.R. did not itself change so as to become in crucial respects a liberalized society, which is to say if it did not cede the ideological battle, war between the two superpowers was thought to be, in the long run, inevitable. Once again, the Soviet Union was described in the totalitarian terminology of the 1940s and 1950s.

Moscow did not grasp the irony. Its doctrine of the inevitability of conflict, officially discarded during the post-Stalinist 1960s, made a return to international politics as a doctrine put forward within the U.S. government. The link of causation was direct. Members of a generation of American specialists on the Soviet Union learned too well to take Trotsky, Lenin, and Stalin seriously, and proved unable to take these men's successors any less seriously—paying them the compliment of believing them, too, to be men of steel, of austere revolutionary commitments, prepared to commit any crime. This tribute, however, was an extravagant one, since little in the conduct of the Soviet Union in the 1970s and early 1980s, before the accession to power of Mikhail Gorbachev, revealed its leaders to be other than aging and unimaginative men, obsessed by the security and power of an overextended Soviet Union—scavengers of influence among the debris of colonialism in Central America, Africa, and the Middle East. During the years of détente, these Soviet leaders had actually shown themselves painfully eager for "normal" relations, in which, despite the meanness of Soviet political society, its economic failures, its technological backwardness, they could conduct themselves as members (as Richard Nixon once said of himself and Chairman Leonid Brezhnev) "of the most exclusive club in the world." There was a period, when Nixon was the American president and Kissinger his foreign policy lieutenant, that this goal seemed not only possible but all but achieved.

Richard Nixon found Leonid Brezhnev congenial; he is said to have been convinced that only the two of them could understand each other, and could understand the burden of leading a superpower. During this time of good relations, Henry Kissinger observed that "the problem of our age is how to manage the emergence of the Soviet Union as a superpower." He coupled this with gloomy reflections upon what he saw at that time as a "self-destructive isolationist course in American life" and the danger that the United States was on its way to becoming "an isolated fortress island in a hostile and turbulent global sea, awaiting the ultimate confrontation"—both trends supposedly following from a failure of nerve among the liberal elites of the country. During his custodianship of American foreign policy, the United States even interested itself in regularizing the Soviet Union's control of the East European nations, a relationship deemed "inorganic" and "unnatural" by a State Department official, who described the instability within the Soviet bloc as "a far greater danger to world peace than the conflict between East and West." It was said that American diplomacy should "strive for an evolution that makes the relationship between the Eastern Europeans and the Soviet Union an organic one." The State Department subsequently insisted that nothing had changed in American policy toward Eastern Europe, but, of course, the words were not to be called back.

Such an American concern for improving the Soviet imperial position was not as odd as it might seem today. It could be interpreted as a further development in the American official impulse toward interventionism—as a kind of apotheosis of interventionism in which officials felt impelled to correct and manipulate the Soviet Union's use of its own power in the Soviet Union's own best interests, as seen from Washington. But there is perhaps another, more fundamental explanation for this preoccupation with improving the position of the Soviet Union. Like the Austrians and Russians of the Holy Alliance (in the era of Metternich's counterrevolutionary policy), Americans and Russians during the years of détente understood themselves to be established powers in a time when new political and ideological trends posed disorienting threats to the existing order. We and the Soviets were at the pinnacle of world affairs, united in being jealous of the right to conduct our rivalry without uncontrollable and even revolutionary disruptions within either camp. The Soviet leaders, in fact, were among the most stubborn defenders of Richard Nixon against the forces within the United States that brought him down. According to the director of the Soviet press agency, writing at the time, Watergate was merely "given the appearance of a conflict between the executive, in the person of the President, and the legislative power, represented by Congress." There was, he said, "a very definite brainwashing of public opinion . . . both on radio and television." Club members stand by one another.

During the noontime of détente, at the beginning and into the mid-1970s, the American relationship with the Soviet Union became to a significant degree an alliance to perpetuate status and self-esteem—qualities that surely rank among the less creditable interests of governments, and of those who make their careers in government. Heretofore, being president of the United States had been a great distinction, but did not confer one of the two available places in the most exclusive club in the world. In the days of Roosevelt, Truman, and Eisenhower, the club had more members than two. At the height of the Second World War, there was a "Big Four" on the Allied side, and Hitler, General Tojo, and Mussolini on the other. The presidents who succeeded FDR took Winston Churchill, Clement Attlee, Harold Macmillan, Charles de Gaulle, Konrad Adenauer, and Alcides de Gasperi quite as seriously as they did the Malenkovs, Bulganins, Kaganoviches, Molotovs, and other apparatchiki who jostled for Stalin's power after he died. Only when an adulatory press made Kennedy and Khrushchev the "Big Two" was the world's most exclusive club really brought into being. After that came the grand intoxications of presidential power in the United States—all those Marines standing at attention and those trumpeters on the staircases at parties, the helicopters and the fleets of private jets, the Margaux '66, and the Lincoln automobile shipped to Moscow by the Nixon administration as a personal gift to Brezhnev, leader of Russia's revolutionary alliance of workers, peasants, and intellectuals.

Membership in the club was warmly welcomed by the leadership of the Soviet Union, for whom it also represented a geopolitical reassurance. The claim repeatedly made by the Soviet government and Soviet officials was that Russia was entitled to a formal status of equality with the United States in international politics as well as in military affairs. Russia was said to be entitled to as large a role in the Middle East or Asia as the United States. By implication, spheres of influence should be acknowledged. An equal and balanced naval and military position should be recognized. The Soviet Union had earned this status, Soviet officials said, and was determined to maintain it at any cost. The unspoken wish of Soviet leaders really was to exercise a condominium with the United States over world affairs. The roles of the older great powers—Western Europe and Japan—seemed irritants to the Soviet Union, of less interest than they were even to Washington. The Soviet leaders concentrated on the United States. It was their challenge, but also their measure.

The claim to equality was used to justify the Soviet military buildup of the 1970s and 1980s, aimed at giving Russia strategic parity with the United States—an objective that Moscow subsequently claimed to have achieved. At the time of the debate over intermediate-range missiles in Western Europe, Yuri Andropov said that "military strategic parity" existed, and that "this parity is a reliable guarantee of peace, and we will do everything to preserve it." He went on to say, in an interview with Pravda in March 1983, that it was the United States that wanted to create "qualitatively new systems of conventional weapons," and searched for ways of "unleashing nuclear war in the hope of winning it."

Anxiety underlay the anger. The Soviet Union could not sustain an arms race with the United States that broke into radically new technologies without inflicting a desperate cost on its civilian society. The Soviet demand that parity be acknowledged rested on an assessment of its actual economic and industrial situation. The big scientific espionage program of the 1970s and 1980s was an effort to find abroad what the Soviet Union could not easily develop at home. (The French Interior Ministry, following a mass expulsion of Soviet diplomats and journalists from France in April 1983, cited "a systematic search throughout the national territory . . . for scientific, technical and technological information, particularly in the military domain.") The demand that the Soviet Union be treated by the United States as an equal world power clearly was charged with psychological as well as political weight for the Russians. It revealed their awareness that Russia is not a society like others. It reevoked what has been a central problem in modern Russian history.

A persistent question for Russian intellectuals throughout the nineteenth century was whether Russia belonged properly to Europe and European values or constituted a separate civilization, which could afford indifference to the West (or required such indifference to survive). Nineteenth-century European Romanticism, by its rejection of industrial and capitalist values, reinforced Russian intellectuals' criticisms of Western European civilization. The very material backwardness of Russia, and thus the survival of the "organic" peasant community, was held to have saved Russians from Western man's alienation from the sources of existence. The romantic view within Russia was that "we do not march step by step with the European civilization, we are running a race with it and we shall soon surpass it if we have not already done so. . . . It is not our role to be the echo of a civilization which lies in ruins and agony and of which we see perhaps already the convulsions announcing its death but to produce ourselves a new, young, strong civilization, a genuine Russian civilization which will renew old Europe." This was the opinion of Nikolai Ivanovich Nadezhdin, a leading historian of the arts, a liberal, writing in the 1830s.

Slavophiles said much the same thing. They counted Russia's millions, added to those the Slavs of Central and Southern Europe, marveled at Russia's natural variety and its huge size, described Russia's spirituality and its intellectual and artistic gifts, and concluded (as in a famous statement of 1838, dedicated to the education of the future Czar Alexander II): "Who can compare with us? Whom will we not force into submission? Is not the political destiny of the world in our hands whenever we want to decide it one way or the other?" The decline of Europe, divided, corrupted by individual liberties, was a condition "by which our greatness—as light by shadow—is still more enhanced," the statement held. "The untiring attention with which Europe follows every step by us, the incessant suspicion of our slightest move, the muffled grumbling of jealousy, envy, and malice . . . are they not the most convincing proof of Russia's strength?" The writer is Mikhail Petrovich Pogodin (1800–75), of the University of Moscow. A colleague called the West the "carrier of a terrible and contagious disease, surrounded by an air created by its dangerous breath"—a rotting corpse.

The belief in Russia as "a world by itself, alien and superior to Europe and at the same time suffering from Europe's hostility and arrogance," reappeared and triumphed after 1917. Leninism provided a secular iteration of the belief in the saving mission of Russians in a world of unbelievers. The conviction that Moscow had become the last and culminating center of Christianity, the "Third Rome"—which is to say, capital of humanity's possibilities for redemption—seemed to find a secular fulfillment in Communism.

This mixture of defensiveness with an overbearing conviction of national mission survived through the 1980s, remaining a serious factor in Soviet policy and Soviet relations with the West. As Edmund Stillman has argued, throughout its modern history Russia has been a reactive civilization, responding to what has come to it from the West, taking from the West solutions to its own most urgent problems—quite brilliantly, but as yet without a conclusive synthesis of these imported ideas with its own needs. Russia, of course, was not yet a unified country at the time of the West European Renaissance. It was "neither European nor Asiatic . . . Christian, but its Christianity had come to it from Byzantium and not from Rome," the English historian G. N. Clark has noted. "The emperor used the title of czar, the most distant of all the echoes of the name of Caesar, but his despotism was of the Oriental type. He was nearer to the Moguls than to the Bourbons. . . . Until this period [the seventeenth century] Russia was external to Western civilization. It had been important to the maritime powers as a field for commercial exploitation, and to its continental neighbors as . . . a possible field for conquest."

Invaded by Swedes and Poles, challenged in the east by Manchu China, seventeenth-century Russia seemed headed for colonization by the more dynamic states in the West. Peter the Great saved it by making over the Russian monarchy and its army on the model of contemporary, absolutist Europe. But Russian society itself was largely untouched; a Europeanized state apparatus, army, and court were simply superimposed. The aristocracy was forbidden Muscovy robes and beards, and its sons were pressed into state service. By the next century, this elite had been augmented through the development of a mercantile and professional class. From that came the great nineteenth-century intelligentsia—Dostoevsky, Pushkin, Gogol, Tolstoy—divided between loyalty to Russia and the allure, or rejection, of a modern Western Europe of secularism, science, ideology, and inner conflict. What was eventually discovered in Europe was a revolutionary doctrine to apply to reactionary Russia—and in 1917 the émigré Bolsheviks applied it.

Russian inadequacies found theoretical and political compensation during the 1920s and 1930s in the messianic belief that the revolutionary Soviet state, under attack as it was, was an outpost of the future. It was a further help that the Russians were increasingly ignorant of much outside Russia's borders. The cosmopolitan upper classes in Russia did not survive the 1920s, and the cosmopolitan revolutionaries were mostly murdered in the 1930s and 1940s. Those left in control of the country were working-class autodidacts, whose whole experience was inside the party and inside the Soviet Union. Perhaps the most significant accomplishment of détente in the 1970s was to allow a large number of Soviet officials and academics again to travel outside their country and to see their own society in a new perspective—not a satisfying one. The result was an official class prepared to support the reform proposals of Mikhail Gorbachev.

The "normalization" of Soviet society under Nikita Khrushchev, after the death of the czarlike Stalin, released immense pressures, freed a million suppressed desires; but fatefully posed the issues of recognition and status. Under Khrushchev, and then under Brezhnev, Russia sought recognition as a great power, not as merely a revolutionary power. The subversive diplomacy that had characterized the Soviet Union from the time of Brest-Litovsk was largely abandoned. Dignity was sought, whereas a revolutionary power despises dignity as a bourgeois concept. Khrushchev himself acquired an Italian tailor. The simple soldiers' uniforms, open collars, workmen's dress, of an earlier leadership were no longer seen.

In becoming a conventional power, the Soviet Union submitted itself to conventional norms of measurement. These, however, were not favorable. The Soviet Union had emerged from the Second World War already a great power in certain important respects. Its extent was large; so was its army. It already dominated the Central Asian regions annexed in the past, Outer Mongolia, the Baltic states taken in 1940. The nations of Eastern and East-Central Europe had forcibly been annexed to the Soviet zone of interest. The Soviet Union became a nuclear power and a space power, and it built a deep-water fleet, as czarist Russia had done. On the other hand, a major part of the Soviet economy remained (as it remains today) primitive, starved of technology, incapable of producing consumer goods on a scale or of a quality to compare even with Eastern Europe, to say nothing of the West. Soviet agriculture remained equally inefficient, incapable of feeding the country properly, even though imperial Russia, before 1917, had been a food exporter.

All this revived the old problem, the central one, of Russia's relationship to the West. Russian leaders of the 1970s and 1980s claimed parity with the United States, but they could not sustain such a claim except in certain narrow areas. "Parity" represented one more attempt to find reassurance that the internal doubt was no longer justified. But neither the United States nor the other major world powers could confer upon the Soviet Union a standing it manifestly did not command on its merits and accomplishments. The United States could not, if it wanted, present the Soviet Union with co-domination of the world, which is what Brezhnev seemed to ask.

The Soviet Union could not sustain such a role even if that role were somehow to be bestowed upon it. It lacked the requisite political and moral gravity. Its standing in the world still derived from its radicalism; it was a revisionist power in Asian, African, and Latin American eyes. To Europe and North America, it was reactionary. In either case, it lacked the authority conferred by great accomplishments, by success. At the same time, it no longer radiated the glamour of revolution and subversion, except to the most backward. It was not, by any but military measures, an advanced state. It was the most important of the Third World powers. As such, it faced Russian civilization's old problem, still unresolved, of what to take from the West and how to deal with its challenge. Leninism promised to cause Russia to leap ahead of the West, shortcutting the bourgeois-capitalist stage of social development so as to reach the penultimate stage of socialism, and then attain Communism— perfected human society, where the state would wither away. That was a fantasy. Ideologists of the Brezhnev period claimed that the Soviet Union had reached the next-to-last point in the evolution of human institutions, that of "mature socialism"—one step away from Communism. After Brezhnev, that was no longer mentioned.

An unrealized, and unrealizable, ambition is potentially destructive. A messianism that fails produces a self-loathing for having failed. The pessimism of Russian society after the humiliation of the Russo-Japanese War and the German victories at Tannenberg and the Masurian Lakes created the climate for the insurrections of 1905 and 1917. The political elite of that time could find no effective way to reform the system, and at the same time they were terrified of the masses, who had lost confidence in them. The situation of the Soviet leaders of the 1980s bore comparison with them. They were bound to an ideology that could no longer be held to describe either the reality outside Russia or the reality within. They could not reject this ideology or break free of it without eliminating the source of their own legitimacy as the governors of the country. Malenkov, Khrushchev, Brezhnev, Andropov, all tried to square the circles of modern Russia: to combine initiative with central direction; revolutionary commitment with actual stability, even stagnation; international advance with nuclear stalemate. Gorbachev seemed condemned to do the same. The plight was made worse by the party's claim to infallibility. Nothing could be introduced unless there was a way to demonstrate that it was really always there. Error had to be explained as deviation from doctrine, and reform as application of the neglected dicta of Lenin.°

°The rest of this chapter appears as it did in 1989, without amendments of tense such as those made in the text of the previous pages.

In fact, the extraordinary political and moral adventure that began with Lenin's passage in a sealed train across the battle frontiers of the Great War, to the Finland Station in revolutionary Petrograd, nears its end. The Bolsheviks overturned a weakened Provisional Government and seized control not only of Russia but of the Western political imagination. Now it is Gorbachev's effort to reconcile Lenin's legacy with its disastrous outcome in contemporary Russia that holds the world's attention.

The Revolution radiated abroad an idea of redemptive change while Soviet society itself changed only painfully, and by the time of the agricultural collectivization, at the end of the 1920s, and the famine that followed, it had changed for the worse. The revolutionaries, and their admirers, lived for the future; the present was scarcely worth attention and was to be discarded. The challenge the Bolsheviks offered to the West seemed more than a political phenomenon, something rather like a mutation of society, and the converts it won abroad were, ultimately, moral converts. The young revolutionaries in Asia and the West, people who committed themselves to the Comintern, underground work, agitprop, labor organization, spying, political penetration, did so with exemplary selflessness, a quality that was at the source of their extraordinary influence on their times and the tenacity of their grip on the modern political imagination—however badly it all ended. Whittaker Chambers wrote that, even when he broke with Communism, "the world I was leaving [looked] like the world of life and of the future. The world I was returning to seemed, by contrast, a graveyard." It is inconceivable that such a thing could be said today.

The explicit purpose of the extraordinary Soviet Communist Party Conference held in Moscow in the spring of 1988 was radical reform of the structures of the Leninist state and of the Soviet economy. The implicit message of the conference was that the whole enterprise has been, in a way impossible for them yet to articulate, a terrible mistake. It has brought them to an impasse. They have to find some way to make up for the appalling waste they have inflicted upon themselves, and on others, during the last seventy years, and to find political and economic terms on which they can continue.

Gorbachev presents himself as a reformer, but he has begun something that calls into question the Soviet system itself. The true challenge facing Gorbachev is not to "reform" the system and the economy. It is to discover a new basis of legitimacy for Soviet society and its government. Before that Party Conference, a Soviet official in Paris said that the significance of glasnost is that of the search by the Soviet elite and people "to recover the moral foundations" of their society. He argued that they could find them in a return to sources, to Leninism. They will discover, however, that Leninism is incapable of providing that renewed moral foundation; Leninism itself is the source of what went wrong. Leninism has undeniably possessed a moral force; its declared purpose, to give power to the people whose labor creates society's wealth, has evoked passionate and selfless response from millions throughout the world. But Leninism also insists on the leading role of the Communist Party, and this has proven, in practice, to result in unaccountable and despotic government by a self-nominating and self-perpetuating oligarchy, which has not even success to justify it.

Mikhail Gorbachev envisages a "socialist state of law" in which the government will govern and the party would become what it was originally meant to be, "the vanguard" of Soviet society. The structural changes he obtained in 1988 in the way the U.S.S.R. is governed bring a new and open form of parliament, elected from multiple candidacies—a body supposed to become a second center of power, separate from the party, naming from its members a bicameral Supreme Soviet to remain in session throughout the year and decide "all legislative, administrative, and monitoring questions," as Gorbachev described it at the special Party Conference. This Supreme Soviet, he said, should have a president—himself.

Gorbachev described what he wants as reform, but it is reform to strengthen his own position. By combining his party office with supreme state office, legitimated by the nationally elected Congress of People's Deputies and its Supreme Soviet, he has become even more difficult to challenge. This, however, is not democracy. Gorbachev wants a one-party state in which public opinion finds genuine expression within that one party, and where the party's leaders and members conduct themselves as a responsible and principled elite. He wants a government exercising autonomous authority, obeying its own laws, doing justice within the terms of its own constitution. He believes in "democratic centralism," which means disciplined obedience to what the government and the party have decided. He wants respect for diversity of opinion and for religious belief—the latter a significant step because it concedes a place in Soviet society to a rival claimant to the moral leadership of society, promoter of a rival conception of the meaning of human existence. Gorbachev called for these reforms in the year of the millennium of Christianity in Russia and at a time when the Orthodox Church is experiencing what a French scholar calls "a formidable intellectual ferment and renewal in which the principal theme is the 'unyielding person' [*la personne irréductible*]." He wants free debate and has sponsored the legal rehabilitation of the great Communist Party dissidents condemned in the state trials of the 1930s—Bukharin, Zinoviev, and Kamenev, now acknowledged to have been "innocent before the law, the state, and the people." He has made important concessions of relative autonomy and political pluralism to the Baltic states. He says that the Soviet Union had come to the edge of "an abyss" when he arrived in office. In 1986, at a gathering of editors and writers in Moscow, he said of the necessary changes, "If not we, who? If not now, when?"

These are fundamental questions, but they are questions of historical accountability. The question not asked, but which has to be asked, is what will become of the Soviet Union and the Soviet system if it acknowledges its intellectual and moral foundations to be untrue? The forces set at work by Gorbachev in the Soviet Union, and in Eastern Europe as well, are revolutionary forces and have acquired a momentum that is independent of Gorbachev's own fate. He may himself prove the Kerensky of this revolution.

It is a revolution of a rare kind, launched from above, by a leader of government, in response to the alienation of the most dynamic elements inside his society, its creative minority—most of them, in contrast with other revolutions, inside, not outside, the structure of state privilege. It is a revolution disguised as radical reform, meant to save the system. That it cannot remain mere reform, however, follows from the fact that the intellectual foundation of the system is discredited. Gorbachev refers to Lenin to justify his program, but the program undoes Leninism.

Marxism rests upon a belief in the possibility of unitary, "scientific" organization of society and economy. It is one of several early- and mid-nineteenth-century general theories of society and history, written with the confidence in scientific social analysis that was produced by the Enlightenment, within the particular context of the early Industrial Revolution. It was the product of a time and a place, Western Europe, when the old monarchical and agricultural order was disintegrating and was being replaced by industry, industrial towns, the proletarianization of labor, and the beginnings of mass political organization and participation. This was a period of displaced hierarchies, with aristocracies and the traditional "estates" of society giving way to money power and the forces of social mobility, meritocracy, and plutocracy. It was a time of great advance in scientific investigation of the physical universe, inspiring confidence that human society was equally susceptible to scientific analysis and, eventually, manipulation to produce a better human order.

Between the 1840s and the 1870s, when Marx wrote his principal works, it was possible to believe in the existence of a unitary, deterministic principle of society, and to believe in the possibility, once that principle was discovered, of a perfected, classless, egalitarian social order in which man's ancient struggles over property—and over nation and religion, "bourgeois" and reactionary institutions—could be ended, and a new order of general happiness installed by "history" itself. The power of Leninism as a political movement derived from its implementation of the explicit messianism and utopianism of Marxist thought.

Today, virtually all this has to be recognized as naïve and untrue. This recognition is at the source of what has been happening in the Soviet Union since Gorbachev came to power and began to encourage long-suppressed forces of realism and renewal in Soviet society to express themselves. Marxism provided powerful insights into the roles of money and labor in society. It changed the way we look at the world. It remains a powerful analytical instrument. But its premises are untrue. Soviet society is organized on the basis of a Victorian interpretation of society and history, very much of its time, interesting and historically important, but false—all but useless as a guide to policy, and wholly inadequate as a description of the world as it actually exists. It has led the socialist bloc to an impasse.

The intellectual difficulties in reconciling Marxist principle with even those pragmatic and market-oriented economic adjustments Gorbachev envisages are very great. Marx's most celebrated contribution to economic thought was the theory of "surplus value," created in the productive process by the discrepancy between the value invested in a product by the workman's labor and the value returned to him in wages. The difference is appropriated by the entrepreneur as profit or interest. The Soviet system claims to have abolished this. Marxism argues that, in principle, the value of a product is not what it brings on the market but (as Eduard Bernstein interprets Marx) "consists in the labor expended on it, and is measured according to the time occupied by the labor employed on its production." But even in the Soviet Union this is now an irrelevant point, since the cost of labor is arbitrarily assigned out of social and political considerations and is actually unknown. One of the chief problems of economic management in the Soviet Union is that no one really knows the cost of anything.

Gorbachev proposes that responsibility be delegated, norms of cost-effectiveness and plant and industry profitability imposed, but within limits defined by the central authority. The Soviet Union's commitment to "scientific socialism" inveterately implies ultimate direction from the center, "scientific" national planning. Ideas of market forces, profit as the criterion of efficiency, and competing economic interests (or classes?)—expressions of bourgeois economic thought and the product of bourgeois conditions and practice—can be accepted in the U.S.S.R. only within a framework of socialist assumptions that contradict them. Gorbachev himself has somewhat obscurely described the purpose of his economic reform—in his speech in 1987 commemorating the seventieth anniversary of the Bolshevik Revolution—as "to assure, during the next two or three years, a transition from an overly centralized command system of management to a democratic system based mainly on economic methods and optimal combinations of centralism and self-management. . . . This presupposes a sharp expression of the autonomy of enterprises and associations, their transition to the principle of profitability and self-financing, and the investment of work collectives with all the powers necessary for this."

The goal of "optimal combinations of centralism and self-management" is a purely verbal solution to an urgent practical problem for the Soviet leadership, heritors of Marx and Engels's injunction that the proletariat, having become the ruling class, must "centralize all instruments of production in the hands of the state" in order to bring about the final defeat of the bourgeoisie and consequent elimination of all class divisions. Gorbachev is determined to renew his system but is constrained to do so in terms of a doctrine that, although it purports to be the most advanced and scientific description of reality that exists, actually cannot account for how the modern industrial economy and industrial society work. It is a doctrine that has amply demonstrated its inadequacy as an organizing principle for the Soviet and Soviet-bloc economies. Every serious person engaged in the direction of the Soviet economy grasps this.

Yet how can the doctrine be abandoned? It is what legitimates the party's rule—and Gorbachev's own position. It is fundamental to the existence of the Soviet state and to the leading place of the Communist Party in Soviet society. Generations of the Soviet elite committed themselves to Marxism-Leninism as the truth. Millions died because of it.

It is not that the Cold War is over. Marxism-Leninism is over. It no longer is of serious interest; it is a formula of words—a formula necessary to Gorbachev and to the Soviet leadership, but without inherent interest. Whatever happens now in the Soviet Union's competition with the Western powers, there is no connection with that "struggle for the world" which both East and West conceived it to be from 1918 to the mid-1980s. The Soviet experiment is ending as the victim not of Bolshevism's enemies but of the movement's own contradictions.

It was supposed to have worked the other way. It was the capitalist West whose "inner contradictions" were supposed to have condemned it. But a lot of things were supposed in the messianic, prophetic, internally consistent intellectual propositions of Marxism-Leninism—and by those who opposed it but in doing so accepted its intellectual categories. The Italian novelist Ignazio Silone, who moved from the Bolshevik revolutionary's position to that of the Christian revolutionary, wrote in the 1940s that history's final battle would be between the Communists and the ex-Communists. No one else could meet the measure of this near-theological struggle. In Western eyes it was something like Paradise Seized/Paradise Lost—Stalin a Mephistophelean figure, the Soviet people at war a heroic host. The audacity of the terror, the blatant lies, the deliberate defiance of "bourgeois" morality, the global ambition and utopian promise, gave the whole thing Miltonian dimensions—made it a challenge not only to the historical order of mankind but to the moral order as well, a thrilling challenge to those in the West who took up the Cold War. In fact, the Soviet Union was failing—failing to feed itself, failing even to keep up with the nonmilitary industrial and social progress of the East European countries it controlled. It was on a track leading to the crisis that has been admitted, with exemplary honesty, by Mikhail Gorbachev.

To say, though, that this episode in modern history is all but over leaves one with the enormous and virtually entirely unconsidered problem of what will follow. Until very recently, it was thought exotic or fanciful to suggest that the really serious problem the world confronts between now and the end of the century is how the Soviet Union is to be disengaged from the hopeless ideological engagement that weighs upon its internal affairs and its economy, and from an ultimately unsustainable politico-military overlordship in Eastern and East-Central Europe. Gorbachev is rocking the Soviet Union loose from its anchorage. His problem is that the nation has no usable past, no model in its history for an alternative, constitutional, representative political and social order. The revolutionary option has been explored and exhausted. Russians, though, are most unlikely to look abroad for a new lead. This is the reason the Soviet leaders cling so desperately to Leninism—to the "true" Leninism, the "real" Leninism—as the starting point for reconstructing a place to stand. Yet even in Moscow people have begun openly to concede, and to document, that Lenin began the practices of terror and forced labor, and the concentration camps which Stalin later expanded; that the "personality cult" began with him; and that Lenin perpetuated a Russian authoritarianism which antedated Bolshevism.

It can be argued that czarist society was evolving toward a West European standard of constitutional monarchy when the First World War struck everything down, and that the Bolshevik Revolution was actually a political trauma, reactionary and obscurantist in effect, halting a constructive political development. If one takes the language of Gorbachev and his fellow reformers to mean what it means in the West—"pluralism," "democracy"—they could be said to be attempting, by indirection, to restart that evolution. But neither in Leninism nor in czarism is there the liberal or constitutional political precedent the U.S.S.R. needs—one to which people might refer in attempting to find a new course.

The past, instead, is a burden. The Soviet Union lives in an uninterrupted historical epoch: an epoch that started with the storming of the Winter Palace, and has since passed through the Cheka, the OGPU, the NKVD, the KGB; through Dzerzhinsky, Yagoda, Yezhov, and Beria; through the collectivizations, the camps, the purges, the Moscow Trials, continuing to the persecution of "the Jewish doctors"—which only Stalin's death halted.

Public policy in the Soviet Union suppressed the truth about the terrible but decisive episodes of Soviet history, and the nation continues to be governed by people who find no alternative to resting their claims to legitimacy upon their continuity with this past, about which everyone has for years lied, yet about which everyone knows the truth—or a part of the truth, or enough of the truth to recognize the extent to which the present rests upon a construction of deliberate and desperate lies about the past.

Stalin's lies were not a success, despite his rewriting the history of the Russian Revolution, and then, as Hannah Arendt wrote, "destroying, together with the older books and documents, their authors and readers." As an American official in Moscow remarked in the winter of 1987, "Any peasant will show you the graves." Any village, as part of its collective memory, knows what was done to it during the agricultural collectivizations and the artificially induced famine of 1929–33. A peasant's parents or grandparents were its witnesses, or its victims. The collective reprisals inflicted by Stalin upon villages, or upon whole nationalities, because of their recalcitrance before party directives or their acquiescence in German rule when the Wehrmacht first came—all this is part of living memory. In July 1987 there were demonstrations near Red Square, which the police tolerated, by Crimean Tatars—members of a whole people transported from the Crimea to Asia by Stalin because he believed they had collaborated with the Nazis.

Intellectuals know what went on. The record was kept in unpublished, officially unpublishable novels and works of history that have nonetheless steadily found their way to readers, both abroad and inside the country. Unreleased films and unstaged plays also record the Soviet past. The moral burden of the past, the responsibility it imposes on the present, is the subject of Tengiz Abuladze's noble film *Repentance,* first suppressed in the U.S.S.R., then, after three years, released, then made the official Soviet entry at the 1987 Cannes Film Festival.

Truth is prevailing over totalitarian obscurantism even in Soviet state policy. The vital element in what is described in the Soviet Union as glasnost, or openness, candor, accountability, is an attempt to bring the underground knowledge that Soviet society possesses of its past into public view, in order to reinforce the political authority of the government of Mikhail Gorbachev. By recognizing the validity of individual memories, the present government is attempting to turn the moral force of historical truth to its own advantage.

Thus, the official history of the party is being rewritten. Major figures in the Revolution and the early development of the party and of the Soviet state, such as Trotsky and Bukharin, are once again discussed. The costs of collectivization—an issue on which there has been silence since the time of Khrushchev—have been described with unprecedented candor, acknowledging that millions died and that the whole thing had been an economic disaster. Stalin's war role is now harshly criticized in the official press, especially his refusal to believe evidence of the impending German invasion in 1941, and his earlier purge of the high command. A suppressed letter sent to Stalin in 1939 by Feodor Raskolnikov, a diplomat who subsequently went into exile, which condemned the purges and called Stalin an "Oriental despot," and which now has been published in the U.S.S.R., gives a precise accounting of what the purges cost the Red Army on the eve of the war—three of five marshals shot, one in ten colonels shot, et cetera.

It commonly is argued that Gorbachev wishes to "democratize" Soviet society. The term is one he himself uses. There is no evidence, however, that he wishes to do so as the term is employed in the West. He wishes to make the Soviet system more rational and more efficient—able to make better use of its human and material resources. He wants realistic plans, managers who take responsibility, workers who stay sober and produce. He wants better technology and better management methods. It is in order to have this, not to "democratize" the Soviet Union, that he has found it necessary to address the problem of history. He must restore a relationship of trust between party and public. To restore public confidence in Soviet leadership, it is necessary that the leaders tell the people the truth, and that people acquire confidence that they are being told the truth. Any approach to telling the truth about the history of the Soviet Union, however, or reconsideration of the roles of Trotsky or Bukharin, implicitly raises the question of whether the Soviet Union should have gone in the direction they wanted rather than in the way it did go. An honest account not only of the colossal injustices and crimes of Soviet history but of the unforgivable inefficiency and waste with which Soviet affairs have been conducted since 1917 inevitably poses a question about the Revolution itself.

The Soviet record since 1917 has in crucial respects been one of retrogression. This has been disguised inside the Soviet Union only because of the intellectual isolation in which the country has lived since the late 1920s. After Lenin, the country was ruled first by a semieducated party intriguer and manipulator, Stalin; then, after a short interval, by Nikita Khrushchev, of peasant origins and, again, semieducated, but with the intelligence and decency to begin to free the country from the consequences of Stalinism. After Khrushchev, there was Leonid Brezhnev, who had worked as a pipe fitter while studying at technical college, and then made his way as a cautious party careerist. Mikhail Gorbachev comes from a similar background, but he is university-educated. His sponsor, Yuri Andropov, rose primarily through the state service, not through the party, and Gorbachev, as John Lukacs observed in *Foreign Affairs* in 1986, has surrounded himself with people identified primarily with government rather than with party affairs—a shift that is of significance in the long-term division of power. These people are educated, well traveled, familiar with the non-Soviet world, and able to compare what the Soviet Union has become with what the rest of the world is really like.

Unlike their predecessors, Gorbachev and his people grasp the dimensions of the problems they confront and the handicaps that the party's own errors and the crimes of Stalin have imposed upon them. They have to believe that their system is intrinsically superior to that of the West, provided its energies can be unlocked. If they do not believe that, or hold that they believe it, their own positions will be deprived of legitimacy. They are where they are only because of their party's claim that it is a historically ordained vanguard of the progressive forces of society, a leading actor in a great dialectical process that will end in a transformed humanity. Since this is not the case, it is difficult to see how Gorbachev and his colleagues can come to grips with their nation's terrible past without destroying their own authority. How can the dilemma be resolved? One fears that it cannot.

It seems more reasonable to think that in the end there will have to be a break in historical continuity in Soviet Russia, as there was in imperial Russia in 1917. If Gorbachev successfully compels his nation to confront its past, he may simply provoke a crisis in the system, ending with its rejection of him. A subsequent reactionary restoration would result—as he foresees—only in continued economic, social, and political decline, and the Soviet Union's eventual loss of international influence. The alternative to that seems to be a crisis in which the party's own legitimacy, its right to rule the country, would be challenged. A revolution put the party into power; there is no real reason that a revolution should not put it out.

It is true that revolutions rarely, if ever, happen outside conditions of extreme tension or external pressure—military defeat, political or economic crisis—or in their immediate aftermath, when established authority is discredited and people suddenly believe that liberating change is possible. Nothing like that exists in the Soviet Union at present. Thus, if Gorbachev fails, the hypothesis of continued relative decline seems more plausible.

Reform in Russia has in the past consistently failed, or proved inconclusive. The "Westernizers" were always defeated. Gorbachev stands in the line of Westernizing intellectuals and reformist czars; but none of those before him could secure for Russia the open, nonarbitrary, "legal," "democratic" government Gorbachev says that he wants. That they failed does not mean that he has to fail, but the size of the problem must not be underestimated. There simply is no precedent in Russia's history for what he has undertaken. The change he and his associates propose attempts to justify itself by reference to an intellectual system that has failed in the practical order and is intellectually discredited. To break with that system would leave Gorbachev and the reformers without a place to stand, a fulcrum from which to move society, or a justification for their own power.

The Leninist adventure is over. What has begun? That is the crucial question.

The question was soon answered. Mikhail Gorbachev's attempt to salvage the Communist system through reform produced, instead, its collapse.

One purpose of chapters 3 and 4, as I wrote them more

than ten years ago, was to convince readers in the Soviet Union as well as in the West that the situation of the countries of Central and Eastern Europe not only was very dangerous and needed to be changed but that it *could* be changed, to the benefit of the Soviet Union as well as to that of the people living in the Warsaw Pact countries. My appeal for a reasoned diplomatic solution to the situation in Central and Eastern Europe was overtaken by what actually happened—all but miraculously without violence, except in Romania.

What did happen allowed the Central and East Europeans to rid themselves of Soviet occupation or control in a matter of months, once the Berlin Wall was down. They were left free to make of themselves what they wanted, which they have done, not always with very successful results; but that is what happens when people are free to do what they want.

The Soviet Union in Mikhail Gorbachev's time was a stagnant and blocked society, but nonetheless it fed and housed its people, educated them (well), provided them security, and could conduct itself in the world as a superpower, which militarily it was. Mikhail Gorbachev and his associates were serious men and women attempting to rescue Russia and its people from the consequences of their terrible history. They deserved a better outcome than what has happened.

Despised now in his own country, largely ignored elsewhere, history will be kind to Mikhail Gorbachev. He could not know where glasnost and perestroika were leading. He did know that his nation had to confront the truth about what had happened, and about what the system had become. This was essential to establishing a moral foundation for reconstruction.

One easily forgets how promising, how hopeful, the situation in Russia seemed as the Gorbachev reforms were launched. He was himself vigorous, intelligent, and, most of all, confident, in command of a society that still believed itself in control of its national destiny.

The contrast with Russia's situation now, in the new millennium, is shocking. Boris Yeltsin, who during the final years of his presidency seemed another Brezhnev—arbitrary, feeble, an invalid—has been replaced by the hard-eyed men who surrounded him and who have placed in power one of their own. Vladimir Putin won electoral ratification thanks to a civil war of doubtful origins and great brutality. The prospect, one fears, is no longer one of progress and further reform but of robber capitalism's permanent installation in the economy and of restored authoritarianism, or Caesarism. Georgi Arbatov, former director of the United States and Canada Institute of the Soviet Academy of Sciences and an adviser to Mikhail Gorbachev at the time of his reforms, was asked in October 1999 what he saw in Russia's immediate future. He replied, "Nothing good."

The saving grace is that the Russian people have themselves democratized, in a manner of speaking. Their outlook and expectations have dramatically changed, however swindled they have been by what were meant to be reforms. This may prove of greater significance than what has happened at the top. The great risk is that Russia's people will conclude that, as on previous occasions in their history, their accommodation to the West has led them to betrayal. They and their leaders opened themselves all but totally to Western norms and advice—whatever the malfeasance and corruption in the course of this great change—and while one result of this has been democratic structures and open debate (provisionally so; press and television have come nearly completely under the control of rival "oligarchs"), the other result has been a national tragedy. The West can easily be seen, after this, as having proven a "carrier of a terrible and contagious disease."

In 1989, the nation's weakness was not simply a matter of

material backwardness. I mention the Soviet diplomat who said on a public platform in the West in the mid-1980s that his country was experiencing "a spiritual crisis" and that glasnost represented a search by the Soviet elite and people "to recover the moral foundations of their society." Hearing those words then revealed to me the true proportions of what was under way in Russia. No Soviet official would ever before have said such things. But the search of which he spoke has yet to be completed.

That was what led Mikhail Gorbachev to decisions of great courage: to accept defeat in Afghanistan and end the war there, to consent to the reunification of Germany and peacefully withdraw Soviet forces from Eastern Europe, and to promote reformist forces throughout the bloc (even sponsoring the coup that became an armed uprising in Romania). These were realistic, if desperate, responses to the condition of Communist society then, and they were very considerable gambles as well. He lost the gamble, personally, but Russia won—if provisionally. It acquired a democratic political structure.

The Gorbachev reforms rested on the mistaken belief that he and his fellow reformers had (could scarcely not have had, given who they were) that reform could be accomplished by a purification of the Communist system, the creation of a "socialist state of law." The project failed. Had Gorbachev an alternative? If so, that would not have been apparent until afterward. He chose his course and followed it with courage. He freed Central and Eastern Europe without attempting to find advantage in doing so, other than the advantage provided by acting realistically. One can compare his realism and ruthlessness in ending the war in Afghanistan with the performance of Richard Nixon and Henry Kissinger on Vietnam, who enlarged, and prolonged by seven years, a war that their administration had been elected to end and that they had promised to end. Gorbachev cut his losses, and gained respect for Russia, rather than losing it.

He was unseated in 1991. Boris Yeltsin intervened when a coup d'état was attempted, and seized the imagination of the West by terminating the Soviet Union, setting free its component republics, and renouncing Marxism. The U.S. government threw all its power and influence behind him, pressing upon him the prevailing American orthodoxy, which claimed that the impartial market would not only transform Russia's floundering economy but install law and democracy as well. Washington insisted that Russia privatize its industry and banks even though no legal, social, or intellectual structure existed in Russia to underpin a modern market system. The result was devastation for Russia's society.

Mr. Gorbachev had set loose quasi-revolutionary forces with what was meant to be a program of centrally directed, "planned" devolution of economic authority. One can ask whether, flawed as that plan was, it might have provided a more constructive transition out of the command system, toward an accountable industry and banking system as well as toward representative government, than the shock treatment actually administered. The Chinese example is inconclusive. China's economy has progressed at a rapid pace, but it continues to depend on foreign (chiefly overseas Chinese) capital and technology, and remains fragile. China has not yet met its political crisis, which will arrive when party rule ends.

The Russian state that emerged from the debris of the Soviet Union functions within the structure of a democracy. Nations are responsible for what they become, and certainly the rampant malversation, swindle, and wholesale theft of national assets that went on during the 1990s were all committed by Russians, with the connivance of other Russians. The economic conditions that allowed, or even invited, this to happen were the result of choices made by Gorbachev's successors, under the influence of Western advisers convinced that the general principles of market economics are universally applicable, whatever the social and institutional realities of a particular case.

Alan Greenspan, chairman of the Federal Reserve, in a talk at the Woodrow Wilson Scholars' Center in Washington in 1997, acknowledged that he had failed to appreciate that economics is not a sovereign science, and that political and cultural factors are fundamental to a society's economic behavior, saying that he had believed that dismantling Communism would "automatically establish a free market entrepreneurial system." He said that after 1989 he—or "we," as he put it—discovered that "much of what we took for granted in our free market system and assumed to be human nature was not nature at all, but culture. The dismantling of the central planning function in an economy does not, as some had supposed, automatically establish [market capitalism]." Mr. Greenspan is not unrepresentative of the American economic community. His remark amounted to an admission that Russia's economic condition today is in part the product of a crucial professional deformation among Western economists, educated to ignore all but a narrow range of material or mathematically defined factors in an economy's functioning.

Mr. Greenspan's was a version of the liberal illusion, that of mankind's essential innocence and natural virtue, whom society corrupts. (Many self-proclaimed conservatives, like himself, are among the liberal illusion's committed believers, if unbeknownst to themselves.) One might think it self-evident that a society's historical culture has a deep influence on economic behavior and values, in both practical and intellectual ways. It was not evident to the most influential Western economists of the post-Communist decade (nor during globalism's promulgation to the less-developed parts of the world—which is another story). Nor was it evident to American government officials and their colleagues in international financial and research institutions—the IMF, World Bank, OECD, and so on. If a society lacks an established culture of commercial law and obedience to law, an entrepreneurial culture and tradition, the experience of modern commerce, and a civil society capable of imposing an indispensable social discipline upon business and businessmen, there can be no "automatically established free-market entrepreneurial system."

That is why Poland, Hungary, and the Czech Republic made relatively successful transitions from Communism. All were relatively sophisticated industrial and commercial societies before Communism was imposed on them at the end of the 1940s. They had governments of law, anchored in Western political philosophy, a history that connected them to the development of Western culture, religion, and political institutions since the Middle Ages. Freed of Communism, they knew how to become citizens again—and even capitalists.

In Russia, only the beginnings of a modern economy existed in Saint Petersburg and Moscow when the Bolshevik Revolution took place, seventy years before the Soviet collapse; and those involved were in any case mostly murdered in the years after the Revolution. Russians for decades afterward were taught that property is theft, capitalism is exploitation, and individual wealth is not "earned" but stolen. It is scarcely surprising that Russian capitalism after 1991 became what its new practitioners had been taught to believe it had to become.

Russians during the past century repeatedly suffered profound moral, political, and intellectual ruptures within their society and in its relations with the rest of the world: the Romanov system's discredit in the Russo-Japanese war; the First World War, with its defeats and its millions of casualties; the collapse of the Westernizing reform government of the February Revolution; the Bolshevik Revolution and the Civil War that followed; famine, Gulag; a second exhausting and devastating invasion and war, conducted without quarter or pity; and, finally, Communist society's collapse. That was followed by a willing conversion to the proclaimed values of the West, with ruinous and humiliating consequences. This development, filled with auspices, brought Russia to where it is today, at another "beginning, from which other things will now begin."

# NATIONALISM

5

The intractability of the Russian problem and the inaccessibility of the Soviet Union to Western influence after the Second World War produced a forty-year stalemate in the relations of East and West in Europe, which ended only with Gorbachev's coming to power in Moscow. During those years the United States increasingly looked toward the non-European world as a zone both of threat and of potential resolution of what it interpreted as the global challenge of Communist totalitarianism. Asia above all seemed vulnerable to the contagion of Communism—the victory of Mao Tse-tung in China in 1949, and the wars in Korea and Indochina, seemed demonstrations of that. At the same time, Asia seemed accessible to American counteraction. There, as later in the Middle East and Latin America, Communism had successfully allied itself with national movements. But Washington resolved that, given American support, the initiative might be reclaimed by non-Communist national forces. From this belief came a series of American economic and politico-military interventions in Asia, and subsequently elsewhere in the non-Western world, that set the United States against radical national movements, deeply involving it in situations it proved poorly equipped to understand and unable to dominate. In the event, four out of the five American presidents between John Kennedy and George Bush were to be damaged or wrecked by attempts to dislodge or dominate radical nationalism in a non-Western country, or by the consequences of illegal measures taken by presidents or their agents to achieve such ends despite congressional and public opposition. The presidencies of Lyndon Johnson, Jimmy Carter, and Ronald Reagan all had their final months ruined or disrupted by essentially the same error, and that of Richard Nixon had been damaged by it before his ultimate downfall.

Such repeated and disabling collisions with radical national movements in Asia, the Middle East, and Central America are aspects of something more important, which Washington, because of its obsession with the ideological conflict with Communism, failed to grasp. The gross political disruptions dominating the twentieth century have actually resulted from defective or unsatisfied nationalism—from the struggles of societies to become nations, to acquire the maturity and "national security" that come from a confident political identity, a cultural autonomy, a homogeneity of population, and, finally, clear and secure borders. Both of the two world wars exploded out of such national insecurities in Central and Southeastern Europe, as Germans, Serbs, Croats, Bosnians, Czechs, and Poles all struggled to affirm, or simply to establish, national identities still territorially indistinct or culturally insecure.

Contemporary events in the Middle East have echoed what happened in Central and Southeastern Europe during the late nineteenth century and the first half of the twentieth. A series of struggles is today taking place to create nations out of the raw materials of premodern society and out of political traditions antedating the modern state. The interventions in this process of both the former Soviet Union and the United States have rested on misconceptions of what actually is going on: the two major powers misidentifying proto-national struggles as having something essential to do with Soviet or American ideas—interpreting them as conflicts of political values directly related to the Soviet and American ideologies. This miscomprehension resulted in irrelevant and destructive policymaking on the part of both powers. The real issue—by no means the only one, but the basic and neglected one—is that of political immaturity, a striving for maturity.

One may speak of this maturity as a more or less homogeneous society's possession of a fixed place, with fixed and acknowledged borders; a recognized history and distinctive national culture; and an absence of what in the political vocabulary are called revindications—claims on others' territories, claims on populations held elsewhere, claims to be satisfied only at the expense of others. A primary characteristic of a mature nation is that it is a satisfied nation, an achieved nation.

In Asia, Japan and China are ancient and fully achieved nations, even though one is a great industrial power and the other is still in crucial respects a premodern society. In Western Europe, England and France are fully achieved, mature nations. The British union of Scotland and Wales with England might be considered less than fully achieved, yet its reversal is scarcely imaginable. In any case, Scotland, whether or not there is ever to be an independent Scotland, is itself an achieved and mature national society. Welsh nationalism, more than Scottish, is vestigial, like the nationalisms of Catalans, Bretons, and Basques in France and Spain. Ireland is an ancient and achieved nation. The separate existence of a Northern Ireland under the British Crown derives from the presence there of Unionist Protestants, a residual colonial population, whose eventual fate is likely to be that of France's settlers in Algeria after Algerian independence, or that which the whites face in South Africa. As long as these minorities resist reconciliation with and assimilation into the majority in their societies, their positions are provisional and their futures contingent. France is an achieved nation even though the French are not a homogeneous people. Normans, Burgundians, Catalans, Gascons, Provençals, are all different, but the French nation to which they belong was achieved, with a distinct culture, and approximately the borders it possesses today, more than a thousand years ago. Spain and Italy are unions of mature provinces, kingdoms, or cities: Castile, Seville, Catalonia; Venice, Tuscany, Lombardy, Sicily, et cetera. The individual parts may resist the political or economic domination of the center, but the cultural identities of the Spanish and the Italian nations are in no doubt.

Questions of nationhood become more urgent as one moves eastward. Those that preoccupied Europeans in the nineteenth century essentially involved how peacefully to give valid and stable political form to the national societies—the ethnic, linguistic, religious, and cultural communities—that emerged from the premodern (or potentially postmodern?) political institutions or relationships of the Hapsburg and Ottoman empires as those empires fell. There is as yet no answer.

In 1918, when the Hapsburg Empire had failed, a romantic American political conception, that of universal national self-determination, brought about the creation of a Czechoslovakia that incorporated Slovak and German minorities; Yugoslavia (or the Kingdom of the Serbs, Croats, and Slovenes, as it was initially known), an uneasy confederation of ex-Hapsburg and ex-Ottoman nations with Montenegro; an independent Poland; a new, truncated Austria; and an autonomous Hungary.

The Ottoman Empire had been a polyglot affair whose frontiers extended at one time or another as far as Vienna and Gibraltar—from the Indian Ocean and the Caucasus to the Atlantic—incorporating a great number of ethnic, religious, and political communities or entities of one or another kind under a flexible Ottoman political overlordship. Its components in the Near East had included Armenia, which was subsequently divided up among the Soviet Union, Turkey, and Iran, and today remains a factor of actual or potential tension for all three. From the Ottoman collapse came the eastern Mediterranean Arab states (including Palestine), Saudi Arabia, and the Persian Gulf principalities (all of them made mandates of the League of Nations or protectorates), as well as an independent, secular Turkish state.

Until 1918, for most of these societies the primary functions of the modern nation-state—defense, the conduct of foreign policy and diplomatic relations, the direction of industry and the economy—were performed, within the limits of the time, by the sultanate in Constantinople. On the other hand, the ordinary lives of the people who made up the Ottoman Empire had relatively little to do with Constantinople, with which relations usually were distant. In Europe, predominantly Muslim societies—such as traditional clan societies in Albania and peasant agricultural societies in Bosnia and Herzegovina—coexisted under Turkish authority with Christian Serbs, Greeks, Bulgarians, Moldavians, and Walachians as late as the early twentieth century. An Albanian dynasty ruled Egypt under nominal Ottoman suzerainty, and there were quasi-autonomous Ottoman states in the Maghreb.

As Turkish rule failed, the new states that emerged claimed the attributes of modern nationhood but could only inadequately sustain those claims. Monarchies were invented by the Western powers for Romania, Serbia, Greece, and Bulgaria. German princes, unemployed nephews and nieces of the Russian and English monarchies, were invited to pack up and make the arduous voyage to primitive capital cities in Europe's south and east, there to rule peasant populations whose languages they could not speak. As late as 1913, the polyglot English aristocrat and traveler Aubrey Herbert, a sometime British spy, was offered the crown of Albania. Romania's last two kings, Carol and Michael, were direct descendants of Queen Victoria, Czar Alexander II, and Hohenzollern princes. A witness to the Romanian monarchy's collapse, R. G. Waldeck, said of the dynasty: "They all went a bit haywire under this violent sun and the deep blue skies. They could not take it. They overdid everything."

Parliaments on French or British models were set up in these countries, but political power usually continued to function by indirection through networks of personal or clan obligations established under the sultanate—to the disapproval or despair of Western observers. Field Marshal Mackensen, who was the German commander in Romania in the First World War, said, "I came to Bucharest with a troupe of conquering heroes, and I leave here with a troupe of gigolos and racketeers."

Alien minorities were incorporated within the frontiers of virtually all these countries, and nearly all claimed some bordering territory. Ex-Hapsburg Hungary kept up a claim to Transylvania, in Romania, where there are two million ethnic Hungarians, provoking Bucharest to accuse its Warsaw Pact neighbor of falsifying history and reviving "theses of the Nazi era." Romania would claim Bessarabia if it dared (it is part of the Soviet Union).* Greece has claimed all of Cyprus; Turkey invaded and occupied a third of it in 1974. Bulgaria has persecuted its Turkish minority, and Turkey, Iraq, and Syria all repress Kurdish minorities. Iraq seems to have tried to exterminate its rebellious Kurds, at the end of the Gulf War. Armenians demand an autonomous Armenia.† Albania would, if it could, claim Kosovo, the Albanian-populated region of Yugoslavia; the Serbs are inclined to regard Albania as, by rights, a Yugoslav dependency.

The borders of the ex-Ottoman Arab states are arbitrary. There was a nationalist movement in Egypt after the Napoleonic invasion; Egypt, after all, had been a nation since antiquity. The national idea that developed in the eastern Ottoman Empire was that of "the Arab nation." The "Arab revolt" against the Turks in the First World War reflected a belief in the possibility of—as Edward Atiyah writes—"one Arab kingdom east of Suez . . . inspired by dreams of past glory and intended to recreate as much of the Umayyad or Abbasid Empire as was possible." This was an unrealizable project, in view of the reality that "Arabia had not changed much since the time of Mohammed . . . whereas Syria and Iraq had several millennia of urban civilization behind them [and] Mecca and Medina . . . were still medieval and theocratically minded, untouched by the Western influences that had been at work for nearly a century in Syria." Arab society was then, and remains today, largely unready for the forms of national existence characteristic of Western Europe and North America. The pressures upon it, internally generated as well as external, to conform to an inappro-

*In 1991 it became independent Moldova.
†In 1991 Armenia became independent.

priate modern model have been a powerful force behind the violence marking the region in recent years, behind popular alienation from the West, and behind the Islamic-fundamentalist reaction that has emerged from Iran, whose essential quality is to reject the modern secular state in favor of a romanticized conception of the political order of classical Islam.

Israel, whose installation in the Middle East was a catalyst for the violence from and among the Muslim states, is itself a political phenomenon rooted in the romantic secular national movements of nineteenth-century Central Europe, given terrible and transforming impetus by the Holocaust. It, too, remains an incomplete nation, with insecure borders and a large and hostile Arab minority population; under constant military and terrorist pressures; and experiencing intense internal controversy over the eventual course its society will take—whether secular and politically pluralist or theocratic. Palestine, which was a political entity but never a nation before 1948, has acquired the attributes of a modern nation now that Israel exists and there no longer is a Palestine. It has a recognized leader, a parliament, an army, a foreign policy, and diplomatic representation throughout the world—everything except a country.

In Africa, nearly all the existing states are not real nations but political units that were artificially defined in the colonial period and survive today because of a consensus among Africa's ruling elites that any attempt to change and rationalize borders would produce chaos. This is not a consensus likely to last; but because Africa is not a major factor in international geopolitics and economics, the incipient troubles there are not as dangerous as those in Central and Eastern Europe and in the Middle East.

The Latin American countries as they exist today also derive largely from the administrative demarcations of colonial empires. The machinery of royal administration in the Spanish colonies was fully formed before the end of the seventeenth century; the old viceroyalties of La Plata, Peru, New Granada, and New Spain are recognizable in the boundaries of today. South America is thus composed of relatively mature nations with serious internal problems but few international ones. The Falklands War aside (the islands were an issue of contention between Spain and Britain as early as the eighteenth century), the last international war in South America was the Chaco War, between Paraguay and Bolivia, from 1932 to 1935. The problems of South America are nearly all social and economic in character, and are partly the result of the general failure, at least until fairly recently (and real change has yet to be confirmed), to deal satisfactorily with the absolutist political and intellectual legacy of Spain and of Iberian Catholicism—to which, in the nineteenth century, were added absolutist or doctrinaire forms of European republicanism and liberalism. Reforms have repeatedly broken down.

Central America, where crisis existed in the 1980s, is different. The viceroyalty of New Spain extended from the Isthmus of Panama northward through Mexico into California, Texas, and New Mexico. These last, of course, were lost to the United States, and Mexico underwent not only conflicts with the United States but also French occupation and repeated civil wars. The "United Provinces" of Central America severed themselves from Mexico in 1823, but their history thereafter has been of separatist struggles among Costa Rica, Guatemala, Honduras, El Salvador, and Nicaragua, alternating with attempts to reunite them, usually under Guatemalan or Nicaraguan domination. From the mid-nineteenth century on, there have been repeated United States military and political interventions. What has been taking place there in recent years is clearly nothing new, and results from the fact that the nations of Central America remain unachieved, immature.

The achievement of nationhood is a product not only of time and circumstance but usually of war and suffering as well. The political terrain of inchoate or incomplete nationhood in what came to be named the Third World proved peculiarly unfriendly to the United States and the Soviet Union—capitals of the "first" and "second" worlds—when they displaced the struggle they had begun in Europe to this new front in the 1950s and 1960s. Washington's failure to understand the nature of proto-national struggle, and Soviet ideological misconceptions about national development itself, led both superpowers to launch themselves into competitions that they were to lose, at considerable cost to themselves (as in Vietnam and Afghanistan) and at even heavier cost to the people of these regions, to whom they attached their misconceptions.

In Europe, the Cold War presented real risks to those who took part, with real gains to be made. It was a struggle for military and political control of Eastern Europe, Yugoslavia, Greece, Austria, and the newly divided Germany. It was a competition for dominant influence over the docks, railways, trade unions, political parties, press, and intelligentsia of certain countries of Western Europe. It was a strategic struggle as well as an ideological one, and both sides were conscious that it might result in war. The struggle outside Europe in the event proved bloodier, provoking direct or indirect American and Soviet involvement in a score of local wars, but it was also essentially irrelevant to the balance of power in world affairs. Japan and China were major factors in the world balance, but Europe remained the decisive arena of that conflict.

The West won the initial battles in Western Europe, and the Soviet Union in Eastern Europe. After 1953, however, there was a notable lessening of tension. The Soviets ceded the disputed territories of Austria—then under four-power occupation—and Greece. Yugoslavia imposed its own neutrality. Stalin's successors, Bulganin and Khrushchev, during a well-publicized tour of Asia in 1955, launched the doctrine of "competitive coexistence," which said that Communism would compete peacefully with the West. This policy was a significant shift from the orthodox Stalinist doctrine that war was inevitable between an ascendant socialist system and the weakened and desperate capitalists. The new doctrine also rationalized the reality that the new leaders of the Soviet Union did not want war, feared war, and had concluded that they had to get along in practical ways with the Western powers. Détente followed competitive coexistence, producing the political accommodation, arms control, and trade that was achieved by the Soviet Union and the United States in the 1960s and early 1970s. The transfer of Soviet-American rivalries from Europe to the Third World expressed a Soviet retreat from revolutionary commitment—a retreat that was indicated in the subsequent ideological revisions. Under Stalin, the postwar nationalist leaders in Asia—Gandhi and Nehru in India, Sukarno in Indonesia—had been attacked as obstacles to true revolutionary change. After 1955, they were described as progressive figures, if transitional ones, in a process that would eventually lead to a true socialism. The Soviet government now sought alliances with Nehru's India and Nasser's Egypt.

The United States found this new political competition congenial, because Americans were as firmly convinced as the Marxists that a great new historical evolution was under way now that the age of empire had ended. Doing away with European colonialism had long been an American ambition. That accomplished, Americans believed that the critical rivalry was between two models of future development for the new nations—Marxism and liberal democracy. The United States would compete with the Soviet Union (and, as it was then thought, its Chinese ally) to demonstrate which system was better at giving people freedom and prosperity. Americans had little doubt about the outcome. "The world has divided like an amoeba into two opposing systems of ideology and power—one based on free choice, the other on the subservience of the individual to rigid dogma." That was George Ball, speaking in 1965, as Under Secretary of State. The idea of an epochal struggle over the nature of society in the emerging non-Western nations gratified the old American sense of national destiny to serve as model for the world.

American confidence in this mission, however, was to be crucially shaken by the war in Vietnam and its aftermath. The belief in global ideological confrontation between Communism and democracy to settle the fate of the world remained a fundamental American foreign-policy assumption, but it became a source of frustration as events in Southeast Asia, Iran, the Middle East, and

Latin America went against Washington's hopes. There were three reasons for this frustration. The first is simple: American ideas of government and economy are the product of a Western intellectual and political history, and of fundamentally American conditions, which do not exist elsewhere. There are lessons for others in what has happened to the United States and in what Americans have done, but the American national experience is not normative. A second, and related, reason for frustration is that liberal and meliorist programs of change and reform do not ordinarily fit the conditions that have existed in most of the former colonies in recent years. Americans offer counsels of reason and moderation to meet conditions of disruption and intolerance. Washington proposes evolutionary change to compete with the promise of cathartic revolutionary change. But the rationalism and conservatism of what Americans offer are no adequate response to the impulses of revenge and violence that have dominated societies like Vietnam, Cambodia, and Iran, still in shock from their political and cultural conquest by the European powers during the years of colonialism. Finally, the United States seeks peace and order. Its ultimate aim is stability, while the Soviet Union's tactical interest has been perceived as instability throughout the Third World. Thus, the United States is nearly always drawn to support a party in power—a liberal party if possible, but an illiberal one if necessary, including the Shah of Iran, a succession of generals in Vietnam, and a variety of military figures in Chile, Brazil, Central America, and elsewhere. Americans prefer, in principle, to support a "third force," between reaction and radicalism, but third forces have proven hard to find and weak in action. Challenged, they usually yield to more radical forces of the right or the left—forces possessing fewer scruples, a greater will to gain and use power, a greater willingness to kill. All this is hardly surprising. The virtues of liberalism are not warlike; they are the virtues of accommodation, compromise, amelioration—and in radically disrupted or revolutionary situations these are usually losing qualities. Starting out on the side of progress and reform, the United States often finds itself with the repressive right.

The truth, though, is that in the twenty-five years before 1989 neither the United States nor the Soviet Union had a great deal of success in the ideological battle in the non-Western world. The competition produced as much disappointment for the Russians as it did for the Americans. At one time or another, such different countries as Egypt, Syria, Iraq, Indonesia, India, Chile, Zanzibar, and Guinea were written off to Soviet or Chinese Communism by the Western press or the State Department, yet in the end, despite having taken Soviet or Chinese aid and having cooperated in one degree or another with the Soviet or Chinese governments, each of these countries went its own way. (In the mid-1970s, for reasons that had nothing to do with China's own policy commitments, Washington suddenly ceased to perceive Chinese Communism as a threat.) The Soviets proved to have no more control over what happened than the United States had in the case of its own protégés— the Shah's Iran, South Vietnam, pre-civil-war Lebanon, Nicaragua, Panama. Communism has "taken" in the Third World only when it was the vehicle of national revival and of rejection of colonialism, as in China, Vietnam, and Cuba. In Afghanistan—an inaccessible country on a sensitive Soviet border, where Moscow might have been expected to be able to impose the kind of rule it wanted—the Soviet Union gave massive military support to a regime that purported to be a Marxist government but was really a throwback to something familiar from Eastern Europe in the 1930s and Latin America in the 1940s: a junta of radicalized officers and intellectuals who wanted the swift and total remaking of a backward society. Moscow's heavy-handed intervention was not a success.

To speak of Afghanistan, however, is to take note of the new activism and openness that developed during the 1970s in the Soviet Union's interventions outside its established zone of direct political and military control in Europe. This changed policy was inaugurated with the introduction of Cuban combat troops into Angola in 1975. Intervention was extended to Ethiopia, with Soviet transport and equipment in support, as part of a striking expansion of the range of Soviet military capacity. East Germany subsequently enlarged its role in Africa, working with the Zambian, Mozambican, and Ethiopian governments, among others, and in the pre-independence struggle in Zimbabwe and in Namibia (South-West Africa). The intelligence services of the Soviet Union and certain East European countries for years tried to influence various radical or self-proclaimed Marxist movements and governments throughout Africa, but their programs became much more ambitious in the 1970s, and the introduction of foreign troops—there were more than thirty thousand soldiers in the Cuban expeditionary forces in Africa—made a quantitative difference in the scale of killing but changed nothing fundamental. In the late 1980s the U.S.S.R. began a retreat from Africa.

There is, of course, a long history of indirect foreign political interventions by the Soviet Union since the October Revolution. The rationale for these was international proletarian solidarity—the Communist International, not the Soviet government, was acting—and this rationale was generally tolerated, even though everyone knew that the international movement was totally subordinated to the interests of the Soviet Union. When international Communist interests had to be sacrificed, this was done summarily—most memorably in the Nazi-Soviet pact of August 1939. In the past, the conventions of Communist internationalism imposed certain restrictions on Soviet behavior, notably in barring the employment of troops. Forms were observed that allowed the Soviet government to disclaim responsibilities that might prove inconvenient to Soviet national interest. In important respects, these forms, under Brezhnev in the 1970s, were abandoned. The conflict in the Third World thus was sharpened, just at a time when the United States had drawn back, as a consequence of its Vietnam experience, and when serious progress in arms-limitation agreements had begun to seem possible. The change exploited American uncertainty in the post-Vietnam and Watergate period in a way that made the ripostes of the Reagan administration—in Grenada,

Nicaragua, and El Salvador—all but inevitable. It was a disquieting shift. When President Carter protested in 1979 to Brezhnev at the provocative turn taken by Soviet policy, he was curtly informed that "détente has not abolished the class struggle." But it was not the class struggle that the Cuban Army conducted in Angola and Ethiopia, nor the Soviet Army in Afghanistan.

The conflict between the United States and the Soviet Union or China in the Third World represented a retreat or diversion from direct conflict and nuclear risk. Except for the Vietnam War, violence had tended to be clandestine and limited. Both the United States and the Soviets acted through proxies. The United States government's usual practice has been to meet political intervention with political intervention, proxy with proxy. In 1975, Secretary of State Kissinger initiated a program of substantial American investment in the Angolan guerrillas of Holden Roberto and Jonas Savimbi to fight the forces supported by the Soviet Union and Cuba, consistent with what had been done in the past in other places, but Congress stopped it. Congressional hostility to this kind of intervention derived from the experience in Vietnam, but was also justified on larger grounds—not least the moral. There was distaste for secret wars and the use of proxies; later, in Central America, these restrictions were relaxed to a degree, and the conduct of war by proxy again intensified, most notably through the Reagan administration's support of the Nicaraguan "contras." In this use of proxies, a kind of complicity grew up between the American and Soviet governments, and even between the two peoples, spared final responsibility for what their governments did, themselves evading a suffering that was imposed on others on their behalf. The moral meaning and consequence of this use of others has not been edifying, but it had the usefulness of sparing the world (as well as the two superpowers) the risks of an engagement from which there might be no retreat. Such allies were dispensable, disavowable. The Soviet Union, for example, readily ignored the bombing of Hanoi. That was an awkward matter, but the lives lost were not

Russian, and while the bombs fell, Moscow dealt on larger matters with the United States, to mutual advantage. The United States survived its defeat by the Vietnamese Communists, as the Soviet Union remained at a discreet distance. On the single postwar occasion when the Soviet Union and the United States were directly engaged, in the Cuban missile crisis, there was an intelligent concern on the American side to limit the resonance of the American victory and to yield something in compensation, in this instance the American missiles installed in Turkey.

Conflict by proxy, however, has turned other people's wars into bigger and better-armed affairs than they ought to be. Unsophisticated armies engaged in what should be mere demonstrations, shows of ornamental ferocity, parades of strength, skirmishes in Africa or Central America, have been taught the methods of large-scale killing and given the weapons to accomplish it. This has amounted to a superimposition of Soviet and American geopolitical perception and ambition upon other countries' wars. It is not a new practice; there were more French troops at the battle of Yorktown than there were American, and the American Revolution was, to contemporaries, a belated sideshow to the Seven Years' War between the major European powers—Britain and France at it again, with exotic colonial auxiliaries. Proxy warfare permits disavowal, but also provides for moral as well as military inflation and escalation. It follows that by attributing large ideological and geopolitical significance to such a struggle as that in Central America, as before in Vietnam, the United States risked making the intrinsically insignificant become truly significant. The fate of the United States, Cuba, and the Soviet Union was symbolically engaged, even though the struggle in El Salvador, say, could just as well have been dismissed by the U.S. government as a matter between El Salvador's forty families and their rebellious peons. At another time, this conflict would have been ignored, and some other affair chosen for the test of great-power commitment. The Salvadorans, like the Nicaraguans, were unlucky.

No one in Washington appears to have taken much notice of

the Communist Party's coup d'état in Kabul in 1978, which might have been thought a more important affair than El Salvador ever could be, a quite undisguised extension of Soviet national power. An expression of American concern might have prevented what followed, but Washington was interested in other matters in 1978. To an unpleasant degree, what counts is what people at a given time think counts. It is a political version of philosophical idealism: things have their reality in the mind of the observer. Vietnam was a great struggle in the Cold War because the United States chose to nominate it as such, and then proceeded at reckless cost to make it so, to its own misfortune. In a sense other than that usually assumed by conservative polemicists, the American defeat in Vietnam was self-inflicted: the test was chosen, and the United States threw itself into it, without serious regard for the reality to which the test had been affixed.

These affairs, however, the great powers notwithstanding, eventually find their decisive meaning within their own geographical limits. Who rules Chad counts for Chad, whether it is Hissene Habre or Goukinni Oueddei. It counts for El Salvador who is in charge there, as it did for the Nicaraguans to have their Sandinistas in succession to General Somoza. It may be doubted that it seriously matters to others. The outside powers do not create the struggles in those countries, any more than the Soviet Union or China was responsible for the struggle for power between politicized northerners and southerners in Vietnam after 1954, in which Americans became incidental victims. Outsiders were not responsible for the Gulf War, or the wars between Muslims and Hindus on the Indian subcontinent in 1947, between Muslims and Christians in Nigeria-Biafra, or between Islamic fundamentalists and secularizers in Lebanon. Communal, national, religious, and ethnic passions are in too generous supply in the world.

The distance between Washington and Kabul, Teheran, San Salvador, Beirut, or Damascus, ordinarily measured in miles, can more usefully be measured in a second dimension, that of historical and cultural time. Foreign policy deals across time as well as across space. Teheran, for example, is a thousand miles from the open sea, more than six thousand miles from Washington, and in another dimension of time. There is more in this than merely the observation that the Ayatollah Khomeini was always to Americans a "medieval" figure. Certainly there was something in him that suggested Peter the Hermit preaching the First Crusade. There was something in him that reminds one of Cromwell or Calvin. Such are men for whom the most important things do not exist in secular time. They believe that common life is ephemeral, and that justice is eternal. Temporal happiness is illusion or temptation. Compromise is betrayal. Truth is more important than feeling. Obedient to God, doing God's will, any of these men, threatened with foreign attack, military reprisal, or war, might welcome it as Khomeini welcomed war with Iraq—as a shortcut to paradise, the longed-for meeting with destiny. God will snatch up his own and impose his own revenge upon the infidel.

A man such as Khomeini is our contemporary, yet he acts in dimensions that are closed to us. Darius Shayegan, an Iranian intellectual and philosopher, has said of the premedieval and pre-Islamic resonances in Khomeini's Iran: "Khomeini stirs the collective unconscious of Iranians. . . . There are precedents of radical confrontation in the religious and political history of Iran which go back to the beginnings, in the tradition of the great 'Magi' before the Achaemenian Age, before Islam. Consider the Manichaeanism of Khomeini, the way in which he presents everything in black and white, good or evil, without compromise—that's much more Iranian, or Persian, than Islamic." Manichaeanism, the belief that evil is an active principle in human affairs and that Satan is coeternal with God, was specifically an Iranian heresy. It arose from the collision of Christianity with Persia's native Zoroastrianism, a religion of the unresolved conflict between good and evil powers, and of the force of the elements. Zoroastrianism was also ethical and activist, and so resisted the doctrine of submission that dominates Islam. The Islamic cult of the Assassins, which deliberately practiced murder, arose in Persia. The Islamic clergy in Persia has repeatedly assumed a political role—in the twentieth century, by supporting the revolution of 1906, by conferring the crown upon Reza Khan, the army officer who founded the Pahlevi dynasty in 1925, and by rejecting his son in 1979.

Miscalculation of the dimension of time contributed to the American failure in Iran in another respect. Washington thoughtlessly assumed the quasi-colonial role that Britain had previously held with respect to the Iranians, at just the point when they had begun their recovery from more than two centuries of national decline and foreign domination, first by the Afghans, then by the Russians and the British. When the United States was ejected from Iran in 1979, it was made the victim of resentments of domination and humiliation that had only incidentally to do with the United States and had virtually nothing to do with the narrowly political and ideological interpretation made of the matter in Washington.

It is one of the perceptual defects of Western government and press to assign Western-style motives to what people do in non-Western societies, as if these were universally relevant. Iran's troubles in 1978 and 1979 were thought to have come because the Shah's policies were insufficiently progressive. People were then confused to discover that his most effective opponents were the mullahs, and that what they wanted for Iran was piety, decorum, theocratic government, and a halt to social and political liberalizations. Joseph Kraft said at the time that "except for a tiny handful . . . almost no Americans perceived the formidable political impact of religion in Iran." This is true, and it is an indictment of the policymaking community in the United States. Along similar lines, the brutal massacres of the Khmer Rouge after the Communist takeover of Cambodia in 1975 reenacted something cataclysmic in Khmer history. The Khmers had engaged repeatedly in near-suicidal wars from the twelfth century onward, eventually producing near-ruin—the abandonment of major cities, and the partition of their country between the Thais and the Vietnamese. The threat, or promise, of the return of oppression is always present in such societies if the membrane of convention is destroyed. People still discuss the Cambodian upheaval as if what happened there were a product of Marxist thought; but when a people inflicts genocide upon itself, it does so as a consequence of great traumas, such as Russia experienced in the period that included defeat by Japan in 1905, the Revolution, and the famine of the 1920s—and such as Cambodia underwent, thanks in part to the U.S.-Vietnamese invasion, after 1970.

In Mecca, in 1978, a young prophet attempted to impose himself as the "expected Mahdi," the inspired leader who, according to the Hadith, the recorded sayings of Mohammed, is to appear at the beginning of a new century with a mission to purify Islam. Tradition has favored the fifteenth Islamic century, which began on November 20, 1979, for the expected Mahdi's appearance. On that morning the Great Mosque in Mecca was seized by followers of this young prophet. Tradition also said that the people of Mecca would try to kill the prophet but that he would escape, eventually march on to Jerusalem, liberate it, and go on to defeat a false Mahdi from Persia. The Jidda correspondent of *The Times* of London wrote at the time that "the niceness of the setting of present events is being remarked on here." This claimant Mahdi did not escape.

The Saudi Arabian episode was a further demonstration of that continuing puritan reaction against Westernizing changes that has become a force throughout the Islamic world, involving a part of the university intelligentsia as well as more conservative elements in society. The present dynasty in Saudi Arabia itself arose in puritan reaction against its predecessor. The people who seized Mecca in 1924 in the name of orthodoxy and of Abdul-Aziz ibn-Saud, the present king's father, came from the same tribes that would be involved in the 1979 affair. Western commentators call this puritanical orthodoxy "Islamic fundamentalism"—a term that is reassuring, because such a definition of the problem implies a solution. For an American to describe the claimant Mahdi in Mecca or the Ayatollah Khomeini and his successors as "medieval" is to imply that education and progress will solve the problem they present. Time does away with old societies; progress replaces fundamentalism with a modern way of life. These crises, then, are accidents, errors, in what is, in the larger plan, an unstoppable process.

Americans nearly always make use of simple models of social change and politics, related to our own national experience and values. Thus, even sophisticated people analyzed 1980s South Africa as if it were Alabama at the time of the civil-rights struggle, or Central America as if Communism were the serious issue there, or Angola and Ethiopia in terms of liberation struggles and the national popularity of rival political leaders—as if the majority of Angola's or Ethiopia's population knew the names of its leaders, or even knew that they were being led. The hero of John Updike's African novel, *The Coup,* observes of his country that "conquerors and governments pass before the people as dim rumors, as entertainment in a hospital ward. Truly, mercy is interwoven with misery in the world wherever we glance."

The American notion of the United States as the "new" world successor to the "old" world, which is Europe, has affected the American approach to Asia, Africa, and the Middle East since the Second World War. We have chosen to call those states "new nations," and for a considerable time we tended to regard them as closer to us, in an important way, than the European states that had been their colonial rulers. Like us, we felt, they had cast off Europe to make for themselves a future that we had already explored, and toward which we led. But these supposedly new nations are actually much older than Western nations, even in terms of conventional linear history, and at the same time, by virtue of cultural differences, they exist on a different plane. The societies of Egypt, Iran, Iraq, Saudi Arabia, Libya, Morocco, Turkey, India, Afghanistan, Burma, Cambodia, China, are fundamentally different from Western societies today, and, indeed, they are not like what Western civilization ever has been. They are not following us, somewhere on a road we have already traveled. They are in a different place, with a different past. It is not wholly unreasonable to think that they may have a different future.

•  •  •

A great nation's foreign policy involves power, money, trade, oil, and arms, but it proceeds from ideas. Because Americans do believe in the universality of time and progress, the U.S. government has conducted a policy that supported progressive and modernizing leaders in the Third World, and has financed industrialization and social changes that were meant to make other societies more like American society—all this being understood to be a matter of speeding progress so as to bring peace. The late Shah of Iran was thought by many Americans to be a progressive man— admittedly authoritarian, an absolute monarch, but then Kemal Ataturk, Napoleon, Bismarck, and Mao Tse-tung were authoritarians, too. All spilled blood and jailed or killed their enemies while reforming their societies. Americans have steadily argued, along the lines of the domestic conservative-liberal division, over whether the United States should support right-wing modernizers (like the Shah) or left-wing modernizers (like Salvador Allende Gossens, Houari Boumedienne, Colonel Nasser, or Pandit Nehru). We usually chose modernizers on the right. But the American debate never admitted a doubt that our national interest lay with modernization in the Third World. Even today, in Central America, Africa, the Far East, Saudi Arabia, Egypt, thousands of Americans—officials, businessmen, volunteers, idealists—are hard at work helping to modernize economies and societies. Not long ago, some of the same people were in Iran, and before that in Vietnam. They are, they believe, doing good. Most of them do not question the purpose of modernization. How can an American question modernization?

Modernization is not even the answer for that part of the less-developed world which is itself Western, or largely Western, in cultural origins, and inside our dimensions of cultural time and space. One visionary or another has been trying to provide a "modern" politics for Latin America since the lapse of Spanish and Portuguese power in the early nineteenth century. Their bones rustle in the winds of history: José Martí, José San Martín, Bernardo

O'Higgins, Simón Bolívar, the greatest of them all, who said on his deathbed that he had "plowed the sea." Each made some difference in his time, as Fidel Castro has made a difference, but Latin America remains largely what it was.

Washington and Moscow both believe in the march of history, and yet Latin America has too often marched backward or not marched at all. The Spanish and Portuguese colonial capitals were splendid and prosperous cities when their rivals in North America were shabby settlements. At the beginning of the nineteenth century, Latin America was richer and more populous than the United States; its future appeared brilliant. But the ingredients of progress seem to have been lacking. In agriculture, there was peonage—the hacienda system. There was no industry; the mercantile system precluded that. Latin America was a place of mines and monocultures, a source of raw materials and a market for Europe and, later, for the United States. In *The Age of Revolution*, E. J. Hobsbawm argues that the liberalization of Latin America's political economy in the mid-nineteenth century "remained as artificial as the liberalization of its political system," and adds that "in substance, parliaments, elections, land laws, etc., notwithstanding, the continent went on very much as before."

The inherited political tradition was that of Renaissance monarchy, acting through colonial regents. The intellectual and moral traditions were also absolutist—those of Iberian Catholicism, a religion of ecstasies, certainties, the Inquisition, damnation. It imposed a struggle "even against life itself," Miguel de Unamuno has remarked. "And against death. This is the meaning of Saint Teresa's ejaculatory prayer, 'I am dying because I cannot die.'" The materialism and liberalism of the United States, and its aggressive secularism alternating with an aggressive Protestantism, are as repellent to the traditional Church as they are to Fidel Castro; a Vatican diplomat has said that Castro, "from the ethical point of view, is a Christian." The alliance of a later generation, between revolutionary Latin American priests and Marxist guerrillas—an alliance of ascetics, loathing capitalism—has a natural foundation.

Spain and Portugal themselves failed to follow the evolution of the rest of Western Europe during the nineteenth century. They swung from absolute monarchy to revolution and back again. Nothing between proved lasting: liberalism failed; no culture of compromise, realism, and parliamentary accommodation was able to emerge. Iberian reform became a matter of elites and conspiracies, in an older tradition of secret bands of the enlightened bestowing progress upon the backward masses. The enlightened were often liberal-minded soldiers. Thus, reform marched by military coups and pronunciamentos. The populist version of this in Latin America was the unlettered leader, the people's soldier, who imposed himself by force of personality and stood up for the peasant against the landowner, the possessor. Such leaders have often ended badly, but they have included Mexico's Emiliano Zapata and Pancho Villa—and also Juan Perón and Fulgencio Batista, both of whom accomplished notable social reforms. The Latin American Indians, the mulatto poor, have tended to remain passive in most countries except Mexico.

While the United States, under James Monroe, declared in 1823 that the Americas were "no longer Res Nullius," a political emptiness to be filled by the European powers, Latin America's political positiveness remained, and remains, unformed. The great liberation movements themselves—of "Great Colombia" by Bolívar, of the Argentine by San Martín, of Chile by O'Higgins—were "the work of small groups of patricians, soldiers, and gallicized évolués," Hobsbawm writes, "leaving the mass of the Catholic poor white population passive and the Indians indifferent or hostile. Only in Mexico was independence won by the initiative of a popular agrarian, i.e. Indian, movement marching under the banner of the Virgin of Guadalupe, and Mexico has consequently ever since followed a different and politically more advanced road from the remainder of continental Latin America." Not even Fidel Castro's uprising was a popular one, nor is it a success. He and his followers were another band of visionaries imposing revolution from above, picking up the pieces—to popular acclaim—after the previous government had collapsed of its own corruption and ineptitude. Castro's conquest was moral, not military.

An important problem of historical and political judgment is presented by Latin America, where such impressive possibilities have always existed and so little has happened. Before the First World War, Argentina, the most advanced of the Latin American nations—demographically a European society—was one of the world's wealthier countries and was commonly considered the natural leader of South America. By the 1980s its economic wealth per capita was lower than that of Gabon or Bulgaria. It was a formerly developed country. Brazil has prospered since the Second World War, but Chile has retrogressed. Latin America as a whole seems to be of less consequence to the world, less creative (except in its literature), less seductive to the world's imagination, than it was a hundred years ago. Its battles, the Cuban novelist Alejo Carpentier has one of his characters say, "because of an incredible chronological discrepancy of ideals . . . [seem those of] people living in different centuries." A second character replies, "You must remember that we are accustomed to living with Rousseau and the Inquisition, with the Immaculate Conception and *Das Kapital*." United States policy toward Latin America, however, has acknowledged only Karl Marx and the late twentieth century.

To believe, as has been the case for official America, that foreign interventions make or unmake revolutions, such as those of Central America (or before, of Southeast Asia), is to deny the responsibility of these states and these peoples for themselves. Governments under internal attack, like El Salvador's in the 1980s, are held not to be responsible for their situation, since foreigners support the insurrection against them. The rebels themselves do not act for themselves but for the Soviet Union and its allies. The Nicaraguan Sandinistas have been perceived in Washington (President Reagan's Washington, certainly) as mere Soviet proxies. The only truly responsible agent on that side thus becomes Cuba or the Soviet

Union, and the only recourse, the finally responsible agent to counter the challenge, the United States.

One might think that for a government, even a Third World government, to lose control of a part of its territory to an uprising by a portion of its own population large enough to jeopardize that government's survival would represent something authentic in the experience of that country—something that is not satisfactorily explicable in terms of the actions of outsiders, or, on the other hand, readily soluble by any outside agent. Clearly, the foreign sponsors of dissidence and subversion, suppliers of arms and equipment to a rebellion, can have an important effect, but it is not apparent, or even reasonable, that the effect will be decisive—as the United States found out with the Nicaraguan contras. It is always easier to create disorder than order. Simply by its assault upon the structures of authority and by its disruption of ordinary life and the economy, a rebellion accomplishes its initial purpose, which is to make a show of power and to expose governmental vulnerability. Governments, however, have an advantage of their own. They are there, and have to be displaced. Even unloved governments provide a measure of order and continuity, the context for everyday life. People do not readily abandon a stable order for the unknown. It is unreasonable for them to transfer their allegiance to an insurrection, or even to acquiesce in one, unless their government has itself become a source of disorder and insecurity in their lives, or of an arbitrary violence. The neglected reality is that it is not in the least easy to mount and sustain a revolutionary uprising. Most fail, including most of those with which the Cubans and the Soviet intelligence services have associated themselves. (Ask poor Che Guevara.) The neglected principle is that governments, like those individuals who undertake an insurrection, are themselves answerable for what happens to them, and there is a fatal penalty for failure.

Another common analytical mistake is to invoke history, not in order to illuminate the present, but in order to deny its autonomy. Present events undoubtedly resemble things that have happened before (everything has happened before), but nonetheless they are also self-sufficient realities. It is obvious that, for many in the American political community, the struggle over Nicaragua seemed an opportunity to refight and win the Vietnam War. These people sought to demonstrate once and for all how those who opposed the war in Vietnam, and argued that it could not be won at a proportionate moral and political cost, or said that it should not be fought at all, were wrong. This time, in Central America, under Ronald Reagan, a new and resolute U.S. government meant to demonstrate the will to win that had been lacking in Vietnam. It failed.

At the time of Vietnam, of course, many of those responsible for that war's planning and conduct were themselves carrying out another retrospective rectification of history: correcting the errors of Munich. They argued that the revolutionary Communist movement in Indochina and its sponsors in China represented a threat to democracy equivalent to Hitler's a quarter of a century earlier. Secretary of Defense Robert McNamara said in 1965 that China's ambitions made up "a program of aggression . . . that ranks with Hitler's *Mein Kampf*." Secretary of State Dean Rusk spoke of "the world cut in two by Asian Communism, reaching out through Southeast Asia and Indochina," and added, "From a strategic point of view, it is not very attractive to think . . . that . . . hundreds of millions of people in the free nations of Asia should be under the deadly and constant pressure of the authorities in Peking, so that their future is circumscribed by fear." That was in 1967. Much the same things were later said in Washington about what was happening in Central America. It now is evident that the only people who suffered from the war in Vietnam were the Vietnamese, the Cambodians, the Laotians—and the Americans. The only government whose power was enhanced was the one that won the war—that of North Vietnam.

The truth is that history constantly presents new problems in the guise of old, and the Central American crisis has been, for the countries involved, the product of an imperfectly achieved Spanish inheritance, the experience of North American and British exploitation, and the expression of a feeble but outraged nationalism. Mexico is the principal regional nation that can be said to have truly found itself—after a heavy cost in European domination, declared and undeclared wars with the United States and the loss of major territories, and then a bitter civil struggle and peon uprisings that culminated in the institutions (nominally revolutionary, actually conservative) that have governed Mexico ever since (but were challenged in the years following the 1988 presidential election). Nothing remotely like this happened in the smaller countries to its south; each has remained more victim than agent of its own fate, except for sterile quarrels with one another. Under United States and Cuban sponsorship, these quarrels were given an ideological gloss in the 1970s and 1980s that made them seem part of the movement of the vast forces of global geopolitics.

The American view of the disorders of the Third World has typically interpreted them in terms of East-West conflict, and has justified intervention as essential to block the other side from taking over "that vital and strategic area of the earth, or, for that matter, any other part of the earth"—as President Reagan once said of Lebanon. Under both Republican and Democratic administrations there has been something more as well: a reaction to the challenge of disorder itself. Reagan spoke with feeling about chaos when he announced his invasion of Grenada. He said that he did it to forestall further chaos: chaos, the void—in Greek, χαος, "unformed matter." The American struggle is with disintegration itself. The challenge is very great; the possibility of success is nil.

It is curious that a government as sophisticated as ours, in a nation as sophisticated as the United States, should make the repeated error of attributing political phenomena of evident historical and social complexity to simplistic external causes. This error has underlain American policy from the time of Vietnam to that of El Salvador and Nicaragua—and it would be a miracle if it does not continue to affect the policy of administrations to follow. The criticism is therefore not that the United States puts itself on the "reactionary" side, or supports military rule, or the rich, or the status quo. In fact, the United States nearly always has ineffectually tried to find more or less progressive "third forces" between the hard men of the right and those of the left. The intention is to evoke progress, democracy, and liberation in Central America, Africa, the eastern Mediterranean, and Southeast Asia. In one way or another, the United States, Cuba, and the Soviet Union are all engaged in the arduous pursuit of such abstractions.

They have all failed until now, but not before doing a great deal of harm to countries that deserved to settle their own accounts. The Cold War, as it was conducted from the mid-1950s in the non-Western world, saw Washington repeatedly confuse specific and tangible problems with a generalized ideological threat, and to respond to them with ambitious but problematical remedies on the same scale, such as the political reconstruction of an entire nation, or the conversion of Third World nations to liberal market economies. This is by no means the error of conservative administrations only. The mistake has equally often been made from the liberal side, in which the remedy to Communism is looked for in U.S.-sponsored human rights programs, land reform, a new international economic order, or—for the tough-minded—mounting "an effective counterinsurgency program aimed at expropriating the revolution from the Marxists" (the words are those of an associate of the Carnegie Endowment for International Peace).

Nations, Bismarck once said, with melodrama, are made in blood and iron. One must add that the blood and the iron must be native for the mixture to work. It seems a truism that if a government is incapable of governing—of controlling its own territory and imposing order among its population—when it has been given reasonable assistance, sufficient to compensate for external assistance given to its internal enemies, it then becomes necessary to question not only whether that government will survive but whether it deserves to survive. There must be a will to survive and to prevail, and this is not available in aid packages from abroad, nor can it be supplied by foreign military and political counselors. This is a rule that applies, impartially, to Afghanistan as well as to Vietnam.

"Foreign countries . . . supply the arms and the Salvadorans supply the bodies," the archbishop of San Salvador remarked at the time when civil war in his country was deepening. That, alas, has been the story of many more countries than El Salvador. In the end, however, these wars stubbornly remain the property of those who begin them for their own reasons, wage them, and in the end settle them for their own reasons and in their own ways, however long that takes: Asians, Africans, and Latin Americans have more time for waiting than either the United States or the former Soviet Union.

The achievement of nationhood is a product of time as well as circumstance, and time is the one thing the makers of American foreign policy do not conceive of having at their disposal. It is all but useless to preach detachment, or patience with history, to American governments committed to action and problem-solving. Nonetheless, one would think a record of four disrupted American presidencies a considerable lesson in the futility of interventions meant to dominate or check long-term historical forces of the kind at work in Vietnam and Afghanistan, and evident amid the uproar of the Middle East, the Persian Gulf, and Latin America. A great power has the resources to influence such things, and to survive them, but it is unable to stop history. Throwing military power against forces of this sort, at work within turbulently unachieved nations, has done nothing except damage the superpower involved.

Vietnam, for example, only recently assumed its modern national form. The Annamese, drifting southward, occupied Cochin China, in the southernmost part of Indochina, only in the seventeenth and eighteenth centuries, following the breakdown of the rule of the Khmers and the Chams—civilizations under Hindu and Indian influence. The French annexed the region between 1862 and 1893. The lack of cultural assurance or security among

Vietnamese elites is evident in the fact that before the end of the century nearly half a million had been converted to Christianity in Annam alone, out of an estimated population of six million. The "nationalist" reaction against the French, and subsequently against the United States, was a cultural as well as a political upheaval, related to the need of the Vietnamese to define a social and political civilization still inchoate. This upheaval had begun to take political form by the first decade of the twentieth century, influenced by the Japanese defeat of Russia in 1905—a victory of Asians over Europeans. The United States entered the Vietnamese struggle late and ignorant, and was eventually violently rejected as an alien and irrelevant factor in the Vietnamese people's own crisis, which is still unresolved.

The Soviet Union moved into Afghanistan in 1979 to reinforce a failing "revolution" that had been launched by an internally divided Afghan Communist Party, in fact no more than a vehicle of elite disaffection. The "masses" of Afghanistan entered the affair only in response to the new government's attempts to impose social changes that challenged the prevailing values and religious beliefs. The reformers proved to have even less of a connection with the vital forces of their country than South Vietnam's generals had with theirs. South Vietnam's leaders had represented both the strong Catholic minority in their country and the Westernized middle and professional classes who had run it under the previous colonial system. Theirs was serious support, even if their movement was a minority one destined to be overwhelmed by the popular nationalism the Communists were able to mobilize against them. The Afghan Communist elite was much narrower, cut off from popular forces, committed to an ideological interpretation of society that had little actual relevance to Afghanistan. Their program, in some respects admirable, was unrealizable, the product of false ideology. They could not succeed on their own and the Soviet Union found that military force could not impose them. They, too, have been rejected; given modern arms, the Afghan forces of resistance were able to make Soviet military occupation unacceptably costly.

American and Soviet policymakers dealt with these affairs in almost complete innocence of the cultural stakes at play, as if each were a matter of ideology and national power, winnable by coercion and money, or, when these failed, by the application of military power. The forces at work, to Washington's surprise—and Moscow's—were discovered to be unamenable to these methods: "unreasonable," or reasonable only by a different calibration of reason from the one employed by the superpowers.

Four years after *Barbarian Sentiments*, I wrote a book on nationalism's origins, character, and implications,* which argued that nationalism has been the most powerful political force of the nineteenth and twentieth centuries and was likely to prove the most powerful of the twenty-first as well. This still seems to me sound.

Nationalism was certainly the force that dominated the final decade of the twentieth century, the principal force in the collapse of the Soviet system in Central and Eastern Europe, and a contributing factor in the breakup of the Soviet Union itself. Nationalism inspired the terrible Balkan wars of Yugoslav succession. The century closed on brutal clashes of nationalisms in Indonesia and the Caucasus.

If I were to write the present chapter again, I would not express the pessimism I did about Latin America. Since 1989 liberal politics have progressed and the economic condition of the region has been ameliorated. The literature of Latin American civilization has achieved remarkable influence in Europe and North America. In Eastern Europe, newly democratic Hungary and Romania handled the Transylvanian issue with tolerance and good sense. The Palestinians began the twenty-

*The Wrath of Nations: Civilization and the Furies of Nationalism* (New York and London: Simon & Schuster, 1993).

first century in reasonable expectation of possessing a state, if a feeble and truncated one.

The variety of nationalism that did the most damage during the past decade was ethnic nationalism, and this is worth a further comment since a new and dangerous idea has been contributed to international political discussion by Professor Samuel Huntington of Harvard, who holds that wars between civilizations will in the future take the place of wars of nationalism and nation-states as we have known them in the past. He suggests that an international Islamic integrist movement has developed which, were it to be armed by China, might in the future attack the West.*

One might think this threat was of less than world-historical importance, given the implausibility of a "Confucian-Islamic" alliance, and given the division and weakness of the Islamic world. Taliban in Afghanistan, "Wahabi" in the Caucasus, and unreconciled Palestinian militants—all financed from Saudi Arabia, where American troops have been stationed since the Gulf War—seem scarcely likely to threaten Western industrial civilization. Nonetheless, the Huntington thesis has exercised considerable influence, in part because it offered an opportune paradigm of conflict for an American policy community that, with the end of the Cold War, was in search of theoretical formulations of future conflicts capable of relegitimating the huge material and intellectual investment American society has made in the apparatus of national defense and international engagement.

The fundamental nationalist idea, that every "race" deserves its own nation, emerged in modern history in the nineteenth century and was initially considered a liberating conception, allowing the suppressed linguistic and cultural communities of the Hapsburg and Ottoman empires to find

---

*See Samuel P. Huntingdon, *The Clash of Civilizations and the Remaking of World Order* (New York: Simon & Schuster, 1996).

political expression. It eventually became the influential modern doctrine of universal national self-determination. But what was a liberal cause in the nineteenth and early twentieth centuries was subsequently to veer into an ethnic nationalism that declared that every people should have its own state, *excluding all others*. The great British liberal historian Lord Acton called this development "a retrograde step in history." He added, "The combination of different nations in one state is as necessary a condition of civilized life as the combination of men in society. . . . A state which is incompetent to satisfy different races condemns itself."

Professor Huntington's reformulation of international relationships in terms of civilizations rather than political nations implicitly confirms the notion that "race" and nation should coincide, for it conflates cultural identity with political identity. This conceptual error is capable of exercising a dangerous influence on international relations because of the effect it can have—and has had—on popular attitudes as well as on the policy assumptions of governments.

Civilizations are not political societies that possess governments to decide, act, and make war. Imperial Britain, France, Portugal, and Spain were members of Western Christian civilization, but their empires were created by trading companies and governments acting upon national imperatives. Moghul India was a part of Islamic civilization, as Iraq is today, but Islam was not Moghul India, and it is not Iraq. These are individual political units within a civilization.

The argument that the wars of nation-states (and of ideologies) that we have seen in the past are now to be replaced by struggles between civilizations ("the next world war, if there is one, will be a war between civilizations," Huntington writes) has also been influential because it offers a plausible general explanation for much that is going on in the contemporary world, and responds to the anxieties many in the West feel about Islamic fundamentalism, and about the supposed linkage of Asian economic progress to "Asian values" unlike those of the Western democracies.

It also has seemed persuasive because it is familiar. The notion of civilizational clashes, racial war, the threat of the Horde, the Yellow Peril, has been with the West since the discovery of worlds beyond Western borders. The non-Western world and Europe have been in tension since the fifteenth and sixteenth centuries, when Europeans first explored and mapped the oceans and regions of the world until then unknown to them, part of the larger Renaissance movement of scientific and intellectual exploration.

There was no Western power advantage when Europeans first made contact with Asia's societies. China was a more sophisticated and better governed society than any in sixteenth-century Europe. However, in the seventeenth and eighteenth centuries, Europe acquired modern science and new technology, reinforcing the conviction it already possessed of moral superiority over "backward" and pagan societies, hence of its right to rule the others.

The consequences of this have provided the principal theme of modern history. In this respect, the "clash of civilizations" is four hundred years old, as old as imperialism. What seized Huntington's attention is that population movements, immigration, modern transportation, technology, and communications have confronted societies much more closely with one another than in the past, extending and intensifying these tensions, and that the non-Western societies have acquired the power to strike at the West. The clash is no longer one that the West automatically wins. The Gatling gun (or its successor, the nuclear or biological weapon) now is common property.

It must also be said that Huntington's scheme is familiar for another reason. It is not actually about civilizations at all. He made a list of today's major powers, or power and interest groupings, and called them civilizations: North America, the

European Union, Russia and its Slavic and Orthodox neighbors, Japan, India, China, and the Islamic world. In this respect his is merely a banal "futurological" exercise in writing conflict scenarios, devoid of serious historical or cultural content.

Islamic fundamentalism—radical Islamism is a more accurate term—was Professor Huntington's great preoccupation in his book. Like many, he failed to acknowledge that the radicals are only one controversial and contested faction at work in Islamic religion and politics today, and that their concerns are mainly directed inwardly rather than outwardly. They aim to reconvert the Islamic people to a rigorous practice of their religion and establish theocratic governments that will protect religion and impose Islamic laws. They make war on what they consider heretical Moslems. Their attacks on the West and kidnappings of Westerners have been retaliation against what is seen as Western interference in Islamic countries, or have been meant to liberate Islamist prisoners abroad. Their sole interest in the West is to expel its political, commercial, and cultural influences from Islamic society. They have no interest in conquering nonassimilable infidel populations.

The Saudi Arabian businessman Osama bin Laden, said to have been responsible for bombing American embassies in Africa, subsequently made into a celebrity terrorist by the Clinton administration, does not want to conquer America. He wants "infidel" American troops withdrawn from proximity to the Islamic Holy Places in Saudi Arabia. That is a perfectly comprehensible demand. Indeed, Washington ought to respond positively. The existing U.S. policy of intrusive military and political presence in Saudi Arabia and the Gulf region is a virtually exact reproduction of the American policy that provoked radical religio-nationalist upheaval in the Shah's Iran two decades ago. If persisted in, it will assuredly produce the same eventual result in Saudi Arabia. One sometimes thinks that no one in power in Washington seems able to learn from the past, or perhaps it is that none of them know what happened in the past, history, even recent history, being no longer studied in most American schools.

The influence of the Islamic integrist movement in the Moslem world is in part a reaction to the failure or corruption of the secular Arab nationalist and socialist movements of the 1950s and 1960s. The conflict between Islamic movements and Israel and the United States, and the terrorism practiced in that struggle, has an even simpler cause, the installation of a Western state in what had been Arab Palestine. The "civilizational" aspect of the conflict is strictly the result of the political and territorial dispute.

It cannot be stressed enough that tensions between Islamic states in the Near and Middle East and the Western countries are the straightforward result of Israel's creation, conflicts of material interest, notably over oil, or the hangovers of colonialism. Other parts of the Islamic world—Islamic Turkey, Indonesia, Pakistan, Malaysia, the Moslems of India, China, Central Asia, the Philippines, those of Albania, Bosnia, Macedonia, and Kosovo—may have problems with Western governments and Western society, but these are not the Arabs' problems, and are rarely connected to Islamic fundamentalism or the Islamic religion as such.

The fundamental danger in thinking of civilizations as political agents is that this moves culture and religion from the periphery of international politics to the very center of the stage. And this, regrettably, is like putting race once again at the center of the world-historical stage. It substitutes a cultural entity, the civilization, which has no responsible political existence, for identifiable and responsible political actors: states, governments, leaders, individuals. It disregards the political responsibility of nations, and announces historical and political fatality. It implies that we are in the grip of an anonymous destiny.

If we accept the argument that the conflicts of the future will be cultural in origin, we must conclude that they will have no solutions. Cultural war is inherently unnegotiable and unresolvable. If the Moslem is the mortal enemy of the European by being a Moslem, with Americans and Europeans his enemy because they belong to Western civilization, all have lost control over their future. Being a member of Islamic or Western civilization is not a negotiable matter—any more than being a Jew is negotiable.

Membership in a civilization, like membership in a race, is unchosen, uncompromisable, ineluctable. If conflicts that today would be recognized as having negotiable solutions—disputes of territory, trade, resources, political ambition, geopolitics, ideology—are to be reinterpreted as clashes of civilizations, they are denied solution. Wars of civilizations cannot even be won, other than by exterminating another civilization. Hitler considered that he was merely the instrument of historical necessity.

The theory of civilizational conflict implicitly denies that the real conflicts in the contemporary world, like those we will face in the future, have to do with national interests, national expansion, power, money, commerce, territory, oil, history, religious and political ideology, the egos of politicians, and the egos of nations, all of which can be dealt with in practical ways.

They have solutions. Some of these solutions may only come about as the outcome of a war, but it would be war for a defined purpose, and it would come to an end. Wars between civilizations have no end, and no limits.

# 6 | JAPAN, CHINA, AND THE MAKING OF NATIONS

Behind the American failure to grasp the nature of the forces at work in the Third World lies a reluctance to confront the basic question of why it should be that some countries are industrialized, rich, and successful while others are not. The usual assumption is that hazards of resources or climate, the accidents of geography or history, are responsible. No doubt there is a sense in which inequity is an accident. But even accidents have explanations. When the James Watt of popular myth reflected on the behavior of his mother's teakettle to invent the steam engine, the intellectual and moral conditions already existed that were responsible for what followed. Conditions existed in the eighteenth century that, once someone had perceived that the force of steam might be exploited, led directly to the creation of steadily more elaborate steam-driven machinery—and also to that segmenting and rationalizing of work which were quickly understood to be needed to take the best advantage of machinery. Many another teakettle, or its equivalent, had boiled in many another place with no result but tea. Industrialism arose in a society that possessed a rationalist and analytical intellectual system, natural science, preindustrial technology of a high order (the real James Watt was a maker of mathematical instruments for a university), and an activist religion, which held that human history means something and has a purpose that will justify what has gone before.

This, of course, explains only the origins of technological and industrial society. Once the system exists—the machinery invented and the systems of work rationally organized—it might seem that anyone could learn to use it. The Walloons, the northern French, the Swiss, and the Germans quickly followed the new examples of British industrialism. The industrial system rapidly spread through Europe and to the European-populated Americas, and even, in a phenomenal transformation of what had been a closed and feudal society, to Japan. Fifty years after Commodore Perry's arrival with his "black ships" in lower Tokyo Bay, in 1853, Japan was not only an industrialized nation but the paramount naval and military power in the Far East, able summarily to defeat czarist Russia, first at Port Arthur and then, in possibly the most conclusive naval victory of all time, in the Strait of Tsushima, where almost the entire Russian fleet was sunk or captured in the space of twenty-four hours, while the Japanese lost three torpedo boats.

Those who firmly believe in the possibility of Asia's rapid industrialization and a consequent shift of world power from the Atlantic to the Pacific assume that the Japanese experience provides the norm of development, and not an exception. Recalling those bands of conscientious Japanese officials and scholars sent out in the 1880s and 1890s to bring back the West's knowledge and methods—to Germany to study medicine, to France to study law, to England for naval science, railroads, the telegraph, lighthouses—they assume that development is a matter of equipment to be obtained and techniques to be learned: that it is something autonomous, and transferable without pain, or, at least, with only a little pain. They believe that what Japan did, China is about to do. Elsewhere in Asia, and in Latin America and Africa, the argument continues, industrial development must follow naturally from the possession of factories with modern equipment and trained managers and workers. Build the factories, or have them built by crews of technicians from abroad, train the machine operators and the supervisors, send prospective managers to the Harvard Business School or M.I.T., assure access to markets, and a country is on its way to an advanced living standard and a position of economic importance in the world. The non-Western world lacks money, trained men and women, and technology; supply them, the argument goes, and economic development will follow.

Christopher Dawson, the British historian, remarked in one of his books that the great non-Western civilizations are "ways of life in a much more definite and conscious sense than that of any national Western culture," and he added that each of these ways of life "is penetrated from top to bottom by the same system of ideas, so that a man can give theological or metaphysical reasons for the way in which he cooks his dinner." This is not because these non-Western civilizations are simple; they are of vast subtlety and complexity. Nor are they backward by other than certain material standards. China is backward economically and technologically, but in other respects the United States or Britain is backward by comparison with China, India, or Egypt. These Asian or African civilizations are far more coherent, and this is both a strength for them and a wall of resistance to industrialization and economic development along Western lines. Of course, Western industrial society has a coherence of its own, in that it rests on generally held assumptions about accomplishment and mastery as central to the meaning of our lives—about exploration and exploitability of material acquisitions, the value of knowledge, the value of work.

Let me be specific, since the issues come down to practical things. To run a factory requires workers and managers who want economic prosperity badly enough to spend a major part of their waking lives doing things that are often boring, exhausting, and unpleasant. They also need, usually, the ability to read and write, to make complicated plans and analyses, to use sophisticated tools, to understand machinery and feel at home with it, and even to take pleasure in the machines and in the concepts that lie behind them. A dependable supply of such workers and managers exists in the United States, Canada, and Western Europe, because fathers and sons have done this kind of thing since the Industrial Revolution first emerged, during the eighteenth century, in a society whose ancient and medieval engineering and technology had already been of remarkable sophistication. One reason they have done this is that even though Western societies are now secularized, they are the product of a religious civilization that insisted that constructive work in this world pleases God, will be rewarded by God, and advances the development of a history that is understood to have begun in the void from which God summoned matter, and to end in the Day of Judgment, when all will be held accountable for how they have used their talents and dealt with their fellow men. The latter-day political secularizations of this religious conception of history have changed little that is essential to it. Progressive humanists or Marxists, rationalists or scientific optimists, we in the West still go on working as if our immortal salvation depended upon it. Our culture is teleological—it presumes purposive development and a conclusion.

Our sense that we are coming from one place and going to another is evident in our use of the expressions "antiquity," "Middle Ages," "modern times." The Chinese identify their past by dynasties, not by a vocabulary of progression. As John Lukacs observes, our Middle Ages were scarcely at an end before people began calling them the Middle Ages. The term "was first proposed by the German Cardinal Nicolaus Cusanus as early as the middle of the fifteenth century." But then, as Lukacs also remarks, Western civilization's consciousness of its history is unique, having developed, as it did, side by side with an unprecedented sense of the importance of the individual, expressed in a whole new vocabulary of self-consciousness and self-concern. For individuals as for nations, our sense of values has been based on a belief in consequence and development, in causes having effects. Industrialism and technology are, par excellence, phenomena of cause and effect.

An extreme contrast is India's Hinduism, a religion of natural order and resignation, of predestination manifest in fixed castes, with a transmigration of souls in union and reunion with the Absolute Spirit, which is the ultimate reality. It is hardly an accident that so many of India's great modern entrepreneurs and industrialists have come from the Parsi community—Zoroastrians from Persia, believers in the resurrection of the dead, when individuals will be punished or rewarded for what they accomplished in life. The Theravada Buddhism of Burma and Thailand is also deeply nonmaterialist, the religion of a "Middle Way" between (in the words of the Buddha) devotion to "those things whose attractions depend upon the passions, a low and pagan ideal, fit only for the worldly-minded, ignoble, unprofitable," and the practice of "asceticism, which is painful, ignoble, unprofitable." Man must renounce "the craving for prosperity." This is scarcely a religion for technicians, to say nothing of capitalists. Even Islam, a religion of surrender to the will of God, is passive. There was a great age of Arab science, created by the mathematicians and astronomers of the early Middle Ages, but—for whatever reasons—it did not have a sequel. The Middle East and North Africa have had a long and close acquaintance with Western technology and organization, both in preindustrial times, when Islam was at the peak of its strength and had colonized Southern Europe, and in modern industrial times, when Europeans controlled Egypt and the North African states. Yet there has been little spontaneous development on Western models. One suspects that many of the factories and "downstream" oil-refining facilities built in Saudi Arabia and the Persian Gulf states with the oil riches of the 1970s are destined to eventual desuetude—sand drifting in through broken windows to cover abandoned machinery, the people returned to the desert. Indeed, except in Latin America, whose cultural origins are predominantly European, the only places where Western models have been truly successfully adopted are in the zone of China's cultural dependencies—Japan, Korea, Taiwan, Hong Kong, and Singapore.

Such cursory judgments on Asian and African societies do no justice to the ways in which they are rich and original. I make only the point that the religious values, moral assumptions, and social structures of these societies are at best alien, and sometimes hostile, to the values and practices of industrialism and capitalism. This situation cannot be changed by the injection of money, machines, or technical instructors. For these societies to "develop" in the sense in which that term is used at international conferences and by the IMF and the World Bank requires a radical and destructive remaking of life and society, implying a reinterpretation of the meaning of existence itself, as it has been understood by the people who live in these civilizations. What usually is put forward as a simple transfer of resources, techniques, and information is, in fact, a revolutionary enterprise of the most momentous consequence. It is for exactly this reason that colonialism proved, for its victims, so radical and demoralizing an ordeal.

From the beginning of the era of Western exploitation and colonial expansion, societies in Asia, Africa, and Latin America not only saw their political and military power overturned by invaders but have experienced a challenge to the norms of those societies themselves. This has been a challenge at the most profound level, because it involved primordial issues of human destiny and the values of life. From the beginning, it has been explicitly a religious challenge. A fundamental motive of Spanish and Portuguese exploration and colonization in Asia and America was religious—the propagation of Christianity and the salvation of pagans. Without Christian baptism, even the most virtuous pagan was considered barred from heaven, fated to an eternity in limbo, where he would enjoy natural happiness but be deprived of the sight of God. The second wave of colonial expansion, mainly by the British and French, was more openly motivated by political and commercial ambitions but was a religious undertaking as well. Such men as Jean de Brébeuf, Isaac Jogues, and David Livingstone, enduring torture and disease, making terrible journeys into the North American forest or deep into Africa, were obviously driven by something more complicated than simple religious faith. But such were the formal beliefs for which they risked death, and found it. They preached Christianity to Iroquois and Africans, baptized them, translated the Bible into their languages, looked after their sick, taught them the hymns of France, England, Scotland, Germany. Dr. Schweitzer, playing Bach in the tropical forest, was there to serve God. The missionaries still at work today do not, perhaps, possess the old confidence in the justness of what they do, but the nature of their enterprise has inevitably meant insisting to non-Christians that their religions are false, their values deceptive or perhaps damning, their gods idols.

It was not only the missionary who thus addressed the peoples of Africa and Asia. The religious claim made by the West was merely one expression of a self-confident civilization that also possessed high science, formal philosophy, mastery of technology, and belief in its own destiny. Until our time, the people of Western Europe had scarcely any doubt that theirs was mankind's highest civilization and that they had a mission to convert others as part of the grand process of man's enlightenment and progress. The native peoples of Asia, Africa, and the Americas were expected to acknowledge Western truth as against native error. The issue thus posed for them was one of cultural as well as religious apostasy and conversion. One gave up polygamy not only to become Christian but also to become modern and progressive. One ate unclean foods, or fasted while others ate. One took up kinds of work that in the past had been proscribed, or roles in life that before had not been possible. One profited or progressed by means of the foreign presence and foreign institutions, at the price of alienating oneself from one's origins. Conversion could be a step ahead. It could mean rescue from a mean life and low status, a career opened to talent. It could be an act of generosity and service. It represented a decision that the old society, the old culture, was insufficient.

The Western conquest of Asia and Africa proved in crucial respects an intellectual and moral conquest. The missionaries' horror at cannibalism, slavery, infanticide, suttee (the Hindu widow's ritual suicide); their defense of women as better than chattels; their concern for outcasts and the poor; their devotion to education—all this had an impact that forced Asians and Africans, especially the most sensitive of them, into anguished criticism of their own societies. It led them to alienation. The British-born anthropologist Colin Turnbull quotes the man he calls the "lonely African": "I believed in your world at one time, even if I did not understand it, and I tried to follow your ways. But in doing this I lost my spirit. It left me somewhere; perhaps in Matadi. . . . But somewhere it left me, and I am empty.

"In your world you people made me change to your ways, and tried to make me think like you. But no matter how hard I tried you never took me as one of yourselves. To you I was still a savage, and you used me for your own ends. I was content, because I knew that I could never be completely like you, but I thought that my children could learn, and their children would surely be just like you. I tried to bring help to my people by telling them of your ways, and by being their *capita*. But look at them, they do not even pay me the respect due to an old man: to my own people, as to you, I am just a savage. I am alone in this world. You made it impossible for me to be true to the ways of my ancestors, yet I cannot understand the ways of your Bwana Yesu, I cannot believe his beliefs. When I die, very soon, shall I still be alone? Will you talk to me then? Will my people talk to me? Will anyone speed my spirit on its way to some resting place, or shall I be as I am now, alone?"

The West's moral subjugation of the non-European world is even more striking when one notes that originally the technological and organizational advantage of the Western conquerors was very slight, when it existed at all. Clive, Hastings, and Mornington conquered India by political maneuver and with only a handful of soldiers. The numerical odds overcome by the Spaniards in subduing the Incas and the Aztecs are hardly credible. Africa was taken by little bands of men of whom the mass of Africans was scarcely aware. There was never a time in the great age of imperial conquest and colonial rule when the European power occupying a major Asian or African society could not have been ejected through determined resistance on the part of even an important minority of the subject people. India at the time of the so-called Sepoy Mutiny, in 1857, was held by a force itself four-fifths Indian. The English and Scottish regiments were drastically outnumbered. That uprising—"the last determined but ineffective attempt of the old ruling classes, the Marathas and Moghuls, to drive out the British," says K. M. Panikkar, the Indian historian—was put down by a predominantly Indian force in the service of the British East India Company. Muslims were used against Hindus, southern Indians against northern Indians, linguistic groups against one another. Africa was controlled until the 1960s by African troops under European officers. Belgium, with a population one-fifth the size of the Congo's and a territory one-seventy-fifth that of its colony, met no serious opposition. The Belgian record in the Congo before the reforms of 1908 was nonetheless one of the cruelest. So was the Dutch record in Indonesia, a sophisticated Asian civilization, where the Dutch easily held a territory sixty times the size of the Netherlands and a population ten times their own.

It was not that the colonial power had a monopoly on muskets and artillery. Up to the middle of the nineteenth century, the conquered everywhere had—or certainly could have had—roughly the same firepower as the invader, to go with their overwhelming superiority in numbers. When the serious, sustained, and successful uprisings against colonial authority came, after 1945, the development of ordnance had given the colonial powers a vastly larger advantage than they had ever enjoyed when they conquered their empires. The French sent their first military expedition into the Kingdom of Annam in 1858 and were in Saigon by February 1859. When the French were driven out of Indochina a hundred years later, they possessed bombers, radar, napalm, airborne troops, sophisticated radio communications, automatic weapons, long-range naval gunfire, command of both sea and air, and a deep knowledge of the society and its languages. All these did them no good. Thought was even given in Washington to using the atomic bomb against the rebels. Yet the French lost, as did the United States when it came in with its own advanced technology of war— smart bombs, electronic sensors and barriers, computerized intelligence systems, lie detectors, and the heaviest aerial bombardments in the history of warfare. The North Vietnamese by this time had plenty of small arms and artillery, but the shovel, the sharpened stick, the pit, and the tunnel were their decisive tools of war. Their victory was essentially organizational and political, giving them a moral ascendancy over their enemies, including the U.S. government. The crucial difference is that in the 1850s the Vietnamese had darkly sensed that they had to lose, and the invader was convinced that his destiny was to conquer, convert, civilize.

The moral conquest that the West accomplished in the age of imperialism was followed, in the mid-twentieth century, by the moral recovery of the subject peoples and by the colonial powers' loss of confidence in their own mission of civilization and conversion. These changes were caused by objective as well as subjective forces—notably, for the Western countries, two world wars and the experience of totalitarianism and genocide. The pattern of reaction and resistance to the cultural as well as the political intrusion of the West has tended to take three forms, which recur to this day.° One is the reactionary response—to resist change, expel the dangerous novelties from the society, and reaffirm established values. The second is total conversion, cultural apostasy, producing the condition of the "lonely African," or the embittered exile on a foreign café terrace or university campus. The third is to attempt some kind of synthesis. The fact that the last option is the most reasonable response (and perhaps, in the long term, the only feasible one) does not mean that it can be achieved in any given case, or that the two other forms of response will not repeatedly occur.

The reactionary response—evident in contemporary Iran—is seductive because it is direct and uncomplicated, offering relief from stress in an idealization of a past that has been lost because of the corruptions introduced by foreigners. Moreover, it seems

°The Western impact on non-Western societies, and their reactions, was treated at length by the late Edmund Stillman and myself in *The Politics of Hysteria: The Sources of Twentieth-Century Conflict* (New York: Harper and Row, 1964), from which a part of my discussion is drawn.

achievable: you must simply drive out the foreigner, destroy his works, proscribe his ideas, humiliate those who have made themselves his agents and converts. That, at least, is the argument. Such reactionary movements sometimes have been accompanied by symptoms of social disorientation and hysteria, with magical and prophetic elements in the popular manifestation. During India's Sepoy Mutiny, a restoration of the Moghul Empire was proclaimed in Delhi. While the immediate causes of that uprising included such provocations as violation of the dietary conventions of both Hindu and Muslim troops, one British historian of the event (writing at the turn of the century in the eleventh edition of the *Encyclopaedia Britannica*) concludes that a major cause was popular anxiety over what had been the most progressive and humane British innovations: "the prohibition of suttee and female infanticide, the execution of Brahmans for capital offences, the remarriage of widows, the spread of missionary effort and the extension of Western education."

The Boxer Rebellion in China at the end of the nineteenth century resembled what had already happened in India. In this case, a secret society that called itself the Band of Righteous Harmony (mistranslated as the "Fists"—"Boxers"—of Righteous Harmony) arose among the peasant communities following sixty years of accumulating Western humiliations. The movement seems to have begun spontaneously, but was connived at by the Manchu court after the Boxers adopted as their slogan "Cherish the Empire—Exterminate the Foreigners." Serious violence began with the murder of a British Christian missionary in 1899, and by 1900 the Boxers controlled all of northern China and occupied Peking. The driving force was fury at the missionaries, who were held to embody the essential Western threat. Militants were said to possess invulnerability to Western bullets. They did not; and a combined expedition of European, Japanese, Russian, and American troops marched on Peking, took it, and looted it, putting down the rebellion at the cost of fairly indiscriminate destruction. The American commander, Major General Adna Chaffee, said at the time: "It is safe to say that where one real Boxer has been killed since the capture of Peking, fifteen harmless coolies or laborers on the farms, including not a few women and children, have been slain."

The Muslim Brotherhood in the Middle East, a proscribed movement in many places but still of considerable influence, is another such reactionary movement, aiming to restore a lost past. Anwar al-Sadat was its victim. Colonel Muammar al-Qaddafi, in Libya, is yet another reactionary, despite his megalomania, Fascist trappings, progressive language, and willingness to finance secular revolutionaries in the Middle East and elsewhere. He, too, stands for Muslim theocracy in revived and revised form.

The reactionary response to Westernization can scarcely succeed, except in delaying change and eventually making it still more explosive. The abasement of total conversion is equally unworkable, as the Shah of Iran and the Marxist leaders of Afghanistan have discovered. The most reasonable solution to the challenge, if the least easily accomplished, a creative synthesis of values drawn from both native society and the West, was attempted with some degree of success by Ataturk in Turkey in the 1920s, by Nehru and the Congress movement in India after Gandhi (Gandhi is a more ambiguous figure, accepting certain liberal changes but rejecting the Western industrial system), and in Japan. Japan is the great modern success in intelligent but discriminating adoption of Western ideas and practices, but even in Japan this has been done at considerable cost to the society and to the integrity of Japanese civilization. Even today there are those in Japan who think the cost has been too great. (That was one meaning of the ritual suicide of the novelist Yukio Mishima in 1970.) Japan paid for its accomplishment with a half-century of internal political unrest, leading to military government, colonial war in China, the Second World War, and, finally, cathartic defeat—the bombs on Hiroshima and Nagasaki.

The record of Japan after 1868 was initially that of a brilliant and energetic program of study, adaptation, and adoption of everything Western that the Japanese deemed useful: school syllabuses, railroads, armies and navies, diatonic music, banking, double-entry bookkeeping. Government was reorganized on the Western parliamentary model while retaining a monarchy held to be divine. Alliance with Britain was made the foundation of Japan's foreign policy. The Japanese, in the late nineteenth and early twentieth centuries, wanted to be accepted as equals in the company of the major powers of the West. They also wanted an empire: contemporary economic and political doctrine held that an empire was indispensable to a major power.

Japan's imperialism, however, provoked European and American resistance—to say nothing of their racism. Even after Japan sent ships to the Mediterranean to fight for the Allies in the First World War, the Western governments, Woodrow Wilson's American government among them, refused to include a declaration on racial equality, sought by Japan, in the Charter of the League of Nations. The liberal West refused to accept Japan as an equal. Japan then, in the 1920s and 1930s, rejected the liberal West. It chose an illiberal model, a form of the militarized politics—the Fascism—of contemporary Europe. Today, when Japan again is a liberal society and government, it still looks for unqualified acknowledgment of equality from the Western nations, and does not always find it. Some of the old forces of exclusion are still at work, as are some of the old provocations in Japan's own conduct. It is not unimaginable that there will be still more trouble between Japan and the West. The accommodation of Japan to a modernity still framed in Western terms, and of the West to Japan, is not even now completely achieved.

There have been grotesque failures of synthesis. Poignant but also sometimes sanguinary examples are provided in the "religions of the oppressed" thrown up in nineteenth-century Africa, Indochina, and China, which were amalgams of Christianity with the older religions or animism of the place. They were often magical or talismanic. Some became very important. The great Taiping rebellion in China, between 1848 and 1865, was led by a village school-master named Hung Hsu-chuan who had been the student of an American Protestant missionary. He professed to be the Celestial King, the younger brother of Christ. The movement he founded called for communal living, collective farming, equality in material possessions, equality between the sexes. It condemned slavery, the exploitation of women, foot-binding, opium. It arose just after the first Opium War, during the worst years of China's humiliation by the colonial powers. It swept northern China and captured Nanking, the southern capital, where the Celestial King ruled for a decade. Millions were killed in the fighting between Taiping and imperial troops. It represented the convulsive attempt of ordinary people to seize from the scarcely comprehended message of West-ern Christian missionaries the ideas and methods of acting that had given the West its power to impose itself on China, and which might then be used to protect China and counterattack Western influence. There are, of course, clear resemblances between the Taipings and what happened a century later in China, with Com-munism. A form of Western ideology was again seized upon by the Chinese to supplant a system in disintegration, and so to defend against the encroachments of the West.

The case of China is extraordinarily interesting, for its history brings into sharp focus the inherent difficulties of introducing Western values into a traditional society. By sheer size, to say noth-ing of political influence and military power, China is an important force in world affairs, expected by many to become one of the dom-inant powers of coming years. Moreover, in many respects, China seems to be a society in which modernization and cultural synthesis might really succeed, as in Japan. China has always been a formida-ble civilization, its classical age contemporary with that of Greece, its Confucian ethic as old, or older, than the Old Testament. China also has a long history of absorbing and assimilating foreign con-querors without a real cultural submission; the Chinese always conquered their conquerors, from the Mongols to the Manchus. China was also Western Europe's clear superior in science and technology as late as the Middle Ages. But China did not then experience the Newtonian revolution; its science did not become modern science. Thus, by the eighteenth century, China had fallen decisively behind the European colonial nations in material power, and in the explanation of things.

Joseph Needham, the great British student of Chinese science, offers a Marxist explanation for this failure. China, from the fifth to the fifteenth centuries, had been the most advanced civilization on earth in applying material knowledge to human needs. That was under essentially feudal conditions. Needham follows Karl Wittfogel's argument in saying that the successful centralization of power in China, produced by way of the construction and maintenance of immense irrigation systems, placed political power in the hands of bureaucrats and administrators. The social ideal in such a society became the scholar-administrator or scholar-gentleman. Merchants and soldiers were despised. As a consequence, the entrepreneurial, innovative middle class that modernized the West never became a serious force in China.

In the late Middle Ages, China remained largely unaware of what was happening in Europe. This was a result not only of distance but of an isolationist habit of mind, and of complacence. Renaissance Europe knew a good deal about China, and China had a marked influence on the taste and sensibility of Europe. But the Chinese regarded themselves as the center of civilization and wanted no outside contact. Under the later Ming dynasty, Chinese were even forbidden to sail abroad without a special imperial license. The Chinese authorities insisted on treating with foreigners in terms of submission and tribute, keeping the Europeans contained within as few trading points and other authorized points of contact as possible. Foreigners were under severe restrictions as late as the 1830s, as they were again in the 1980s. But after the mid-nineteenth century, China's power to contain foreign influence began to crumble. The English had found that opium, produced in

India, could pay for the silk and tea they were buying from China, and forced that opium past Chinese customs or landed it illegally on the coasts, eventually going to war to maintain this trade. The result of China's defeat in 1842 was the Treaty of Nanking, the first in a series of humiliating concessions, providing for British annexation of Hong Kong and occupation of Shanghai, and eventually granting to Europeans and Americans extraterritorial rights: trading ports, free navigation of the Yangtze, exemption of merchants from Chinese law, and broad privileges for missionaries. Further resistance by the Chinese resulted in the Anglo-French punitive expedition to Peking in 1860 and the burning of the Summer Palace. The emperor was compelled to express his apologies to the Europeans for having provoked them to this onerous effort, and China paid indemnities.

The Europeans treated China contemptuously, but also with a sense of irresistible destiny. Europeans were meant to rule, Chinese to submit, and by this process civilization would be conveyed to a China whose history might seem impressive but whose contemporary condition was regarded by Europeans as backward, poor, superstitious, in need of reform. The American involvement with China in the nineteenth and twentieth centuries was missionary and reformist as well. That pagan China needed both conversion and democratization was a very powerful belief in America, animating American leadership as late as the days of Henry R. Luce and John Foster Dulles in the 1950s. It remains a factor in American attitudes today, although the American outlook is now more mercantile than missionary: China is now seen as the last great consumer market.

There were early, abortive attempts at synthesis in China. The young emperor Kuang Hsu launched a series of reforms in 1898, under the influence of Westernized intellectuals impressed by Japan's accomplishments. He ordered missions sent abroad for "careful investigation of every branch of European learning appropriate to existing needs, so that there may be an end to empty fallacies and that, by zeal, efficiency may be attained." Favoritism was banned, the old examination system abolished, the schools ordered to teach such subjects as political economy. A naval college was planned, a translation bureau opened. But the emperor's reforms lasted for just one hundred days, before reactionary forces at the court had them halted.

In the early twentieth century, the predominant intellectual force was the "New Learning" or "New Tide," which was rationalist, humanist, and determined to jettison Confucianism and adopt Western ideas without compromise. In the words of the movement's leader, Chen Tu-hsiu, Dean of Letters at the National Peking University: "Whether in politics, scholarship, morality or literature, the Western method and the Chinese method are two absolutely different things and can in no way be compromised or reconciled. We need not now discuss which is better and which is worse, as that is a separate issue. . . . But if we decide to reform, then we must adopt the new Western method in all things and need not confuse the issue by such nonsense as 'national heritage' or 'special circumstances.' " Chen eventually became the first leader of the Chinese Communist Party—a new and still more radical repudiation of Chinese tradition. When the Manchus abdicated in 1912, in conditions of deepening political crisis, a republic was proclaimed with Sun Yat-sen, a Christian educated in Hawaii, its president, but the country's disintegration was only halted by the military campaigns of the nationalist movement, the Kuomintang, founded by Sun Yat-sen and later led by Chiang Kai-shek.

The eventual success of Communism in China represented an unexpected synthesis of influences. Mao Tse-tung reversed the policies of his predecessors, the Westernizing reformers who wanted wholesale conversion to foreign principles, including the orthodox Marxist and Leninist founders of the Chinese Communist Party. He turned this party, which in its European form was meant to mobilize an urban industrial proletariat, into a movement of the Asian peasantry. Japan's invasion of China in 1937 worked to his advantage: Communism was able to make itself a movement of national resistance, but because it did not bear the main weight of resistance, it was spared those corruptions of power to which the Kuomintang succumbed. Communism in China was thus able to present itself as both progressive and nationalist. In the later years of Mao Tse-tung's rule, it became increasingly Confucian as well.

Still, Communism, even reformed Communism, has not yet proved that it can make China a modern society, even by the party's own standards. It has not proven that it will itself last. Jon Elster, of the University of Chicago, wrote in late 1988, after a journey in China at the invitation of the Chinese Academy of Social Sciences, of his "dominant impression . . . that the Chinese do not know what they are doing. First, the leaders do not know where they want to go. . . . Even if the leaders knew where they wanted to go, they would not know how to get there. Economic theory has nothing to say about the transition from Communism to capitalism, nor is there any precedent from which they can learn. The official metaphor for the reforms is 'feeling the stones with one's feet in crossing the river.' . . . Finally, nobody knows what will be the outcome of the reforms that are actually being undertaken." The Communists have been in power in China not much longer than the time that elapsed between the national revolution in 1911 and the Kuomintang's defeat and retreat to Taiwan in 1949. In its four decades the People's Republic has been through terrible upheavals, factional and ideological struggles, civil-military rivalry, the rivalry of central authority with the provinces. Its future is not assured. The idea that Communism in China has succeeded in giving the Chinese efficient administration and an equitable distribution of food is widely accepted in the rest of the world, but it is hard to know whether this is true. It is said that entrepreneurial reforms are transforming agriculture and the economy. This certainly appears to be true for agriculture. But we still know little of China outside the cities. No one can say with certainty that the present government of China is there to stay—the Celestial Empire reestablished on post-Maoist terms—or whether Mao and his successors will simply prove ephemeral figures in an ongoing dynastic interregnum.

It seems logical to think that China should be able to make a success of industrialization and development, as Japan, South Korea, Taiwan, Hong Kong, and Singapore have done. But as Arnold Toynbee has observed, border cultures often have a vigor the central civilization lacks. If civilization arises from challenge, as he argues, then the first and necessary challenge for societies on the rim of a great and original civilization is the one that arises from their relationship to that larger civilization. This "is implicit in the relation itself, which begins with a differentiation and culminates in a secession." The secession ordinarily comes when the original civilization has lost the creative allure that commanded voluntary allegiance from the people on its borders. The industrialization and Westernization of Japan, South Korea, Hong Kong, Singapore, Taiwan—the peripheral Sinic cultures—might be seen as the ultimate secession from a preindustrial Chinese civilization that has failed to renew itself.

China and the other ancient non-Western civilizations have yet to solve the problem set by the transformation, two hundred years ago, of the quality of Western power. In the nineteenth century an official of the Manchu court observed that "in order to handle barbarian affairs, you have to know barbarian sentiments: in order to know barbarian sentiments, you have to know barbarian conditions." That was a confident statement: the thing could be done. In China today, as in much of the Third World, it is not so clear; the attempt repeatedly has been made and has yet to succeed. If the industrialization and modernization of China could really succeed—the progressive synthesis accomplished—the world would be changed. But to talk of this being done by the year 2000, as China's recent leaders have done, or as some Western observers assume, is absurd. The question still is whether it will be done at all. What current discussion lightly describes as the economic development of the Third World invokes one of the deepest historical movements of our times, cultural and moral in weight, scarcely begun, where failure is quite as probable as success.

The third millennium has begun and China has yet to become the "superpower" it was at the end of the first millennium. The nation (not the civilization) continues to obsess the Western imagination (and the foreign businessman) because there are so many Chinese. But numbers are not power, and population can be a weakness. China survived (or postponed) the economic crisis of 1997–98 because it is not a globalized economy. Its political crises lie ahead, when the Communist Party finally loses its grip on society.

The once fashionable idea that the Pacific Basin would soon dominate the world economy—sharing its domination with the United States, for this purpose a Pacific power—has not survived the crisis that globalism has provoked. Asia, with its political transitions still fragile, its geopolitical balance artificial so long as the United States insists on maintaining large military forces there, did not really need the assault upon its established societies and cultural norms that globalization carried out. The radical and disruptive remaking of its life and society—the challenge to Asians' understanding of existence itself, made by the West's four-century-long intrusion—is ignored or simply not understood by Western policymakers and observers.

Asia's future inevitably will be influenced primarily by Asia's own great powers. Japan is the only one at the present time. It is reasonable to think that China will become one, although at what time and after what further traumas remains to be seen. Taiwan and South Korea—eventually a united Korea, and possibly a Taiwan reunited with China—will be important players, and probably Indonesia, despite its fissiparous potentialities. India, the great democracy of Asia, is pre-occupied by its sterile conflict with Pakistan, but it is a rival to China.

All this is usually taken to justify continuing active U.S. security intervention in Asia. I would argue that whatever this may serve in the short term, the American presence in the long term will prove destabilizing and provoke hostility toward the United States, and possibly conflict. Asians must settle Asia's affairs.

# THE POSSIBILITY OF EXTRAVAGANT WASTE

# 7

"As Europe becomes more helpless, the Americans are compelled to become farseeing and responsible, as Rome was forced by the long decline of Greece to produce an Augustus, a Vergil. Our impotence liberates their potentialities. Something important is about to happen, as if the wonderful *jeunesse* of America were suddenly to retain their idealism and vitality and courage and imagination into adult life, and become the wise and good who make use of them; the old dollar values are silently crumbling, and the self-criticism, experimental curiosity, sensibility and warmth . . . are on their way in. For Americans change very fast. 'Do they?' 'Very fast and all at once . . . and nothing ever changes them back.' "

So wrote Cyril Connolly in October 1947, introducing a special issue, devoted to the United States, of his London literary magazine *Horizon*. The words, no doubt extravagant and intended to encourage the evolution they described, nevertheless expressed a foreign, especially European, view of the United States that has been one of the most influential political ideas of modern history. The United States has been seen as a society of unlimited possibility, of changed men and redeemed history. It is a view of the United States that since 1947 has been sustained with mounting difficulty. Connolly's are words that an American today must read uneasily. So much was expected.

In that same issue of *Horizon*, the philosopher William Barrett quoted Archibald MacLeish: "It is a difficult thing to be an American." The European has a known and articulated tradition to which he reacts, even in opposition, but the American, Barrett said, "has to explore his own personal relation to the American fate," confronting "something much more indefinite and amorphous; something which exists, certainly, otherwise how should he be so persistently haunted by its challenges and opportunities; but which, just as certainly, is not yet defined, and to that extent does not yet quite exist but has to be made, and so may never be brought to exist at all; so that the American imagination, otherwise so young and innocent, has been persistently haunted by these darker shadows of possible failure, extravagant waste, final abortiveness."

What Barrett wrote was a prescient statement with political implications, for the fate of the American, unlike that of the European, is inevitably a political fate. In this, the United States is unique. The men who founded the United States of America justified their creation, and their rebellion against the British Crown, as establishing a new and different kind of political society, making obsolete the kinds of government that existed before the American Constitution was drafted. The nation today rests upon a political compact or treaty among people of increasingly diverse ethnic origin and religious belief, or lack of belief, but who have in common a political vocabulary and constitutional system: and it is that which justifies the national existence. The United States could as easily have been established in Australia or New Zealand, or any other large and mainly unoccupied tract of land in a reasonably habitable part of the world, as long as the Constitution was the same. If that Constitution should be abrogated, or if the political system that it established should fail or be overturned, then there would be no point to the United States. It would cease to be what it was intended to be, and we all might as well go back to where we came from.

What we have meant to the rest of the world has incorporated this special political character of national mission into a larger perception of America as the New World. The Cleveland Museum's exhibition, mounted for the bicentennial, called "The European Vision of America," superbly illustrated the successive myths of America that were believed—and, indeed, proposed—by Europeans. America first was Eden, land of spices and springtime, of native peoples of sublime beauty and innocence. Then came exotic America, whose fauna and flora—turkeys, toucans, cacti, armadillos, flamingos—reinforced the perception of America as Another Place, wholly remote, vast, where everything no longer possible in Europe could occur or be created, all imagination gratified. There followed republican America, classically virtuous, propounding with enlightened elegance a self-government as yet only imagined in Europe. Then there was generous immigrant America, refuge and opportunity. The exhibition ended with a view of the scaffolded Statue of Liberty standing in the foundry yard of Gayet, Gauthier & Cie., in Paris, ready to be taken apart and shipped as republican France's gift to America. But, of course, there was a sequel—the savior America of the two world wars, rescuing liberal, democratic Europe from Europe's self-inflicted calamities, guiding it toward the recovery of the 1950s and 1960s. What these successive visions of America have had in common is the conviction that America is a place where constraining reality—indeed, history itself—is defied and the limits of Europe do not prevail; where optimism is realism. The perceived faults of America have been seen abroad as the faults of American virtues—inexperience, idealism that might overreach itself, naïveté, lack of gravity, lack of manners. But hardly anyone allowed himself to doubt that one day "the wonderful *jeunesse* of America" would have become "the wise and the good." This picture of America has been vital to the modern world and to modern politics, especially since 1945, as the United States has become so closely engaged in world affairs.

Until this century, the myth of America was more important than American reality, with which foreign societies had little actual contact. Since 1917, and especially since 1941, that has changed. American action has had to redeem the myth. The fathers have had to be saved by their children. The military liberation of Europe by America implied a cultural and moral reanimation of a civilization in crisis and exhaustion. Having passed to America its germinal culture, Europeans expected that civilization to be handed back, purified of whatever it was within it that had proved corrosive. Stephen

Spender, in his 1974 study of British-American literary relations, wrote: "Today . . . America has the advantage over Europe. European thoughts are American thoughts . . . the result of the great, inevitable, ever-predictable shift in wealth, power and civilization from the eastern to the western side of the Atlantic." This—nakedly, even abasingly—was the consolatory belief of Europeans in the afflicted mid-twentieth century. "France is destined to be protected, either by Germany or by the Anglo-Saxons"—such was the reported conviction of André Gide in the first months of the Second World War. Gide expressed his despair in a France already in moral crisis, broken by events. Spender, whose book derived from lectures given at Cambridge in 1965, wrote from a Britain that, after its supreme effort of the war and postwar years, was slipping, in its turn, toward abdication—the last of the European nations to do so. For the British, as thwarted victors in the war, more than for anyone else in Europe, a belief in the United States as their benevolent successor became a terrible, sustaining, need.

An important development occurred, however, in the United States during the 1960s and the 1970s. The American Idea, of unlimited possibility and the transformation of humanity, no longer convinced some Americans themselves, even though it continued to dominate the national rhetoric. This was not simply a consequence of the war in Vietnam, although that war provoked an anguished reconsideration of the national experience and of what American political civilization had become. Even among the men associated with the heroic age of American postwar policy came such reconsiderations as the following, from George Kennan: "I do not think that the United States civilization of these last 40–50 years is a successful civilization; I do not think that our political system is adequate to the needs of the age into which we are now moving; I think this country is destined to succumb to failures which cannot be other than tragic and enormous in their scope. All this, of course, is not an easy thing to live with."

The claim that the future of the United States is in doubt provoked both political and intellectual counterattack, of course. The rally of those who came to be called the neoconservatives aggressively reaffirmed American worth and American primacy. In successive elections in the late 1970s and the 1980s, Americans elected or reelected presidents whose principal, even sole, qualification for that office was their ability to make Americans feel better about themselves and about their country. There was a competition in reassurances to Americans, first that the country was still a "good" country, and then that it was strong, its future bright, its leadership intact. This very insistence suggested, however, that doubt about these things persisted, and not just among an alienated element of a liberal intelligentsia.

America's has been a brief empire, begun in war in the 1940s, confidently consolidated in the 1950s. We attained our Augustan age—as Robert Frost had dangerously prayed—in the Kennedy years, a gleam of decadence to be glimpsed behind the brilliance; and afterward terrible and crazy things happened and the empire began rapidly to come apart. The Nixon administration inherited what might be called a post-Diocletian disarray: collapsing frontiers, an irresolute but colossal bureaucracy controlling incompetent political agencies, client states, armies of foreign mercenaries; and at home, an embittered and scared people fed up with it all, lacking a shared sense of purpose. The failure in Vietnam was the climax to a decade of less comprehensible hazards and frustrations. Afterward there was something like a paroxysm of disillusionment and reaction, producing in succession the apologetic presidency of Jimmy Carter and the nationalistic one of Ronald Reagan. The country was in a dangerous mood, because the immense moral and emotional investment made in foreign policy and foreign engagements over a period of forty years had produced nothing like the results that had been expected. The nation's future, its solvency and competitiveness, seemed cast into doubt—its "decline" even proposed—as a consequence, it seemed, of the rival dynamism of the allies it had for forty years defended. The American commitment to liberal internationalism, made with a sentimental but perfectly genuine idealism, risked finishing in disillusionment, and those impulses that fed the isolationism of the 1930s began to reemerge.

The overall conception of American foreign policy in modern times ultimately derived from a Protestant conception of the United States as the secular agent of God's redemptive action. Woodrow Wilson said that our world role came "by no plan of our conceiving, but by the hand of God who led us into this way." Until the 1960s, it was held with little dissent that the United States not only provided an example to other nations but was the leading nation on a progressive scale of historical development. The essential argument over the proper conduct of American foreign policy, from the time of George Washington's Farewell Address to contemporary debates over policies in the Americas, the Middle East, and Western Asia, concerned whether the United States should act directly to change or influence the fate of others—an interventionist and activist policy—or whether it should hold itself aloof and guard its own institutions so as to provide others with an example of justice and good order, thus influencing them indirectly. The enabling assumption, that the United States is an exemplary society and a model for others, was never seriously questioned until the 1960s and 1970s, and even then inconclusively, the challenge aggressively denied; and yet doubt remained.

When questions arose, there was no history to consult. Thomas Paine had said that "the case and circumstances of America present themselves as in the beginning of the world. . . . We have no occasion to roam for information into the obscure field of antiquity, nor hazard ourselves upon conjecture. We are brought at once to the point of seeing government begin, as if we had lived at the beginning of time." In the 1960s we might have thought ourselves seeing the approach of the end, but still without reference to others. It is true that Americans know, and care, little about history, even our own, and less about the experience and reality of others. Classical political thought has nothing to say to us, according to Jefferson himself: "So different was the style of society then, and with those people, from what it is now and with us, that I think little edification can be obtained from their writings on the subject of government." Knowledge of other countries was thought equally irrelevant. To Americans, excused from history, everything has been thought nationally definable, knowable, resolvable, usable; and what happens, or is thought, in France, Italy, Germany, or Japan, like the history of what has happened to them, or even quite where they lie on the map, has been considered matter for specialists. They are thought to have little or no relevance to America.

The political rhetoric of the United States has continued to employ the old vocabulary of American exceptionalism, national mission, American preeminence. Yet there is no longer an intellectually responsible ruling idea of Americanism, a fully acceptable formulation of this justificatory national purpose—to say nothing of a national policy to advance it. There no longer is a clear ethnic identity. The white, Protestant, generally rural self-identification of the 1930s and 1940s is today as remote as the moon. The Pilgrims and Puritans of New England, the Transcendental thinkers and high-minded Unitarians and Congregationalists, the genteel Protestants of the South, believers in Jeffersonian obligation and yeoman values—all now are routed. The passionate camp-meeting preacher remains, the itinerant revivalist become vulgar mass-media personage, who implies that salvation on offer is merely the condition of being an American. American Catholicism, released by the Second Vatican Council from the need to be Latinate and un-American, enthusiastically turned itself into something scarcely distinguishable from just another American Protestant sect.

The old elite had been so confident. Henry Adams, of Washington and Boston, son of statesmen and divines, wrote to a friend a century ago: "As I belong to the class of people who have great faith in this country and who believe that in another century it will be saying in its turn the last word of civilization, I enjoy the expec-

tation of the coming day." The century achieved, the national condition has proven more complicated.

Americans are at an axial point in the national relationship to the
world, unwilling to admit that the United States is not a unique
nation. We are ready to despise the world again, as we did in the
past, our friends and clients perhaps more than our official Soviet
enemies, since with those enemies it has been possible to feel a kinship of power and isolation, while our friends and clients are impor-
tunate, implicated in our own disappointment, increasingly our
rivals. Our allies and clients are accessible to our anger. We can do
something about them: which is to punish them for having cooperated in our disillusionment and for having become cynical about us
and about our motives. Our enemies possess, we assume, the power
to release us from world engagement. It is our friends who block
us, reproach us, cling to us, impose their moral claims upon us.

America's has been a fleeting empire, forced upon us in emergency, extended with idealism—already being abandoned. Even
Poland's empire, which briefly ran from the Baltic to the Black Sea,
lasted longer. America's has been an unserious empire, of unexam-
ined ideas and uncalculated ambitions, a solipsistic nation's means
for reacting to an external world whose very particularity has
seemed threatening. Perhaps it is to America's credit that we never
wholly abandoned ourselves to a real imperialism even while prac-
ticing it, hotly denying that we were anywhere outside our borders
except for the briefest time and the most disinterested purpose.
Even our imperial pomp was unconvincing. The militarized ceremonial of latter-day Washington provided neither Roman grandeur
nor Nuremberg menace. There has always been about it the air of
show biz, evidence of the efforts of the Hollywood pals of our presidents, a glimpse of drum majorettes and the high-school band.

It is clear now that the internationalism of the last quarter-
century was simply a transmogrified nationalism, and no true passion to rule spice kingdoms or dominate the exotic. We wanted
power, but we also wanted people to concede us that power by

right; we laid a claim upon the century as ours, but as a function of our altruism and the universality of our values. Denied that, our will to empire was broken. It had to be that way, because we remain an isolate and morally isolated people. We could never accept others dispassionately for what they are, because that would have implied an equally dispassionate judgment upon what we are. But can we now return, containing within these continental limits our energies and crackling tensions? Can we deal with our real selves, with all of our inner distress, our national uncertainty—our unrealized national purpose? We do not possess the privilege of a return to innocence.

The outlook [in 1989] is not entirely reassuring. This could prove a dangerous period because both the United States and the Soviet Union are taking risks on the basis of ideas and commitments no longer fully believed. The Soviet Union is in the course of an implicit repudiation of Leninism, which contains within it revolutionary potentialities. There is an American taste for national aggrandizement, now in check, which the rhetoric of idealism masks. There are European and Japanese dynamics at work, rich in possibilities for trouble.

There is a potentiality for an American nihilism. The Puritan sense of "darkness, quiet, and intrinsic limitation" that animated American society for three centuries is now gone. The Emersonian confidence in the essential benevolence of the universe, which lay behind Woodrow Wilson's liberal internationalism, proved an unsuitable philosophy for the fourth quarter of the twentieth century. Emerson believed in the universality of reason, and of law that enforces itself. In the matter of tragedy, he said, "most suffering is only apparent." His post-Christian identification of the substance of self with God, his moral liberation, his belief that he was beyond conventional creeds, his distrust of altruism, influenced Nietzsche (as John Updike has observed). Nietzsche adapted what in Emerson was complacent and harmless, product of a secure and provincial intelligence, to a harder doctrine of the need for amoral and uninhibited "supermen." It is possible that the sentimentalism of a latterly disillusioned American liberal internationalism could be succeeded in the United States by an unsentimental determination to live "as the world lives," and not to spare those who stand in the way. (Nietzsche himself wrote in his notebooks: " 'Without the Christian faith,' said Pascal, 'you will become for yourselves, just as nature and history will become, *un monstre et un chaos*.' This prophecy we have fulfilled.")

The old utopianism cannot be discarded without putting something in its place. The vision of a world parliament of nations and an expanding system of international law and cooperation was not an ignoble one. It expressed a belief that the civilizing progression that has taken place within Western society—from family and blood obligation to feudalism, to centralized law and social contract—has a counterpart in the relations of nations. It is possible that this is an unjustified assumption. But if Americans give up their older ideas, they must also give up the progressive, moralizing language connected to those ideas, which continues to be employed by conservatives quite as much as by liberals. The day the United States renounced World Court jurisdiction over its conduct in Central America, President Reagan proclaimed "Law Day," saying that "without law, there can be no freedom, only chaos and disorder."

"Because [men] are wicked and would not keep faith with you, you yourself need not keep it with them" was the great Machiavelli's way of saying that one should not practice "unilateral compliance" with the law (to employ former U.N. Ambassador Jeane Kirkpatrick's disparaging phrase). Herbert Butterfield, the Oxford historian, comments that the injunction to "live as the world lives is the ordinary vulgar doctrine that morality does not pay; its only purport is the reduction of the conduct of good men to the standards of the worst." This certainly is not the moral, or immoral, position the United States wishes consciously to adopt. But, then, what is the American position today?

One concludes that the United States is in a state of significant intellectual confusion. The discrepancy between language employed and what actually is thought (not to speak of what is done) approaches scandal. Americans remain moralists, "globalists" in their fashion, prisoners of the progressive tradition, even as they chant the glories of American nationalism. We are not philosophical realists, willing to leave Russians, Nicaraguans, Cubans—or Afghans or Poles—alone if they would leave the United States alone. We are not philosophical pessimists, prepared to argue that international life is mean, and foreign policy a way to make the best of bad choices—in Michael Oakeshott's famous metaphor, to keep afloat in "a boundless and bottomless sea [where] there is neither harbor for shelter nor food for anchorage, neither starting place nor appointed destination." There is an intense and even painful dissociation of the mind and moral sensibility from action, and the result is an attempt to escape. The solution that arises, without its being articulated, is that the United States revert to its natural condition, which is isolationism.

One may reflect upon what has happened to the United States during the last half-century with regret, or with irony; one may also ask if a qualified confidence about the future might be justified. Isolation could be good for the country. The United States might find itself again; resources exist for reconstruction—"that coarseness and strength combined with acuteness and inquisitiveness, that practical, inventive, turn of mind, quick to find expedients . . . that restless, nervous energy, that dominant individualism, working for good or evil, and withal that buoyancy and exuberance"—thus Frederick Jackson Turner, historian of the frontier. But does the will exist? Is there a willingness to be serious, to make sacrifices again, to take our indulgences in hand? Until now, the price of an assumed glory has not been paid. The shadow "of possible failure, extravagant waste," has lengthened. The frontier that remains is the interior one, the most forbidding and mysterious frontier. The country seems still to have about it (again to quote Fitzgerald, writing in 1929) "that quality of the idea . . . a willingness of the heart." But does it, really? We shall see.

# AN AFTERWORD IN THE NEW CENTURY

Few today express doubt about the future of the United States as I did in the preceding pages, writing a decade ago. Despite all that has happened since then, my fears about the American future persist. I will lay them out in this afterword, taking up questions of democracy's inherent vitality and progress in international society, the accompanying development of seemingly irreversible plutocratic mechanisms in the American political system, the militarization of American foreign policy thought and practice, and the resurgence of a naïve utopianism in the country's economic and foreign policy, leading the nation into a debate as to whether its twenty-first century destiny may be to promulgate a benevolent form of world hegemony.

In the American policy discussion of today, democracy is generally understood to be the long-term trend in contemporary history—the "strong force," as against various "weak forces." The prevailing view was given a beguiling Hegelian formulation in Francis Fukuyama's argument that history is over because the liberal democracies, being the highest form of historical evolution, have prevailed. That thesis evoked so wide and approving a reaction because Fukuyama expressed in a coherent, plausible way what "everyone," after the Cold War ended, wanted to believe was true.

In the course of the twentieth century, nearly every alternative to democracy had been tried, defeated, or discredited: Fascism; authoritarian nationalism; the combination of the two with socialism in national socialism, or Nazism; monarchy; the Third World's national liberation regimes (ostensibly a variant of socialism, but closer to Mussolini's Fascism); anarchism (Spain's and, subsequently, that of the student uprisings in 1968); theocracy (in Iran, prospectively elsewhere in the Islamic world, and, in a distorted and corrupt version, in the secular deification of Lenin, Stalin, Mao Tse-tung, and Kim Il Sung and his son, Kim Jong Il).

The victory of democracy seems attested to by the large number of nominal or "cadet" democracies. Democracy has become a matter not only of conviction but of political correctness and even of fashion. The former Communist countries of Central, Eastern, and Baltic Europe are democracies, if sometimes imperfect ones. Russia and other former component parts of the U.S.S.R. claim to be democracies even when they are not. The nations of Asia have parliamentary systems or are constitutional monarchies, except for Burma, North Korea, North Vietnam, and China (and even the last three claim to be "popular democracies").

Nondemocratic governments everywhere now feel compelled to disguise themselves as democracies. The "Democratic" Republic of the Congo must call itself that, and promise elections, even if the elections are empty exercises. China, Iraq, Liberia, and North Korea all have their nominal parliament. In Belgrade, Slobodan Milosevic from the beginning of the wars of Yugoslav succession enjoyed a series of electoral validations as he led his country to the abyss.

In the very recent past it was otherwise. In the 1950s and 1960s, revolutionary command councils, single parties, national fronts, and charismatic leaders were the vogue. The Communist parties and right-wing military dictatorships of the Cold War enjoyed a mutually profitable symbiotic relationship because the colonels or generals in Greece, Argentina, or Guatemala—and the generals who had assumed civilian garb in Indonesia, the Arab world, and Africa—presented themselves as indispensable alternatives to Communist oppression, terrorism, or anarchy, while the Communist Party central committees of Eastern Europe, and their protégés elsewhere, claimed that dialectical materialism proved them the necessary successors to imperialism or Fascism. The Soviet Union's ideological position demanded that a monolithic international Communist bloc exist, even when it manifestly did not.

The United States enjoyed the luxury of military alliance with liberal nations but was inclined to think that lesser non-Communist states were more safely led by generals than by princes or mandarins or left-wing Socialists (as in Cambodia, South Vietnam, and Chile)—and so arranged or approved it. It endorsed military coups in Greece and Central America and came close to promoting one in Portugal in 1975–76. The end of the Cold War rendered all this obsolete, although the acquired bad habits persisted in some intelligence and military circles.

Seventy years ago, democracy was thought a failure in much of the world. Parliamentary democracy, dominated by the middle classes and the model of progressive government before 1914, was widely regarded as having been discredited by the First World War. Its parliamentary forms were held to cloak class oppression and oligarchy. Elections were said to co-opt the citizen by providing the illusion of popular rule while behind the scenes powerful interests manipulated governments and international relations, and arranged profitable wars.

Fascism was fashionable in many Western circles, and was believed to have mobilized the Italian people for positive social tasks and national affirmation. The Swedish filmmaker Ingmar Bergman (born in 1918), son of an austere Lutheran pastor, described in his memoirs, *Laterna Magica* (1987), his attraction to Nazism during the 1930s and 1940s. He later said to a journalist that it was not the program of the Nazis that interested him: "I was impressed by the idealism of the Germans." The discovery of the Nazi camps, which he first thought Allied propaganda, "was a terrible shock." In 1946, he said, he lost his innocence. There were many such idealistic sympathizers of Nazism until its real nature was revealed. The Bolshevik model of society was influential among Western elites, and became even more so during the later 1930s and the 1940s. In some circles of the left, notably in France, disillusionment did not come until the 1970s.

Seventy years ago women lacked the vote in most Western countries. Property qualifications limited the franchise in Britain, as race effectively did in the United States. The hereditary peerage still possessed real political power in Britain. The societies of Asia and Africa that were European colonies were entirely subject to the disposition, paternalistic or otherwise, of the imperial powers. And colonialism was considered a progressive institution by which backward peoples could gradually be introduced to a modern way of life, and only then—if then—be allowed self-determination. Imperialism was scarcely questioned in Europe, even in enlightened circles. Great exhibitions were held to celebrate it and to display the exotic products and crafts of the colonized peoples.

The British Empire, expanded by virtue of the Allied victory in the First World War, reached its zenith in the 1930s. The defeat of the Ottoman Empire placed Iraq and Palestine under British control, making it possible for an Englishman to travel from Cairo to Rangoon entirely by way of nations either subject to the Crown or, like Persia, under indirect but decisive British influence. Beyond Persia lay India (including present-day Pakistan) and Burma, Singapore, British Hong Kong. Elsewhere were British East and South Africa, Canada, Australia, and New Zealand, plus sundry islands and Crown possessions. The empire may have been overextended, but violence was necessary for the overextension to become evident.

The Second World War provided the violence. The Western allies opened their political systems to wider electorates. The welfare state was promised in Britain to reward people for the great wartime struggle. Defeat and crime discredited the Fascist state. Japan's destruction of the American, French, Portuguese, and Dutch empires in Asia, and the blow it delivered to the British Empire, made it impossible to reinstall Western colonial power there after 1945—even though France and the Netherlands both tried, fighting wars in their attempts to do so.

The fact that political respectability today demands that a state present itself as a democracy represents real progress, even though the effective practice of democratic government has probably not greatly advanced. There has been a consolidation of international opinion to press governments and societies everywhere toward more representative politics. It is not a negligible development that even despotism now considers it necessary to sail under the colors of democracy.

How enduring will this change in global political consciousness and public morality prove to be? Most of those in official positions in the Western countries take for granted that the change is permanent, as do most commentators and scholars in the universities and the political policy community. This is an expression of what the British historian Herbert Butterfield named "the Whig view of history": that history has been a progression whose significance has been to lead up to us and to our institutions, and that we establish the terms on which the future will develop.

It is an opinion firmly held in the United States, despite the fact that the nation no longer possesses the representative form of government its founders conceived, and has instead become what might be called a consensual plutocracy. As it construes its laws and its political practice, it is a qualified plutocracy, in that the rich do not rule directly. But indirectly, wealth, mainly corporate wealth, exercises predominant influence over domestic government and over foreign relations, and this condition seems irreversible.

In past periods when money values acquired an unacceptable level of influence, as in the 1920s or in the age of the so-called Robber Barons at the end of the nineteenth century, counterbalancing movements of reform were generated. The great reform movement of the late nineteenth and early twentieth century produced the principal institutions regulating modern American capitalism. Greed (or material ambition, to soften the term) was no less indispensable to making the country's economy and society function than it is today. It motivated an immigrant society. The notion that anyone could become rich and claim the emoluments of the highfalutin elites of "the old country" was often enough validated—alongside the homesteader reality of sod houses, penury, land not made for what the homesteaders grew on it, and the cultural alienation of immigration.

There was opportunity enough to sustain the illusion—which was understood to partake of illusion, but had truth enough—that "in worn out, king-ridden Europe, men must stay where they are born. But in America a man is accounted a failure, and certainly ought to be, who has not risen above his father's station in life." That was how a leader of the New York bar, Charles O'Conor, put it in the 1860s. He was an immigrant who had been apprenticed to a lampblack manufacturer at the age of twelve. However, opportunity's denial was capable of generating social upheavals and demands that had, in turn, to be given political response.

The great boom in the northern states immediately after the Civil War culminated in America's Gilded Age (while the South, ruined, stayed poor until the Second World War). Completion of the transcontinental railroad, and the Homestead Law of 1862, giving federal land in the West to those willing to settle and farm it, opened the Great Plains to the East's poor and to ambitious immigrants. The same period saw notorious corruption in Washington politics and in law and business during the Grant administration, as well as machine politics in the cities, notably the corrupt Tweed machine's domination of New

York. A reform reaction was provoked, which, while it failed to elect a president (Grant won again in 1872), was reinvigorated during the depression of 1873–79. Henry George argued in his enormously influential book *Progress and Poverty* (1879) that the United States was using up the free land that had "given a consciousness of freedom even to the dweller in crowded cities, and has been a well-spring of hope" and was moving toward a rigid economic and social stratification like that of Europe.

The concentration of new industry into "trusts" fixing prices and competition and the discrepancy in income between owners and workers (which approached that which Americans are experiencing in the 2000s) inspired a popular reaction against business. Agricultural depression dampened the allure of homesteading. The Knights of Labor, the first important American industrial labor organization, formed in 1869, acquired more than seven hundred thousand members in the following decade and a half (in a national population of slightly more than 50 million). The financial panic of 1873 produced a crisis in agricultural prices and the organization of "Farmers' Alliances" in the West, which demanded railroad regulation (later, nationalization of transport), abolition of the national banks, a graduated income tax, and Free Silver (meaning unlimited coinage). An informal coalition of Farmers' Alliances, Knights of Labor, and European-influenced immigrant socialist groups with other reformers hostile to business and favoring government social intervention elected five U.S. senators, six governors, and forty-six congressmen in 1890.

Two years later the Populist Party was founded in Omaha by delegates arriving by train and buckboard and on foot. It won more than 1 million votes for its presidential candidate in 1892 (Grover Cleveland won, with 5.5 million votes). This convinced the Democrats to adopt the Free Silver issue, and in 1896 the two parties jointly nominated William Jennings Bryan as their presidential candidate, a man whose oratory combined religious imagery and revivalist emotion with a message of economic and political change. His message was addressed to an audience, as the historian Richard Hofstadter has written, "nursed in evangelical Protestantism and knowing little literature but the Bible, but it launched another 'Great Awakening' which swept away most of the cynicism and apathy that had been characteristic of American politics for thirty years." Bryan the man unfortunately was insufficient to Bryan the image; his heart, Hofstadter also says, "was filled with simple emotions, but his mind was stocked with equally simple ideas." He swept the South and the agrarian states of the West but lost the presidential election.

He lost again in 1900, when more than a third of American farmers no longer worked their own land and 1 percent of the population owned more of the national wealth than all the rest combined. The *Chicago Evening Post* wrote that "it was bad enough to have million-dollar trusts run by a few men, but what is going to happen to the farmer, the worker, and the small businessman when we have billion-dollar combines maneuvered by a handful of men who have never been in a plant and who think of a factory as just another chip in a gigantic financial poker game?" Victory in 1900 went instead to the Republican McKinley-Roosevelt ticket, and Theodore Roosevelt became president within months, following William McKinley's assassination.

Roosevelt led a second and more successful reform movement, that of Eastern patricians resolved to control the excesses of business, paternalistic and hostile to the "mob"—meaning the spontaneous and uncontrollable Populists. The first Roosevelt administration revived moribund antitrust legislation and attacked more than forty large industrial and investment trusts, mostly with success. Roosevelt's second administration obtained interstate commerce regulation, increased government control over railroads, established meat inspection, passed the Food and Drugs Act, and extended timber and natural resources conservation and the national parks system.

While the first Roosevelt's regulation of business was fundamentally supportive of it (as were the measures against the "malefactors of great wealth" of Franklin Delano Roosevelt three decades later—a truth incomprehensible to most businessmen of either time), his values were not those of business. He was a romantic nationalist, a believer in heroic virtues and masterful personal leadership, contemptuous of materialist values. He believed that he stood above class interest. He shared with his fifth cousin, young Franklin, the belief (as Eric Goldman has written) that "a patrician's politics should be reform, and that reform meant broad federal powers wielded by executive leadership."*

He said of his own class, "The wealthier, or, as they would prefer to style themselves, the 'upper' classes, tend distinctly towards the bourgeois type, and an individual in the bourgeois stage of development, while honest, industrious, and virtuous, is also not unapt to be a miracle of timid and short-sighted selfishness. The commercial classes are only too likely to regard everything merely from the standpoint of 'Does it pay?' "

It was a comment that has obvious contemporary relevance. But even if the riches enjoyed by the United States in the twenty-first century were to be taken from it by crisis and depression, as happened in the late nineteenth and early twen-

---

*A notion not so different from that of Herbert Hoover, who was not the conventional supporter of market capitalism most now think him as having been. Hoover emerged from federal service during and after the First World War advocating "a new era of national action, in which the federal government forms an alliance with the great trade associations and the powerful corporations," developing cooperative codes of behavior. He put this into practice as president, and left office with more than two thousand trade associations in existence, many of them with their agreed codes of conduct. "We are passing from a period of extreme individualistic action into a period of associational activities," Hoover wrote. Had he included unions in these associations, the system would have resembled the anticapitalist "corporatism" of Mussolini's Fascism. FDR's National Recovery Administration, killed by the Supreme Court in 1935, added federal planning and compulsion to Hoover's business and industrial cooperation. Hoover, however, called that "fascism, pure fascism."

tieth centuries, reform would meet the enormous obstacles that have been put into place by the institutional choices and constitutional interpretations made by Americans during the past thirty years. It was a distant relation of my own, the sober Calvin Coolidge, who unanswerably observed that "the chief business of the American people is business." American society's alliance of wealth with power began the twenty-first century with new and firmly established structural impediments to reform which the electorate largely ignores, or to which it has proven indifferent.

In 1998, a congressional election year, in nearly 95 percent of all federal elections, the candidate who spent the most won, according to the Center for Responsive Politics. In 2000 the trend strengthened, "the megamillionaires taking the place of daunted multimillionaires," as an academic observer commented about the New Jersey senate race, where the Republican governor and a former governor renounced plans to run again because of lack of money, while a retired Wall Street executive with a reported fortune of $300 million won the Democratic nomination.*

The sums committed to the 2000 presidential campaign, even before the primary elections began, surpassed anything previously experienced, yet the Republican candidate, George W. Bush, spent his entire original campaign fund, which was some $70 million in January 2000, simply to defeat the primary challenge of Senator John McCain. The amount had been expected to finance both his primary and general election campaigns. In March 2000, *The New York Times* estimated that total national campaign spending on the year's presidential and congressional elections would exceed $3 billion, probably

*Charles Lewis, in his book *The Buying of the Presidency 2000* (a collaboration with the Center for Public Integrity, 1999), notes that at least ten of those who declared themselves candidates for the 2000 presidential election were millionaires, including the two who obtained the major parties' nominations. One-third of the Senate is composed of millionaires. Less than 1 percent of the general population falls into that category.

an underestimation. This situation is well-known and much deplored, but the fact that it has changed the nature of the American political system still is not acknowledged.

Money has always been essential to politics in the United States, as everywhere else. What is new is the scale of the sums required, which by their quantity have produced a qualitative change in American political society. As one congressional candidate described it in an unsuccessful suit against the Federal Communications Commission, which regulates broadcasting, an "unconstitutional means test" for political office has been established. Elections are conducted all but entirely by means of paid political advertising, especially advertising on television and radio, and the price of this advertising is such that the cost of election to national office is beyond the means of all but a handful of private individuals. A candidate in such circumstances finds the money where it can be found, which means from groups interested in influencing legislation and policy. That is normal enough in democracies, except that the huge sums now required have created a situation in which those who supply the money automatically acquire an interest in maintaining the electoral finance system as it is. It benefits them directly by giving them a privileged political role, while sharply limiting the influence of others who lack such resources. The effect of this is to make the change irreversible.

There is nothing formally undemocratic about American elections. They simply require so much money that no successful challenge can be made either to the existing electoral system or to the prevailing money values that support it and dominate public life. This situation serves the particular interest of the broadcasting and advertising industries, which during each election profit from a huge transfer of private and public wealth (the latter in government-provided counterpart funds for political campaigns) as candidates and parties purchase campaign broadcast time and advertising space. The campaign "industry"—of fund-raisers, speech and advertisement writers, communications experts, consultants, pollsters, and journalists who live off American elections—also benefits directly. It is part of a powerful coalition of corporate and political interests which defends the rule of money.

Many companies resent the present situation because it amounts to a form of blackmail, in which they have to make campaign contributions, at their stockholders' expense, in order to counterbalance the funds given by their competitors. Lobbies representing special political interests, which formerly exercised influence by mobilizing activists and voters at election time, have now found that contributing money directly to parties or candidates is more effective, since it directly obliges the recipient. This situation has helped to accelerate the decline in electoral participation, which in the United States is now one of the lowest among all the democracies. In the most recent congressional election (1998) it fell to 32 percent, the lowest in a nonpresidential election since 1942. Spending on television advertising nonetheless was at an all-time high, more than $500 million.

Legal restriction of campaign spending is prevented by a disastrous Supreme Court ruling in 1976 (*Buckley* v. *Valeo*), holding that money spent on political advertising is an exercise of constitutionally protected free speech. A ban on broadcast campaign commercials would undoubtedly be struck down under the First Amendment of the Constitution, even if its passage by Congress were imaginable. The erstwhile federal requirement that, in exchange for free use of the public airwaves, broadcasters provide "public interest" programming, including campaign coverage and independent examination of public issues, established by the Federal Communications Act of 1934, was repealed during the Reagan administration, and its reinstatement has been blocked by Congress and is almost certainly a political impossibility.° Political incumbents, who

---

°A further complication is provided by the concentration in recent years of media ownership in corporate conglomerates (such as Disney, Fox, Time Warner, the

tend to benefit most from the system, vote to maintain it, even when they dislike it, because they despair of changing it.

This system is unique among the world's major democracies, and its faults are well-known and much criticized, to no great effect. Two unsuccessful candidates for the presidential nomination in 2000, Bill Bradley and John McCain, made campaign finance reform an important part of their campaign platforms, with the result that their opponents unenthusiastically pledged themselves to reform as well, but none of the proposed reforms would do more than make payments to candidates and parties transparent and limit what could be contributed to "issue" advocacy indirectly benefiting candidates ("soft money"). There have been state initiatives to provide public funds to replace private campaign contributions, and proposals that would require campaign contributions to be rendered anonymous by passing them through foundations or a blind trust, or be transformed into dedicated election currency or scrip, or which would create a public body to receive contributions and distribute them to candidates who forgo other contributions. But none of these—even if their passage by Congress were imaginable—challenges the system's constitutionally protected dependence on paid advertising, which is the fundamental problem and would seem insurmountable.

For all the criticism made by Americans about the campaign system and its effect on the quality of government, it seems to be a system with which the majority of the American people are content. Possibly this is the result of the prosperity

---

Tribune Company, and General Electric) whose business interests may conflict with the news media's formal commitment to provide impartial information. Sumner Redstone, chairman of Viacom Inc., in the course of his bid to purchase CBS, the network whose news service has been the most distinguished in American broadcasting, made the following comment to journalists in late 1999 about the tension between news and business judgments. He said that while "journalistic integrity must prevail in the final analysis . . . that doesn't mean that journalistic integrity should be exercised in a way that is unnecessarily offensive to the countries in which you operate."

of the present decade and would change if bad times arrived. Possibly it results from ignorance: Americans are a parochial people, and many do not know that other democracies do not live their political lives in this way, or that sensible alternatives exist to what in the United States is taken as normal. For many Americans, it no doubt is scarcely conceivable that the founding texts and political institutions of the United States could have become so distorted in contemporary practice as to have fundamentally changed the American political system. Yet the country has deprived itself of the essential legal and constitutional mechanisms of reform, so that even if critics were to turn the alabaster hearts of lobbyists and business executives, inspire repentant politicians to return to the republican virtues of a yeoman America, and convince everyday Americans to turn off their television sets, disarm their children, and go to the polls, it would do no good.

A decade ago it was possible for me to write in the first edition of this book that if American democracy failed, it would do so in a democratic way—"carrying the national logic to the bitter end." I thought it a clever remark. Today it has proven a disagreeably prescient one. The Republic established in 1787 is today governed by the form but not the intent of the Constitution ratified that year, and the people have acquiesced.

A decade ago I would not have thought that the collapse of Communism would increase rather than reduce the militarization of American life. The military now have a larger role in national life than in any country outside the Third World. The country has fallen into what can be described as civilian militarism. Military considerations and modes of thought possess an importance in the country's foreign relations which has no constitutional warrant, and which influences American government to turn to military violence for remedies to international problems for which the only real solutions (when solutions exist) are political.

In September 1939, when Europe went to war, the United States Army (including the Army Air Corps, later the Army Air Force, which did not become a separate service until 1947) numbered 174,000 men. The nation had an old and principled hostility to "standing armies," believed a threat to democracy. That sentiment was explicit in the Constitution, whose drafters delegated to Congress the authority "to raise and support armies," but made that power subject to the condition that "no appropriation to that use shall be for a longer term than two years."

The standing military force of the United States was constitutionally confined to a "well-regulated militia" in the individual states. A militia is a body of civilians who have received military instruction and can be called up for service in a national emergency. In the United States today that militia is the National Guard, normally under the authority of state governors. John Hancock said in 1774 that from a militia "we have nothing to fear; their interest is the same as that of the state."

Today the United States has 1.4 million persons in its "standing army," members of its regular navy and air force included (but excluding the Coast Guard), and a ready reserve and National Guard force of nearly 2.5 million. These forces hold themselves prepared to wage simultaneously two major wars in different parts of the world, even though the United States faces no serious military threat. It is the United States which poses the military threat to others.

The United States in 1999, according to *The New York Times,* still maintained some twenty-three hundred nuclear warheads on alert, with an explosive power equivalent to forty-four thousand Hiroshimas. The scale of existing Russian nuclear forces is undoubtedly smaller, but the command and control arrangements and the weapons' state of maintenance probably make them less secure than America's missiles. In 1998 the Clinton administration programmed more money for modernization and simulated testing of the American nuclear force than, on annual average, the U.S. government spent during the Cold War to build the force.

In his authoritative *History of Militarism* (1937, revised in 1959), Alfred Vagts wrote that militarism is the "domination of the military man over the civilian, an undue preponderance of military demands, an emphasis on military considerations, spirit, ideals, and scales of value, in the life of states. It has meant also the imposition of heavy burdens on a people for military purposes, to the neglect of welfare and culture."

In the former respects, this does not describe America's situation. The military man does not dominate civilian authority in a direct way and has no ambition to do so, although during the 1990s the Joint Chiefs of Staff successfully imposed new limits on civilian authority. When General Colin Powell was chairman of the Joint Chiefs of Staff, he gave an interview to *The New York Times* in which he courteously but firmly set out the conditions (in terms of casualty risks and the political definition of the military objective) under which he and his colleagues were prepared to carry out presidential orders (the "Powell Doctrine"). In an earlier time this would have been regarded as an act of gross insubordination, and General Powell would have been dismissed, as General Douglas MacArthur was dismissed by President Harry Truman in 1951.

Concerning the burden of supporting U.S. military forces on their existing scale, most argue that it is essential in order to deal with a resurgent Russia, or with China, which they see as a potentially hostile state. The United States has no conflict of essential interests with China, merely a rivalry for influence. China has no way to attack the United States other than with strategic nuclear weapons, which it does not possess, may or may not possess in the future, and against which the United States already deploys a massive deterrent force. A conceivable Russian nuclear threat would actually be increased by ending certain existing arms-limitation agreements, as proposed by the

Clinton administration and advocated by the then–Republican opposition, in order to build a technologically implausible but (probably) psychologically and politically irresistible missile defense system. Even though the existing Russian nuclear force is large enough to overwhelm the proposed U.S. limited missile defense system, and a termination of existing agreements would automatically stimulate the modernization and expansion of existing forces there and elsewhere, the seeming promise of invulnerability responds to the nation's essential isolationism.

India and Pakistan have already committed themselves to constructing usable nuclear forces. The NATO intervention in Kosovo, without U.N. authorization and against Russian and Chinese objections, lent weight to the argument that small nations need nuclear forces as a deterrent to great-power intervention (on the assumption that NATO would not have attacked Serbia if Serbia had possessed nuclear weapons). This has added to the unpredictability of international relationships, with ambiguous consequences. It enlarges the rationally incalculable factor in what in the past was a largely calculable relationship of military force and material power. The reason the United States gives nonproliferation a high priority in its foreign policy is that it sees itself directly threatened by proliferation. However, proliferation would actually seem likely to contribute to the stabilization of international relations, since deterrence has functioned among the traditional nuclear powers, and adding "unreliable" players to a nuclear system until now composed of fairly sober governments that have had the time to become "educated" to the dangers of their situation would seem an incentive to even greater prudence than before.

Much is made of threats of attack with weapons of mass destruction by "rogue nations" ("states of concern," as we are now enjoined to call them) or civilian terrorist groups. A federal commission report in October 1999 asserted that the terrorist threat would increase over the next twenty-five years, although it cited little that was specific to demonstrate that this was so. It said that since the United States is unprepared for terrorism, there would be "more pressure on the military to expand its scope into domestic law enforcement, as the line between foreign and domestic threats is blurred."* William Cohen, defense secretary in the Clinton administration, made the astounding forecast that a terrorist nuclear, chemical, or biological attack on the United States is "not only possible, but probable" before 2010. Yet the actual evidence that a major foreign terrorist threat exists tends to be anecdotal and highly, if not irresponsibly, speculative—"scenario-dependent," as military planners say. The domestic terrorist threat in any case is fundamentally a police problem, whatever its sources in foreign relations. The rogue-nation threat is that of an "irrational" one-off attack. If such an attack cannot be deterred by the same measures that deterred Cold War nuclear threats, it is unlikely to be deterred at all. America's bombing of Colonel Muammar Qaddafi's Libya in 1986 did not, as usually claimed, deter terrorism, but according to the assertion of the U.S. government itself, provoked the Libyan government to have a bomb placed aboard Pan American flight 103 two years later, whose explosion over Lockerbie, Scotland, killed 270 persons, most of them Americans.

Also neglected in most discussion is the fact that most international terrorism since 1945 has had its source in five decades of Middle Eastern war or tension. If there were a final settlement of the Palestine-Israel and Israel-Syria conflicts, followed by withdrawal of American bases from Saudi Arabia and the Persian Gulf, normalization of American relations with the Islamic world would undoubtedly follow and the principal terrorist threats could be expected to disappear.

Civilian militarism in the United States consists chiefly in the repeated and uncritical recourse to military measures to deal not only with foreign policy crises but with such civil-

---

*Creation of a new army continental command, responsible for dealing with terrorism within the United States, has already given the military constitutionally unprecedented emergency authority in civil matters.

society issues as terrorism and even the drug traffic (through indirect military intervention in countries, such as Colombia, where drugs are produced). Reports published in late 1999 by the Triangle Institute for Security Studies (made up of faculty members from Duke, North Carolina, and North Carolina State universities) said that "at least since 1816, there has been a very durable pattern in U.S. behavior: the more veterans in the national political elite, the less likely the United States is to initiate the use of force in the international arena." The year 2000 finds Second World War and Korean War veterans gone from American political life and the number of Vietnam veterans in decline. This suggests that in the future the American political class will possess even fewer internalized inhibitions about the use of force than now is the case.

These studies also found that the absence of civilian leaders with military experience has tended to draw military leaders out of their traditional constitutional role as disinterested professional advisers to civilian authority and has helped to turn them into policy advocates and decision-makers. Since civilian leaders with no military experience tend to have a more aggressive view of the utility of military force than do military officers themselves, the latter have come to

> believe that it is their role to *insist* and *advocate* rather than merely *advise* on key elements of decisions concerning the use of force, for instance: setting rules of engagement, developing an exit strategy, and deciding what kinds of military units . . . will be used to accomplish all tasks. . . . [These differences of view] have already caused real friction in policy and decision making and will in the future, and could lead in some instances to unprofessional behavior.

An aspect of this changed balance is that the Pentagon has in recent years established a web of relationships with foreign armies and navies that allows it to conduct what amounts to a parallel foreign policy, not always that authorized by Congress or the State Department (as in maintaining contact with military establishments in Indonesia and Latin America by means of subterfuges, despite congressional resolutions, motivated by concern for human rights issues, that forbade such contacts).

American regular military officers express "great pessimism about the moral health of civilian society." They believe that the country's political leadership "does not share the same values as the American people." As a result, the authors of the report remark that the principle of civilian control of the armed forces has been subjected since the 1960s "to more ongoing strain than at any time in American history." For the first time, the United States has been

> obligated to manage the cultural gap [between civilians and military] whilst the military is large and powerful, yet without an external threat to focus civil-military cooperation. . . . Many of the problems and failures of recent American military interventions originated not in excessive or incompetent civilian meddling but in poor civilian oversight, particularly in failures to insist upon open and candid dialogue with the military, to plan, to ask difficult or unpleasant questions, and to scrutinize military activities so as to connect means with ends.

Another qualified critic, a professor of political science at the U.S. Military Academy at West Point, Don M. Snider, recently wrote (in the Spring 2000 *World Policy Journal*) that "the professionalism of the military has declined since the end of the Gulf War, and markedly so. Whether measured by military-technical (warfighting), ethical, or socio-political standards of professionalism, this decline can be readily seen." This occurs as American foreign policy has become increasingly militarized. Military action seems the policymakers' instrument of choice, even though the essential forces at work in international society today are civilian in nature.

The American military establishment effectively dominates Congress so far as military budgets are concerned, and this dominance is not unwelcome to legislators, since the Pentagon has by now so widely distributed its expenditures that there is hardly a congressional district without a military manufacturer contributing campaign funds or a job-creating military installation comforting the incumbent representative. This is why Congress regularly votes even higher credits than the Pentagon requests, supporting weapons programs and military installations that the Pentagon does not necessarily want.

Military expenditure since the 1940s has also been the principal support of American scientific and industrial research and advanced technological development, providing wide nonmilitary applications. The Pentagon has subsidized high-technology exports and furnishes the United States with an American version of a national industrial policy. None of this could be ended or even sharply reduced without serious domestic economic consequences, automatically generating enormous political opposition.

The end of the Cold War has left the United States with a huge military establishment of unprecedented policy influence, unleavened by an enlisted corps of civilian national servicemen and a cadre of temporarily serving reserve officers—as it had in the past, before the army's post-Vietnam professionalization. One can no longer say what the army's chief of staff, General Fred C. Weyand, said in 1976: "The American army really is a people's army in the sense that it belongs to the American people who take a jealous and proprietary interest in its involvement. . . . In the final analysis the American army is not so much an arm of the Executive Branch as it is an arm of the American people."

American foreign policy since Communism's collapse has sought and found a new rationale in theories of a basic mutation in international society, requiring the development of what President George Bush called a "New World Order." During the Clinton administration this evolved into parallel efforts to establish new, American-led international systems in both the economic and political realms. That administration's program of trade and financial deregulation, the so-called globalization of the world's financial, trading, and manufacturing systems, was directed toward making the world's economy into what, for investment purposes, would be a vastly extended American economy.* Since the Asian economic crash of 1997, the political consequences of globalization have proven less benign than government and academic economists, and the banking and business communities, had predicted.

In American discussions globalization is often presented as the result of a basic system change of autonomous origin. It obviously has been made possible by the revolutionary increase in speed and flexibility of communications that technology has provided, and continues to provide, but it consists essentially of a program for deregulation of the international economy. Such has been the policy of the American government and the international financial institutions over which it has predominant influence, the IMF, World Bank, and OECD.

Any economic policy reflects a certain vision of society as a whole, not only of the economy. It is the product of a dialectical interaction of ideas and interests. The assumptions that underlie the American policy promoting international economic deregulation are recent in origin, and will one day pass into economic history, just as Keynesianism, and before that the orthodoxy of gold, belong to history. The dominant Keynesian economic practices and expectations of Britain and the United States were the product of a particular interpretation of

---

*From the investor's viewpoint, it is better than America's, since the global deregulation that was the principal objective of American international economic policy under the Clinton administration (and undoubtedly will remain that of Clinton's successor) creates a system with fewer obstacles to the free movement of capital than exist in the United States itself. The United States does not have a deregulated economy; its investors and financiers work under strict, constraining rules

economic forces and function, and also expressed certain assumptions about the social obligations of economic actors. Similar assumptions prevailed in postwar Western Europe, where Christian Democratic and Social Democratic movements cooperatively developed what became known as social capitalism, or the "Rhineland model" of capitalism. The Christian and Social Democrats were also mainly responsible for European unification, a model of constructive economic cooperation and liberalized trade.

A different view of economic forces and social responsibilities became increasingly influential during the 1970s, thanks to the Chicago School of monetarist economists and the political writings of Friedrich Hayek and the philosopher Karl Popper. It rejected government intervention into economic matters and placed its confidence in the self-regulating market as the basis for growth and development, attributing to it power to produce social progress as well, identified in terms of wealth. This neoliberal economic doctrine is hostile to the demand that market mechanisms be subordinated to norms of social justice. It holds that the free play of the market, extended internationally by means of deregulation, will have ultimately benign consequences, whatever interim difficulties may appear. A deregulated universal labor marketplace is held to be in society's best interests, whatever incidental injustices it produces, and the workings of unregulated corporate capitalism are held to be constructive in ultimate effect, contributing to the wealth of nations and the eventual enrichment of the individual members of society. All of this ordinarily is put forward as beyond serious challenge. It is now an orthodoxy.

However, it is an orthodoxy that lacks historical depth and whose vision of society is defective. The claim to scientific authority often made on its behalf is unsustainable. There are

---

imposed by the Securities and Exchange Commission, federal and state banking regulators, environmental and labor legislation, et cetera.

ascertainable truths about economic behavior, as about political behavior, but there are no laws in economics (or politics) equivalent to those in physics or chemistry, which allow scientific forecast. Karl Popper himself wrote many years ago, in his famous essay "The Poverty of Historicism," that the growth of human knowledge creates a situation in which "we cannot anticipate today what we shall know only tomorrow." Humans confront a ubiquity of choice. Economics and politics are the study of human experience and human conduct. They are not sciences in the proper meaning of that term.

The conventional argument that deregulation and globalization follow necessarily from technological evolution and organizational innovation fails to acknowledge that deregulation as a program is also the product of an ideology. The objective sources of the globalist orthodoxy must be distinguished from those that are doctrinal, arbitrary, or self-interested. The belief that market forces will automatically enforce the general interest was not the conviction of Western political economists thirty years ago. It originated as the sectarian enthusiasm of a minority of writers and theorists in Britain and the United States, and derives more from their political hostility to so-called big government than from economic analysis as such.

Its principal intellectual progenitor was Friedrich Hayek, whose arguments concerning free markets included the contention that government regulation in the economic sphere is connected in a fundamental way to political tyranny: that it is, as in the title of his best-known book, "the road to serfdom." This conviction was rooted in a specific Austrian political experience and in Hayek's hatred of the totalitarian politics that emerged in Central Europe and the Soviet Union during the 1920s and 1930s.

While the centrally directed economy was integrally connected to political tyranny in Soviet Russia and the other Communist states, no such connection existed in the Scandinavian social democracies of the same period, or in the New Deal of

Franklin Roosevelt, or, later, in the centralized and planned economic structure of postwar and Gaullist France, or in the highly regulated social market capitalism of West Germany.

Hayek's arguments had a particular resonance in the decaying British welfare state that Margaret Thatcher took over in 1979, at a moment when the Keynesian model for international finance was also foundering. Inflation had accelerated under the impact of American economic policy during the Vietnam War and the United States' abandonment of the Bretton Woods system and fixed currency rates. Hayek's arguments against the existing Keynesian consensus found a natural response in business circles in Britain and the United States, particularly in the financial community, and in Britain they inspired the political as well as economic policies of the Thatcher government and its successors. In the United States, with its long native tradition of hostility to big government, these arguments and precedents from Britain provided a respectable rationale for the business-inspired policies of the Reagan, Bush, and Clinton administrations. Under the last-named, the New York financial community assumed a crucial role, influencing the manner and speed with which the United States imposed globalist practices on its trading partners.

Thus globalization, as it occurred, was deliberately produced as a matter of policy by a United States government acting in good faith, in what it considered to be not only the national interest but, by agreeable coincidence, the interest of influential political constituencies as well.*

It was a program—an experiment, even—inspired by a set of beliefs, or, to be more accurate, by an ideology, that was

---

*In February 1999, *The New York Times* published a remarkable series of articles clarifying the Clinton administration's conversion to globalism. It reported the process by which a program for deregulating the international economy was proposed to the Clinton administration (indeed, to Clinton himself while he was still governor of Arkansas) by leading figures in the New York financial community.

political in ultimate origin, and in crucial respects utopian. John Gray, in his book *False Dawn* (London, 1998; New York, 2000), describes the globalization project as the legitimate successor to Marxism, a new expression of that universalizing Western utopian tradition which began in the Enlightenment, and an instance of Western hubris—"the Enlightenment's project of universal civilization in what is likely to be its final form . . . [a] Utopia that can never be realized . . . [and whose] pursuit has already produced social dislocation and economic and political instability on a large scale." Untrammeled secular optimism underlies this utopianism, which puts its values into conflict with those of an integral humanism that insists that the

---

Clinton, at the time largely innocent of economic sophistication, was convinced by these arguments, and when he came to power he made aggressive pursuit of global trade deregulation a major theme of his administration. The political and economic power of the United States was mobilized to promote radical change in the world financial system.

The policy largely succeeded, with consequences yet to be fully felt. Goods and commodities were replaced as the principal components of international trade by stocks, bonds, and currencies. That is to say, the global financial market replaced the global economy. The total worth of the financial derivatives—leveraged financial instruments—traded in 1997 alone was twelve times the worth of the entire world economy.

The *Times*'s account says, "Although the Clinton administration always talked about financial liberalization as the best thing for other countries, it is also clear that it pushed for free capital flows in part because this is what its supporters in the banking industry wanted." When the Asian economic crisis arrived in late 1997, the Western investors who had profited from investment in Asian markets worsened the crisis by speculating against newly weakened currencies, and the U.S. government used its own resources and those of the IMF to rescue them and (as is now generally acknowledged) American and European banks. The countries that were the victims of the crisis were at the same time urged by Washington and the international lenders to adopt measures of austerity that imposed severe economic and social costs on their populations—also a policy that now is widely admitted to have been mistaken. The disrupted Seattle World Trade Organization meeting in December 1999 may be said to have closed the first phase of globalization. The International Monetary Fund, the World Bank, and other international economic institutions have since undertaken reform of the globalization project so as to reduce its exploitative and socially abusive elements.

well-being of the human person is the proper criterion by which economic as well as political policy is to be judged, and opposes programs that do harm in the short run but are justified, according to theory, by the argument that good will result in the long run.

Justice deals with the relationships of autonomous persons with legitimate claims upon other individuals and/or upon society, and with rights to be respected. The various utopianisms of the twentieth century characteristically have rested on faith in human progress and confidence that the growth of knowledge, and technological and scientific enrichment, can provide the ultimately perfected society. Marxism, despite its dialectical materialism, preserved a vestige of classical thought in describing its ideal society in terms of justice rather than wealth. The new utopianism, by measuring itself and justifying what it does solely in terms of wealth production, in this respect represents a retrogression.

A different manifestation of contemporary secular optimism is the argument that the modern nation-state, which replaced the feudal monarchies and "universal empires" of earlier times, is now on its way to replacement. This idea is widely held in academic political science circles, where a pleasing evolution is seen toward a progressive internationalization of political authority on the one hand and strengthened regionalism on the other. The progress of the European Union encourages many to find in it a precedent that in the new century may encourage democratic consolidation in a larger international system, or set of systems. The nation-state in modern times, however, has demonstrated greater competence than any other political agency in representing and defending the interests of a defined community, a people. It seems more prudent to say that what has happened in Europe was the outcome of a singular and profound trauma, the European civil war of 1914–45, and that the eventual outcome of European unification is most likely to be a highly sophisticated and powerful coalition of like-minded states that remain fundamentally sovereign. Even this limited model of union will be difficult to emulate in regions that lack the historical and cultural unity of Christian Europe.

The American government, however, has envisaged a larger consolidation of the democracies, an idea that presumes that the success of the democracies and the economic integration produced by globalism have brought a qualitative or structural change to international political society—a positive mutation in humanity's general political evolution, from which there can be no permanent retreat. The argument made is that the technology that produces a globalized economy breaks down national and cultural isolation and radiates liberal democratic values throughout the world, tending to make national frontiers obsolete. Timothy Garton Ash has written that the Yugoslav wars of the 1990s produced an informal, spontaneous, and eventually very influential coalition of people with liberal values inside the warring ethnic groups themselves, allied with sympathizers in the rest of Europe, North America, and elsewhere to defend those values in the former Yugoslavia. He cites the Tiananmen Square liberty demonstration in China in April 1989 as another spontaneous reaction to internationally communicated ideas and values. This is presented as a qualitatively new development in the relations of peoples and nations, a new internationalism.

While this increase in the influence of liberal and democratic values is a welcome development, I would argue that it nonetheless is a provisional development that needs to be defended because it is reversible. The claim that democracy's triumph is permanent generalizes from the experience of less than a half-century, and forecasts the future by simple projection of a twenty-year trend that began with Mikhail Gorbachev's inaugural attempts to reform the Soviet system from within, which proved revolutionary in effect. Democracy in Russia itself may already have been arrested, since the presidential election of March 2000 merely ratified what had been a form of coup d'état three months earlier, carried out by the entourage of former president Boris Yeltsin.

The claim ignores the evidence of localized wars and traumatic political events in the very recent past, as well as the likelihood, indeed the certainty, that more will occur in the near future (unless history has indeed come to an end). Skepticism is imposed by the entire historical record. The triumph of republicanism in Rome was followed by empire and decadence, and an age of so-called barbarian rule. The history of China, the Chinese themselves say, is cyclical, not progressive. Possibly the unprecedented nature and influence of electronic communications in promulgating the values of democracy and peace in today's world have changed all that, but I doubt it. I remain a historical pessimist, a believer in original sin, with a view of history as a chronicle of tragedies—although, in that, I see a cause for optimism about humanity, whom tragedy ennobles.

Democratic values remain vigorously contested in a large part of what is purported to be a new world order. They enjoy their present eminence in the developed nations (which fifty years ago were warring with one another over just those values) to the extraordinary evils of recent industrial wars and genocide. The new humanitarian and democratic consciousness owes its existence to Hitler and two world wars. Only a naïve historicism or a certain cultural parochialism allows one to believe that democracy has "won" the competition of historical existence. The technology of globalized communications and markets could easily be mobilized in the service of some new ideology that was anything but liberal. It could be elitist, eugenicist; a technocratic despotism, a repressive and censorious regime of what has become known as "political correctness"; it could practice a hegemonic internationalism, a manipulative neocolonialism, or a simple demagogic exploitation of racism or populism for nationalistic ends. There are sinister forces that are confined or dormant now, but modern means of global communication are as adaptable to the manipulation of ignoble emotions or the propagation of hatred as to the promotion of enlightenment—as the Balkan wars of the 1990s demonstrated.

It is also a conceptual error to identify democracy, an affair of elections and popular will, with the just or liberal society. Liberal society, as it has evolved historically, checks the abuse of power and preserves individual liberty through law, a guarantee of rights, and representative constitutional government. The just society is one in which, as Aristotle argued, individuals are rendered their "due," which is to say what is theirs by right, and this presumes they possess an inalienable "due" or right. This principle is prior to democracy, which merely concerns gratifying the opinions of people. Mass opinion is probably more often wrong than right according to the ethical or philosophical standards most would independently apply: thus the conviction widely held in the past that democracy was (or is) potential tyranny. Aristotle talks about that version of democracy in which the people collectively become "an autocrat, a single composite autocrat, with many playing sovereign—not, of course, individually, but collectively. . . . A democracy of this kind, having all the characteristics of an autocrat and being uncontrolled by law, seeks to exercise autocratic powers. It grows despotic; flatterers are esteemed; and the democracy itself becomes analogous to the tyrannical form of one-man government." This is when there is rule of the people rather than the rule of law.

The important distinction is between democratic government and constitutional government. There were constitutional governments and the rule of law before there were modern democracies. Britain did not have universal suffrage until after the Second World War, but it had disinterested justice, private property, separation of powers, and free speech in the eighteenth century, and it had put a limit on monarchical power as early as 1215 (in the Magna Carta). The Western political tradition has more to do with the emergence of law, constitutions, property rights, and even international law than with universal suffrage. The tragedy of Russia and the other states of the former Soviet Union since 1990 is due precisely to the failure of their own leaders, and some of their most influential Western advisers, to understand the importance of this distinction and its implications.

Democracy empowers public opinion, which in principle is an excellent thing. In practice, public opinion is usually uninformed, biased, emotional, and open to demagogic exploitation. Genocide in Rwanda was democratic: the Hutu majority committed and approved it. Lynchings are democratic, in that impersonal mobs willingly commit them. The person to be lynched can be saved only by the application of legal order, by the defense of a person's right to be heard and to have the facts of the alleged crime impartially ascertained, with punishment applied, if punishment is appropriate, in a legal and disinterested manner.

There are illiberal democracies, societies despotically or unjustly ruled by individuals or parties elected or ratified in free elections. Serbia has been the most prominent recent example, a nation responsible for aggression and acts of genocide in the course of the wars of Yugoslav succession that it deliberately provoked. Popularly elected governments in Singapore and Malaysia make a principled defense of authoritarian practices as the expression of "Asian values." There are, of course, many other countries where governments exercise unchecked power but hold elections that are not free.

The question for the future is that of constitutionalism and the rule of law. One can promote democracy without promoting justice, as the Western democracies have tended to do in their relations with the former Communist bloc countries. Elections and privatization of state property were exported to Russia after the collapse of the U.S.S.R., but not the institutions of law and civil society.

The conceptual error of confusing democracy with the rule of law has been encouraged by the very American assumption that the former is the natural mode of human government, thought to spring up automatically when artificial obstacles to it are removed and elections are held. This is another case of the romantic fallacy, applied to politics. Michel Camdessus, former director of the International Monetary Fund, told the Paris newspaper *Liberation* in August 1999, "We did not see that dismantling Communism meant the dismantling of the state." But anyone familiar with the Soviet political system before 1990 could have told him that. It is why Gorbachev set out to reform the Communist Party, not the Soviet state. Camdessus's error was equivalent to that of Alan Greenspan, chairman of the Federal Reserve, who has said that he believed that Communism's collapse in Russia would "automatically establish a free market entrepreneurial system."

The illusion that it is the natural condition of humanity to be governed by the will of the majority as expressed in free elections, and to possess a market economy unfettered by state regulation, lies behind the notion that history is in its culminating stage (even if it has not ended). It is at the root of much American thinking about the future and about America's role as avatar of democracy and capitalism. It rationalizes American messianism.

The idea that democracy and peace are integrally linked is also an illusion. Democracies have in the past been reluctant to go to war, but they have repeatedly demonstrated a taste for total war once they are committed. The First World War was identified by Woodrow Wilson as the war to end war, a goal of such moral absolutism as to abolish the possibility of compromise. The democracies' demand for the unconditional surrender of their enemies in the Second World War was described by the British military historian Basil Liddell Hart as combining "an *unlimited aim* with an *unlimited method* . . . [which] produced a deepening danger to the relatively shallow foundations of civilized life." In 1954 an American naval officer, Ralph E. Williams, wrote of the contrast between the limited war waged in Korea and the Second World War, when "moral hysteria betrayed us into a witless, paranoic insistence that 80 million Germans and 70 million Japanese were our mortal enemies and must be destroyed wherever they may be found and at whatever cost." Something of this spirit still persisted in some sectors of opinion, particularly American military ones, during the Cold War, with respect to the use of nuclear weapons. The great Italian historian Guglielmo Ferrero wrote in 1930, "Restrictive warfare belongs to a class of hothouse plants which can only thrive in an aristocratic and qualitative civilization. We are no longer capable of it."

One might argue that the Western powers' recent interventions in the Balkans have demonstrated the opposite. However, the NATO powers' concern to avoid "collateral" civilian casualties on the enemy side as well as Allied military losses followed from the fact that no threat existed to the Western nations or their populations, so that the issues of conflict were remote and theoretical for the NATO public. Neither fear, nor vengeance, nor ideology was engaged. On the other hand, despite the lack of any direct threat to American national or material interests, Washington policymakers felt impelled to describe the Vietnam War as a crucial episode in an ideological conflict of world-historical importance, threatening the survival of democracy. Torture by American forces occurred, there was systematic assassination of civilians during the so-called Phoenix program, agriculture and forests were destroyed with chemicals, and heavier bombing was conducted than during the Second World War. It was total war, which stopped short only at nuclear weapons. Yet, for those not ideologically engaged at the time, it was not hard to foresee that these measures would fail and that the war would be lost by the United States—with little effect upon democracy's fortunes in the larger world.

An alliance has emerged in Washington since the Cold War's end between avowedly "Wilsonian" liberals, anxious to extend

American influence and federate the democracies, with tougher-minded unilateralist neoconservative believers in U.S. power-projection, who call for American world leadership, aggressively imposed, for world society's own good.

The United States enjoys a hegemonic position in these first years of the new century, both in terms of its economic weight and dynamism and of its formal military power. The technological potentialities of the latter extend to something resembling a doomsday extermination of civilization, yet the exercise of American military power has repeatedly proven to be incompetently conceptualized and directed, and in significant respects irrelevant to the characteristic military challenges of the present day.° Cases in point have been not only the Vietnam War, the maladroit Central American and Caribbean interventions, and the Somalia fiasco, but the interventions in the former Yugoslavia. The display of technologically sophisticated power in Serbia and Kosovo in 1999, when NATO fought a war which proved not to be the war Serbia was fighting, and failed to prevent the ethnic purge of Kosovo simultaneously being carried out, was not a success, and Russian diplomatic intervention was necessary to produce an outcome that left NATO's reputation intact. The Kosovo campaign, well-meant but without coherent political objective or geopolitical vision, reliant on technological power and unwilling to pay a serious human price for its ambitions, offered a true picture of actual American capabilities, which are scarcely those of a determined hegemon.†

The hegemonic spirit nonetheless has underlain the activism and unilateralism evident in much recent American policy,

---

°A paradigm was the episode in 1998 when the response to two terrorist bombings of American embassies in Africa was to dispatch Tomahawk cruise missiles to blow up a modest chemicals factory in Khartoum—a wrong address, as it turned out—and a camp in Afghanistan once used by the CIA.

†One of France's former commanders in Bosnia, General Philippe Morillon, has asked, "How can you have soldiers who are ready to kill, who are not ready to die?"

despite the criticism made of it by some commentators and scholars. It is behind Congress's aggressively unilateralist approach to foreign relations, which also expresses an older American isolationist impulse, unilateralism and isolationism being two expressions of the same parochial sensibility.

Globalization found its political counterpart in the Clinton administration's program to enlarge NATO's membership and extend its operations "out of area" (Central Europe), first to the Balkans and eventually beyond Europe. This essentially unilateralist initiative expressed a conception of extended American influence that has become the principal theme in post–Cold War policy thinking. Some envisage NATO's eventual extension into the former Soviet states, possibly including Russia itself, and on to Central Asia, toward the frontiers of another American-led Pacific strategic system and military alliance. Zbigniew Brzezinski suggested such a scheme in his book *The Grand Chessboard* (1997). Brzezinski also said, however, that this should be a short-term stabilization measure, not a long-term program, and that when multilateral structures were put in place the United States should reduce its commitments and presence—a recommendation which underestimates the inherent expansionism of bureaucracies and the emotional power of the idea of an American political counterpart to economic globalization.

Others in the policy community see no such need for limits and regard the new century as an opportunity for an international reenactment of eighteenth-century America's confederation of the thirteen original colonies into what became the "united states" of America. They would like the industrial democracies—the developed world, or a major part of it—to form a new democratic federal union of which the United States would be the inspiration and the leader.* This

---

*There has also been a call for confederation of the United States with Britain, Canada, Mexico (because of its membership in NAFTA), and possibly Australia

ambition is not always explicitly expressed, but it lies behind Madeleine Albright's characterization of the United States as the "indispensable nation" that, because it "stands taller," scans horizons others cannot see.

An early statement of what its advocates call the new Wilsonianism and others call the case for hegemony was made by William Kristol and Robert Kagan in 1996, in a *Foreign Affairs* article; they followed this with a book and other articles, and recapitulated their case in the Spring 2000 issue of the Washington quarterly *The National Interest*:

> Today's international system is built not around a balance of power but around American hegemony. The international financial institutions were fashioned by Americans and serve American interests. The international security structures are chiefly a collection of American-led alliances. . . . Since today's relatively benevolent international circumstances are the product of our hegemonic influence, any lessening of that influence will allow others to play a larger part in shaping the world to suit *their* needs. States such as China and Russia, if given the chance, would configure the international system quite differently. . . . American hegemony, then, must be actively maintained, just as it was actively obtained. . . . The United States does not pursue a narrow, selfish definition of its national interest, but generally finds its interests in a benevolent international order. In other words, it is precisely because the United States infuses its foreign policy with an unusually high degree of

---

and New Zealand. This has come mainly from conservative circles in Britain, prompted by the Canadian press lord Conrad Black's London publications, with enthusiastic support from Margaret Thatcher and certain more conservative figures in the U.S. Senate. However, unlike other visions of American expansion, it is defensive and distinctly unmessianic in character and isolationist in spirit, inspired mainly by British hostility toward the European Union and nostalgia for the wartime Atlantic alliance. *The Guardian*'s Hugo Young describes it as "the last blast of a perverted Anglo-Americanism which has become a parody of itself."

morality that other nations feel they have less to fear from its otherwise daunting power.

Another recent work, H. W. Brands's significantly titled *What America Owes the World* (1999), suggests that while American "exemplarists" think the country should try to serve as an example of a humane and just society, "vindicators" believe that America's "peculiar obligation" to better humanity's lot may require intervention and coercion. "Human nature is too recalcitrant for mere example to have much lasting effect, and . . . military might, even if it doesn't necessarily make right, certainly can restrain wrong." An analyst at the American Enterprise Institute in Washington, Joshua Muravchik, argues that other nations "know that they have little to fear or distrust from a righteous [America]." He says in his book *The Imperative of American Leadership* (1996) that "aside perhaps from the French, the only people averse to American leadership are the Americans."*

Opposed to this is the view of what Brands calls the "exem-

---

*A striking aspect of the recent debate has been its intellectual poverty. This is an aspect of a larger problem. While the New Deal, the Second World War, and the international crisis produced by the confrontation with Stalinist Russia in the 1940s drew American elites into government service and kept them there, Vietnam was their self-imposed defeat (imposed because of their own generational experience and failure of historical imagination; they thought they were preventing "another Munich"). Chastened, or embittered, they returned to their Wall Street law offices, universities, and foundations. There is a great deal to be said in criticism of them, but they were intellectually serious and understood the world beyond the United States. American foreign policy has since been in the hands of provincial lawyers (Hollywood lawyers, trade lawyers, corporation lawyers) and professors of political science, a discipline that since the 1950s has been interested more in methodology than in foreign societies. The judgment made by David Rieff about a recent book extolling globalization unfortunately can be applied to the outlook of too many Americans professionally concerned with the country's foreign relations: "purportedly hard-headed and optimistic, can-do and open-minded, it is, however unconsciously, callous, ignorant, complacent, nationalistic and contemptuous of other cultures and other philosophical traditions."

plarists," whose most eminent member is undoubtedly the diplomat and historian George Kennan, who observed in 1999, in an interview in *The New York Review of Books,* that "this planet is never going to be ruled from any single political center, whatever its military power." He added that for Americans "to see ourselves as the center of political enlightenment and as teachers to a great part of the rest of the world [is] unthought-through, vainglorious, and undesirable."

One may add that a bid for hegemony would also eventually fail because its objective, however "benevolent," is unacceptable to other nations and is seen as a threat. European nations are already actively resentful of American pressure to block them from establishing a European defense "identity" able to assert some independence of NATO. A European foreign minister remarked in the fall of 1999 that he had found that all his European Union colleagues regarded their most serious current problem in foreign relations as that of dealing with the United States. The president of the Defense Commission of the French National Assembly, Paul Quilès, wrote in the Paris newspaper *Le Monde* in April 2000 about the disquiet felt in the Assembly, and in the French policy community, at the views expressed by Senator Jesse Helms, chairman of the U.S. Senate Foreign Relations Committee, during his encounters with Security Council members earlier in the year. The senator had "maintained that states, above all the United States, which are democratic, and act in the cause of liberty, possess unlimited authority, subject to no external control, to carry out military interventions." Quilès continued:

> If we allow these attitudes to follow their course, the risk is great that the United States, in searching to impose its will, will provoke greater and greater defiance from countries such as Russia and China, and still others. American refusal of collective security; recourse to solutions of force by an increasing number of states; intensification and generalization of conflict

(think of Grozny, first European city to be razed since 1945)—
doesn't this recall something from the past? Are we going to
relive the drama of the powerlessness of the League of Nations?

Senator Helms's views are usually unrepresentative of general
American opinion, but one must say that in this case they are
not. They express a version of the Wilsonian legacy, which as a
whole has been less glorious, more complex, and has proven to
be considerably less successful than Washington's contemporary theorists seem to understand.

William McKinley was the reluctant begetter of American
global engagement when, under pressure from the press and
popular opinion, he made the explosion (undoubtedly acciden-
tal) of the battleship *Maine* the occasion to conquer Cuba.
Then, because it seemed logical, he took Spanish Puerto Rico,
Wake Island, and the Philippines—and for good measure
Hawaii, which had nothing to do with Spain. That romantic
nationalist Theodore Roosevelt, then assistant secretary of the
navy, was the cabinet officer who most enthusiastically promoted the war. Roosevelt believed in the seapower theories of
Alfred Thayer Mahan, who held that colonies were essential to
the commercial power of a modern nation, but he also simply
liked war, which he thought brought out the best in a nation.
Roosevelt would have preferred a war with Germany, but, as
he wrote to a friend, "I am not particular, and I'd even take
Spain if nothing better is offered." He was an expansionist and
imperialist. He did not argue that the United States had some
peculiar benediction to confer upon mankind. Imperialism was
the work of civilizing the benighted races of the world, the
white man's burden, incumbent on all the advanced nations,
and the United States, he held, should not leave the British and
French alone in this good work but should take up its share.
That was the moral and "manly" thing to do.

Woodrow Wilson began as a splendid isolationist, apologizing to Colombia for the United States' having stolen Panama

(to build the canal), appointing the pacifist William Jennings Bryan his secretary of state, and naming political hacks to ambassadorships. He was not a man for the strenuous life. He ate raw eggs and oatmeal for breakfast and took an automobile ride every afternoon.

The successes of his first term were creation of the Federal Reserve System, the Federal Trade Commission, antitrust legislation with tariff reform to reduce the power of the "trusts," and passage of the Sixteenth Amendment, authorizing the income tax. He was a great domestic reformer. His initial foreign policy concern was to cope with the consequences of revolution in Mexico. He occupied Veracruz after an affront to American sailors and sent a punitive expedition under General John J. "Black Jack" Pershing to chase the Mexican revolutionary "Pancho" Villa back into Mexico after an intrusion into the United States. He regarded the outbreak of the First World War as a fit of madness among the Europeans. He sent his confidant and adviser, Colonel (a courtesy title, bestowed by the state of Texas) Edward House, to search for a compromise settlement, although House, strongly pro-Allies but anticipating a German victory, worked on a plan that Germany would be expected to reject, so as to provoke American intervention.

Wilson at the same time was saying, "There is such a thing as a man too proud to fight. There is such a thing as a nation being so right that it does not need to convince others by force that it is right." The latter proved to be untrue. In January 1917 he appealed for a "peace without victory," but after extension of the German submarine campaign, he went to war in April. He did so, he said, in order to fight a war to end wars, to make the world safe for democracy, and to end "power politics," after which the United States would lead the way into a new international order in which war would be abolished.

When victory arrived, and with it the opportunity to realize his vision, he said that America's role in the war had come about by divine agency: "It was of this that we dreamed at our birth. America shall in truth show the way." He was confirmed in his faith by the response of the exhausted Europeans to his peace proposals. When he arrived in Paris to take part in the Versailles negotiations, the crowds greeted him with what one observer called "inhuman . . . superhuman" cheers.

He said that the world turned "to America for those moral inspirations which lie at the base of all freedom . . . that . . . all shall know that she puts human rights above all other rights, and that her flag is the flag not only of America, but of humanity." He thanked God that Americans were not like other men. This conviction of national righteousness was unfortunately linked to an equivalent belief by Wilson in the correctness of his personal judgments, as the distinguished novelist Louis Auchincloss has noted in a recent (eponymously titled) biography. He "could hardly conceive, much less admit, that he could be wrong in judging matters that he deemed within his peculiar sphere of expertise: the education of young men, the upholding of moral values, and [eventually] . . . the establishment of world peace. Thus Wilson, with God and his angels presumably ranked behind him, tended to regard opposition as malicious betrayal."

The myth of Wilson, taught in American schools for eighty years, holds that he was indeed betrayed by a reactionary Senate which refused to ratify the treaty that would have made America a member of the League of Nations, and by doing so made itself responsible for that organization's failure and for the outbreak of a second world war.

This is largely untrue. The issue was Article 10 of the Covenant of the League, which would have mandated the United States (and the League's other members) to take part in any military action against aggression voted by the member nations. The Senate balked (as it would balk today at an equivalent UN treaty clause, and as the Pentagon and the Clinton administration did balk in 1998 when the United States refused to sign the treaty meant to create a permanent war crimes tribunal, to whose jurisdiction American troops would have been subjected).

However, there was a compromise available in 1919, proposed by former secretary of state Elihu Root and drafted by Senator Henry Cabot Lodge, that the Senate attach a "reservation" to its ratification which would say that as the Congress possessed the sole constitutional power to declare war or authorize the employment of military force, the United States would not act under Article 10 without the authority of an act or joint resolution of Congress.

Wilson refused this compromise, Auchincloss says, because this reservation "would wreck the whole concept of world government." But world government (on an American model) was Wilson's private vision. One may be sure that Lloyd George, Georges Clemenceau, Vittorio Orlando, and the other Allied war leaders had no such ambition.

It is hard to explain why Wilson's fundamentally sentimental, megalomaniacal, and unhistorical vision of world democracy organized on the American example and led by the United States should continue today to set the general course of American foreign policy, under both Democrats and Republicans, and inspire enthusiasm for American global hegemony among policymakers and analysts (a hegemony that would bear little resemblance to the high-minded assemblage of nations Wilson imagined; his was the Tennysonian vision, "the Parliament of man, the Federation of the world").

The disastrous consequences of Wilsonian sentimentality during the past eighty years seem to have made no trace on the minds of his modern followers. His naïveté about universal national self-determination contributed to creating conditions in Central and Eastern Europe that in the 1930s and 1940s invited Hitlerian intervention. His influence on Franklin Roosevelt led the latter to oppose Winston Churchill's efforts to exercise "power politics" in Central Europe so as to secure it from postwar Soviet control. It was responsible for Roosevelt's belief that a new League, the United Nations, could resolve postwar geopolitical problems. Even U.S. policy in the Vietnam War was a confused amalgam of anti-Communism and Wilsonian sentimentality: Lyndon Johnson justified his foreign policy as meant only to give others what they "want for themselves—liberty, justice, dignity, a better life for all."

Few in Washington, since Wilson's time, have seemed interested in speaking softly while carrying the big stick, as the first Roosevelt recommended. Both Democratic and Republican presidential candidates in 2000 promised to overthrow the regimes of "rogue states," rally laggard allies, and promulgate American-style democracy under American supervision everywhere within America's reach. That public opinion accompanies them in these extravagant ambitions may be doubted, but the rhetoric is automatic. They know no other. The country is still in the intellectual thrall of the megalomaniacal and self-righteous clergyman-president who gave to the American nation the blasphemous conviction that it, like he himself, had been created by God "to show the way to the nations of the world how they shall walk in the paths of liberty."

The projections conventionally made with respect to the future are usually for more of the same, or, if not that, for more or less of a repetition of something well-known from the recent past (another Crash, another depression, another Hitler, another Munich, another Vietnam). Neither assumption is really very useful, since the sole certainty about the future is that it is, strictly speaking, unforeseeable.

The useful statements that can be made about the future are the general ones: that hegemonic power invites opposition; that political entities seek to aggrandize their power and wealth; that a vacuum of power will be filled; that evil exists in history and reason is not its master—and that a constant in history is the unforeseen rupture that changes everything, as did the First World War.

The United States will undoubtedly remain the most powerful and influential state and social system in international society during the early years of the new millennium. It is the "sole superpower," and its economic system will undoubtedly continue to be the most visible and influential economic and commercial model. The system of global bases and integrated alliances which it built up during the 1950s and 1960s in response to the real threats of the Cold War was for that reason accepted by those associated with it as legitimate, indeed desirable. When the threat was removed by the collapse of the Soviet Union, and by the evolution of Communist China into a rationally authoritarian state, observing more or less normal rules of international relations, this policy of the United States was deprived of what before had been its compelling rationale, and therefore, potentially, of its legitimacy.

Under the influence of institutional and conceptual momentum, these systems of alliances and engagements were nonetheless maintained and extended, even though they had lost their essential justification, with the practical effect that maintaining the apparatus of the outmoded policy became the policy itself. The allies, who previously had been its beneficiaries, began to perceive it as a burden, an interference in their affairs.

This is not, of course, true for the former Warsaw Pact countries, who had never been American allies and were eager to have an American guarantee extended to them, even though Russia had conceded their independence. The history of their proximity to the Russian great power made a new NATO link to the United States a precious one. But in the old alliances, in Western Europe and the Far East, the American presence came increasingly to be seen as a potential infringement of their sovereignty, insisted upon by the United States with less and less evident reason.

Americans were themselves confused as to whether this costly and expanding global engagement was really necessary. New theories of external threat to the United States thus were developed: wars of civilization, generalized Islamic assault on the West, global terrorism, resurgent Chinese or Russian imperialism, international crime, the drug trade. The wretched "rogue nations" were promoted to the front rank of those threatening the U.S. None of this possessed much convincing intellectual or political warrant. The postulated threats were fragile structures of speculation and worst-case scenarios, and some of them—the rogue missile threat and the drug danger in Colombia, supposedly requiring indirect military intervention— were influenced by the commercial interests of military manu- facturers. All reflected the natural survival instincts of the Cold War bureaucracies of government and of the latter's policy aux- iliaries in the civilian community, whose raison d'être had been thrown into question.

The European allies, berated in the past for not doing enough to defend themselves, found themselves criticized when they launched a project for their common defense, now accused of undermining NATO and, indirectly, American influ- ence and privileges in Europe. The Europeans' decision, nor- mal enough, to rationalize and develop their own arms industry rather than buy from America was criticized as creating a "Fortress Europe."

The American government reacted with alarm when an ambiguous new relationship began between North and South Korea which implied the possibility of withdrawal of the Amer- ican army stationed in South Korea. If it were removed, the rationale for American bases and facilities in Japan, notably at Okinawa, would be weakened. Their necessity is taken for granted even though the United States has friendly relations with China, accords it normal trading relations, and has spoken of its strategic relationship with that country as a "partnership." The United States has an obligation to Taiwan, but Taiwan is not essentially a military problem but a political one. America's primary interests in Asia are commercial and economic. Japan, the true (or eventual, when present political inhibitions are lifted) great power of the region, meanwhile spends $40 billion annually to have the most advanced, and one of the largest, military establishments in Asia—a military expenditure more than three times that of China.

Washington is unwilling or is perhaps incapable of reassessing its actual strategic interests in Asia with serious attention to the costs of existing policy. The Asian deployment is defended because it exists, but some in Asia now ask whether it is not an instrument of intimidation. Here, as in Europe, the American position risks becoming transformed from that of welcome defender into burdensome intruder. Washington does not understand that its power risks becoming a destabilizing force. The American position and the prevailing system will certainly both be challenged in the future. The nature and identity of a successful challenge is unforeseeable today, but it is in the nature of a dominant or quasi-hegemonic system to generate challenge, and its own eventual replacement.

That is a basic political reality. Domination can endure for long periods when it is that of an advanced civilization over backward ones (as with Rome). The challenge to the American position will come from societies that are themselves equally advanced—and as a consequence of the entropy of the hegemon itself, its natural tendency toward degradation of its energies: a general phenomenon.

The United States is nearly always taken by foreigners to be invulnerable to the kinds of upheaval that European countries have experienced since the French Revolution, culminating in the great crisis of European liberal civilization that began with the outbreak of world war in 1914. But why should it be invulnerable? A stable and seemingly fulfilled European society, enjoying the most prosperous economy in the contemporary world, fell overnight into a series of sanguinary calamities.

In 1900 the British Empire was "the sole superpower." It had rivals in Europe, as the United States today has one rival in the European Union, another in Russia, and still others in Asia. However, the conventional belief a century ago was that which Norman Angell was to express in a globally best-selling book in 1910, *The Great Illusion*, which held that the common interests of the great powers, and above all their economies, were so closely interlinked and interdependent that war no longer made sense. The existence of empires and the gold standard had made the world's economies and international finance more "globalized" than they are today. The Polish banker Ivan Bloch had made the same argument in 1898 but drew the opposite conclusion: *The Future of War*, was an unhappily prophetic study that foresaw catastrophe.

The destructive forces that were to dominate most of the twentieth century were without influence in 1900, or did not yet exist. Marxism as a political movement was a marginal affair. Lenin was thirty years old, and in 1900 was concluding a period of political internment in Siberia and was about to go into exile. Hitler was eleven years old. Benito Mussolini was seventeen, a budding pacifist and socialist. Fascism and Nazism did not exist. They were unimagined, perhaps unimaginable.

The British, French, Portuguese, Belgian, and Netherlands empires dominated Asia and Africa. The United States was in the process of putting together its own empire from the Spanish possessions it had seized in the Caribbean and the Far East. The Hapsburg system was troubled by nationalism in the Balkans, and the Ottoman Empire was in decline, but all that seemed manageable.

The century began in circumstances of apparent security

more reassuring than those of today. No one in 1900 could have imagined the events which only fourteen years later were to destroy the existing international system, and deal a blow to Western civilization whose effects still are felt, opening the way to the immense and original totalitarian political phenomenon which, after the Russian Revolution in 1918 and Hitler's coming to power in 1932, dominated world affairs for most of the rest of the century.

Responsible political and economic leaders and scholars in 1900 would undoubtedly have described the twentieth-century prospect in terms of continuing imperial rivalries within a Europe-dominated world, lasting paternalistic tutelage by Europeans of their colonies, solid constitutional government in Western Europe, steadily growing prosperity, increasing scientific knowledge turned to human benefit, et cetera. All would have been wrong.

The Swedish writer Goran Rosenberg—writing in the international journal *Lettre Internationale* and referring to the great trilogy by the Austrian writer Hermann Broch, *The Sleepwalkers* (1932)—has recently asked whether Americans and Europeans today might recognize themselves in Broch's description of pre-1918 European society in crisis, "where the value system of 'business is business' is overpowering all other values? Or where genuine human moral problems and choices have been transformed into issues of technical-scientific competence? Where human judgement has been replaced by *Sachlichkeit* ['objectivity']? Where everybody can blame the system, but few can take responsibility?"

At every stage in political history there ordinarily is one system that elites accept as the most advanced, the one toward which others are evolving and which they should emulate. Until 1914 it was the liberal representative republic or constitutional monarchy, notwithstanding criticisms made by utopian and Marxist socialists, and assaults made by a vanguard of literary, philosophical, and religious critics upon its bourgeois complacency and materialism.

After the great crisis of 1914–18—the most important event of the twentieth century—democracy did not reemerge as a compelling model of government until the Second World War and the Cold War had revealed the nihilism of the alternatives. Given a populist cast by the ascendance of the United States, Western democracy then presented itself to the world as the most authentic and humane form of representative government history has known. It entered the twenty-first century, the new millennium, with that reputation intact, but again, as before 1914, under attack for its spiritual sterility.

I concluded this book a decade ago by writing that "there is an American taste for national aggrandizement, now in check, which the rhetoric of idealism masks." The intervening decade has not seen the mask fall, and the national impulse for aggrandizement has found its expression in an American-driven program to remake the international system. The totalitarian utopian movements of the past ended with the collapse of Nazism and Marxism, but the utopian impulse is not exhausted in the United States, where it has always been an element in the national sense of self.

Europeans after their experience in the last century have been content with a modest and prudent program meant to integrate national economies and material interests, in hopes that this might permanently end the destructive European national rivalries of the past. The United States, by contrast, has pursued what it has considered its mission to change the world, a pious and quite unrealistic hope turned into a foreign policy.

America's optimism about world transformation has yet to be broken, which is why the United States is a dangerous nation while remaining a "righteous" one. The puritanism of its cultural origins was intolerant of sinners, and impatient with God's roundabout and unhurried ways. The United States is impatient for progress. As its vision of reform expresses its conviction of singular virtue and national exception, which by happy coincidence reinforces national economic interest and the extension of national power, the risk is the classical one which history poses to power, that of self-destructive hubris, leading to barren tears.

The question with which I concluded *Barbarian Sentiments* in 1989—"Does the will exist . . . to be serious, to make sacrifices again, to take our indulgences in hand?"—still awaits a positive answer. What in 1989 seemed the nation's "indulgences" are no longer recognized as such: the moral framework has shifted. With that, the shadow of extravagant waste has lengthened.

25 August 2000

# ACKNOWLEDGMENTS

I wish to acknowledge, with thanks, my debt to Steve Wasserman, David Rieff, and Paul Golob, for having found the lost chord; and to Lucille Lvoff, who would have been pleased to see this book at last. R.I.P.

I must also thank Elisabeth Sifton, the begetter of this new edition, for reopening a book I had thought closed.

# INDEX